The Politics of the Body

Gender in a Neoliberal and Neoconservative Age

ALISON PHIPPS

polity

Contents

Acknowledgements

This book could not have been written without the help of my partner Jan Selby, who has provided practical assistance, emotional support and an intellectual sounding board which is second to none. I count myself incredibly lucky to have so much to say to, and so much respect for, my partner in life: being in a relationship with him has helped me to tackle this ambitious project. I am also deeply grateful to my colleagues and friends Trishima Mitra-Kahn and Margaretta Jolly and the anonymous Polity reviewers for their feedback on various drafts of the manuscript, to Jonathan Skerrett from Polity Press, who has been enthusiastic and supportive throughout, and to Gail Ferguson for her thorough and rapid editing.

This book is dedicated to two people: first, my friend Lisa Smirl, who passed away at the age of 37 in February 2013. Her courage, grace and humanity in the face of an incredibly aggressive terminal cancer which cut short her own promising academic career left me in awe, and inspired me to be truer to myself in work and in life. Second, I dedicate this volume to my daughter Caitlin Phipps Selby, born in September 2010, who has brought me more joy than I could ever have anticipated. I hope that, by the time she is grown, some of the debates covered here will have moved on in positive ways, and the feminist movement in particular will have found a way to negotiate a fraught and difficult macro-political context. Judging from the passion, thoughtfulness and good grace shown by so many of my feminist students (of all genders), I have great hopes that this will be the case. I would like to thank my students for being the biggest pleasure of my working life, and give especial thanks to Tom Chadwick who provided me with valuable research assistance for this book. Any errors or omissions in the text are solely my responsibility.

Introduction

In the summer of 2010, I was heavily pregnant with my first child. One early evening, as the nights were drawing in, my partner and I attended a barbecue organized by neighbours in Brighton: the predictably cosmopolitan, left-leaning crowd. One couple in particular, directors of a local alternative theatre company, talked us through the home water birth of their third baby, which they had celebrated the previous year. As I shared anxieties about my own impending delivery, the experienced father provided reassurance and various tips on how to deal with the pain without resorting to drugs or epidural anaesthesia. Giving birth should come naturally to women, he said – it was something we had all been designed to do. Furthermore, it was a process which would put me in touch with my strength and my powerful, primal self. My partner, understandably, wanted to know what he ought to do while I was undergoing this transformative experience. 'You protect the door of the cave,' he was told. The incident gave us much to talk about in terms of the juxtaposition between an unapologetically biologically essentialist narrative and its otherwise unconventional source. Although this book is not a personal one, it has been inspired by experiences such as this, which led me to want to explore the contemporary discursive and political terrain around issues to do with women's bodies.[1]

I began this research in 2008 after a discussion in one of my postgraduate feminist theory classes. The episode inspired me to reflect upon the difficulties of positioning for contemporary feminist theory and activism in a political context characterized by binaries and extremes and in which women's bodies have become battlegrounds both material and symbolic. In class, an Iranian student, who had chosen not to adopt the chador, was presenting her view of practices of veiling in her country as essentially oppressive and a reflection of a patriarchal value system. The room was silent while she spoke, in deference to her first-hand experience and also highlighting the discomfort many western students feel around voicing opinions about politically loaded topics in Othered cultures. However, before her narrative was finished, she was interrupted by a white European student, who had come top of the class in the previous term's feminist theory assignment and who gently explained to her Iranian colleague the empowerment she felt could be granted and expressed through the choice to cover one's face, body and/or hair. This incident was fascinating in its reversal of the usual problematic between feminists from the West and women from Muslim-majority societies. It spoke to potential shifts in the political and academic landscape in the West which I felt needed to be set in a broader context.

I chose to focus my research on four contemporary western debates centred on women's bodies which have been marked by controversy and contention: sexual violence, gender and Islam, sex work, and childbirth and breastfeeding. During the course of a number of years embedded in the fields of literature, media and politics around these issues, I found much experiential material which provided alternative stories to those narrated above. As any ethnographer knows, the arena of human feeling, thought and action will always be full of diversity, multiplicity and contradiction. However, as I began to follow different threads and piece together the web of discourses and power relations which constitute contemporary orthodoxies around the issues in question, a number of important common themes started to emerge.

Some were highlighted in existing research, and others emerged as I trawled through a huge variety of primary sources – policy documents and reports, newspapers, magazines, novels, blogs and other media – and conducted informal interviews with key official and unofficial political actors. As I worked, I found myself asking difficult questions: how, in the same period, have left-wingers, academics and other political progressives simultaneously defended powerful men accused of sex crimes, been critiqued for ignoring honour killings and other 'culture-based' forms of gender violence, positioned topless tabloid pictures as empowering, and opposed these same pictures for sexualizing breasts and undermining the breastfeeding which is an essential part of 'natural motherhood'? Exploring these pointed me each time to the same common factor: the contemporary political and economic coalition of neoliberalism and neoconservatism which has put opposition movements very much on the defensive. This, I found, has posed particular dilemmas for feminism, which is currently enjoying a resurgence but has perhaps never operated in a more difficult political and cultural milieu.

This book, then, engages with the current state of feminism in relation to mainstream and popular political discourse and the framework of neoliberalism and neoconservatism in particular. It presents a challenge to emergent retrosexism on both the right and left wing of contemporary politics, as well as what I view as problematic developments within feminism itself: a focus on women's agency and identity at the expense of examining framing structures; a reluctance to moralize or adopt 'victim' positions which can be seen as silencing and which maps onto the omnipresent politics of personal responsibility; and 'radical' movements in the spheres of both sexuality and health which leave unchallenged the role of the capitalist market, the material and discursive framings of contemporary femininities (especially how 'progressive' forms may still be retrograde in their lineage or effects), and the operation of privilege. Overall, I contend that the rejection of neoconservative themes, agendas and institutions has within much feminist thought and action produced ideas and politics which can be seen as neoliberal in their emphasis on agency, 'empowerment' and individual choice. This is a development of Eisenstein's (2010) work on the co-optation of liberal feminism by corporate capitalism, and Fraser's (2009, 2013) analysis of feminism's relationship with neoliberalism, in which she elucidates how elements of the feminist critique of capitalism, namely those focused on cultural and identity-based recognition, have been co-opted in the current political context, while structural and economic themes have been lost or transmuted into individualistic self-betterment goals. My work provides a detailed account of the impact of these discursive shifts in a variety of different topic areas, also showing how it is not just liberal but postmodern, postcolonial and 'third wave' forms of feminism which have been seduced by the market, and incorporating the dialectic between neoliberalism and neoconservatism which has affected left-wing movements in particular, and feminism especially, due to synergies between radical feminist activism and 'law and order' agendas (Brown 1995; Bumiller 2008).

Although many of the issues covered in this book are over-researched and debated, my analysis is genealogical (Foucault 1977) in its concern with how the discussions themselves are constructed: the concepts and rhetorics or 'regimes of truth' (Foucault 1980: 131) deployed, the political allegiances being made, and their contextual conditions of possibility. Following Fraser and Gordon (1994: 310), my approach is based on the conviction that politics has a role to play in defining social reality and that, furthermore, particular terms (or in my analysis, concepts and modes of thought and action) become sites at which identity and experience can be negotiated and contested. Genealogy, then, involves looking critically at the taken-for-granted meanings which populate social and political spheres and uncovering their underlying assumptions. This encompasses starting from particular case studies and progressively taking a wider and wider lens, comparing these to other empirical examples to establish general trends, but also attempting to contextualize these in relation to historical lineages and broad institutional, economic, social, political and cultural discourses and structures, paying particular attention to the circulation of power (Stevenson and Cutcliffe 2006: 715). I adopt Foucault's (1977) view of the genealogical project as a 'history of the present', and there has not been scope in my analysis to undertake a detailed longitudinal mapping of change. However, I have tried to indicate, where possible, how and why key themes and perspectives have shifted.

Chapter 2 explores the issue of sexual violence, focusing in particular on the contemporary anti-victim orthodoxy in academia and its relationship with neoliberal rationalities, and how this is set against the rather problematic alliance of radical feminist activism and neoconservative projects of social control. In chapter 3, the power of neoconservative discourse is again examined, particularly in terms of how the centring of the victimized 'Muslim woman' within neo-imperial projects has led to a focus on agency and resistance in progressive political and intellectual circles. These two chapters look at fields which are characterized by contestation and dispute: in contrast, chapters 4 and 5 tackle areas where there is a more definite orthodoxy at play. Chapter 4 examines the contemporary sex-radical framework which dominates debates about the sex industry, exploring commonalities with neoliberalism in its emphasis on identity, empowerment and choice. In chapter 5, the discussion tackles the 'natural' birth and breastfeeding movements which have emerged in many western countries, asking questions about how these have coincided with neoliberal and neoconservative agendas, sometimes in dubious ways. Throughout, common themes and ideas are highlighted and related back to my overarching conceptual framework. Bringing all these different issues together, an endeavour which has not been attempted before, yields invaluable insights about the nature of contemporary gender politics.

None of the areas covered in this book is neutral – they are all politically and morally constructed. Furthermore, many of them are characterized by 'bad science' residing in frequent claims and counterclaims which are often partial but which also invariably purport to be conclusive. Examining these fields discursively involves an attempt to deconstruct some of the more common or dominant claims and contextualize them more broadly. Such an analysis will not produce the 'truth' about whether practices of veiling and/or professions in the sex industry are essentially oppressive or essentially empowering, whether Julian Assange has committed sex crimes or whether breast is really best. Indeed, Shiner (1982) terms Foucault's genealogical method an 'anti-method' for precisely these reasons: because the search for truth and origins is ultimately destined to fail, and because there is no objective, apolitical method which can help it succeed. Instead, my book may give insights into the web of discourses and power relations which constitutes the contemporary politics of the body. I am aware that this may be seen as a 'truth-telling' by some, and that the sources from which I have gathered my data – policy, politics, popular culture and the media in the United Kingdom and other western countries – are circumscribed. The discussions I examine will not touch everyone in the West and will be limited in their impact in broader contexts, although policies emanating from these arenas may have considerable international reach. I also realize that, in exploring major frameworks and orthodoxies, there will be many discourses I have missed or perhaps flattened out, as I am sketching with a fairly broad brush. Finally, I should check my own privilege at the outset, as a white, western, able-bodied and cisgendered woman married to a man, living a fairly conventional middle-class lifestyle. The analysis I present here, then, cannot be exhaustive or irrefutable: however, the book should be seen as an interpretation of major contemporary debates which may be of interest and provide food for thought.

1

Neoliberalism and Neoconservatism: Framing the Politics of the Body

This book takes the dominant contemporary economic and political rationalities of neoliberalism and neoconservatism as its primary conceptual resource in analysing themes common to a number of different western debates about women's bodies. While by no means the only discourses in play, these two have achieved enormous political, social and cultural power, to the extent that other perspectives and movements have found themselves on the defensive (Brown 2006), and this can be observed in all the fields explored here. My broad approach to investigating this dynamic can be characterized as a *political sociology of the body*, both associating with and differentiating itself from the sociological and political modes. The *sociology of the body* can loosely be described as a sub-discipline concerned with how the body is both material and socially/politically constructed (Turner 1984; Shilling 1993). It covers themes around embodiment, experience, identity, representation and power, and explores how these are shaped by discourse and social structure and refracted by categories such as class, gender, 'race', sexual orientation, (dis)ability and age. In contrast, the *politics of the body* can be understood as the substance and detail of debates about key issues such as the ones covered in this book, as well as others such as abortion, cosmetic surgery, disability and disordered eating. These are often contentious and characterized by claims, counterclaims and controversies, featuring individuals and groups of seemingly diametrically opposed political persuasions. Feminism is regularly implicated or involved, since such debates often pivot around women's bodies (Weitz 1998), even when focused on issues which also affect men.

Working alongside and drawing much from both these modes of engagement, the political sociological analysis developed in this book asks questions about how contemporary discussions of issues to do with women's bodies reflect and construct how we conceptualize embodiment. It also, crucially, attempts to contextualize controversial political debates within a sociological frame. This involves situating them within the social, political, economic and cultural spheres and structures of neoliberalism and neoconservatism, as well as exploring the social construction of the discursive fields themselves. The latter implies a commitment to uncovering whose are the dominant voices and how this reflects and perpetuates existing inequalities based on social categories such as gender, 'race' and social class. Furthermore, it raises questions about how the debates themselves might reflect the concerns of the individuals and groups who predominate within them, highlighting important silences and wondering about the potential effects of taking other perspectives into account. In this endeavour, which might be called genealogical (Foucault 1977), I make use of a number of key concepts and theoretical frameworks, which allow me to conceptualize the broad structural and political context of neoliberalism and neoconservatism and provide useful tools for a more intersectional analysis.

Neoliberalism and neoconservatism: the unholy alliance

First of all, my political sociology of the body is framed by the structures and discourses of neoliberal capitalism. In particular, the shift from Fordist to post-Fordist capitalist production has intersected with and informed processes of embodiment in a number of important ways. Fordism, the system of industrial mass production which employed large-scale, low-cost physical/manual labour, used detailed technical divisions of tasks along a moving assembly line (Pietrykowki 1994: 68; Rayner and Easthope 2001; Smith 2008: 180). The Fordist market was dominated by a small number of major producers, resulting in little consumer choice (Rayner and Easthope 2001). In contrast, in a post-Fordist era we have seen an explosion of market-based choices which has come to inform the social construction of identities, as well as the engagements of individuals and groups with the political sphere. The industrial production of goods in the West has made way for a 'post-industrial' economy based on services and knowledge (Nettleton 2006: 221). Labour has become more flexible and decentralized and many functions have been outsourced, leading to an international societal division of production which has exacerbated existing inequalities (Waters 1995). There is also a greater emphasis on product differentiation by marketing, packaging and design and the targeting of consumers according to lifestyle, taste and culture. The global economy is now dominated by multinational companies, which have a degree of autonomy from nation-state control, and financial markets which have been a product of the communications revolution (Hall 1988).

The growth of service- and knowledge-based industries has had important effects on the social structure and the formation of identities, contributing to the decline of the Fordist (white, male) manual working class and the 'feminization' of the workforce. Theories of an attendant 'crisis of masculinity' (Shilling 1993: 114–15; Gill, Henwood and McLean 2005: 39) have intersected with the neoconservative backlash against feminism to threaten many gains for women's rights and construct a contemporary gender politics which often appears fraught. In general terms, it is now thought that identity no longer derives automatically from one's position in the matrix of production, leading to a greater emphasis on the body which is shaped to a great extent by consumer culture (Giddens 1991; Bauman 1992). The new service industries also engage the body in different ways, for instance the 'emotion work' which requires employees to manage their feelings, body language and expressions in accordance with their employer's requirements, in order to produce the desired emotional state in customers (Hochschild 1983). Some of the new service industries also have particular physical requirements, usually for women employees (Shilling 1993; Davies 2011).

Although capitalism is not a monolith (Duggan 2003), it can be said that in western neoliberal economies the body has become a symbol of value and identity which is largely performed and developed via the purchase of products (Shilling 1993; Carolan 2005). The drive to consume in order to both express and 'add value' to oneself is a key aspect of contemporary consumer culture, which feeds markets that rely upon idealized representations of the body and the elevation of particular prestigious bodily forms through advertising (Shilling 1993: 129). In a context in which consumption is primarily about 'symbolic value' rather than 'use value' (Rayner and Easthope 2001: 170–1), focused on cultural assets as opposed to merely material ones (Savage et al. 1992: 112), we have seen among the privileged a dramatic growth in spending on beauty, fitness and fashion, a rise in alternative health practices and in more extreme 'body projects' (Shilling 1993: 112) such as cosmetic surgeries. These new moralities and practices of consumption are central to neoliberal value systems and can be seen informing many of the debates in this book, evident for instance in prescribed bodily practices which become central to profitable markets, rapidly mainstreaming industries focused on the consumption of sexualized bodies, and most importantly contemporary conceptualizations of 'choice' which have been shaped in newly economistic directions.

In a post-Fordist context, the chief contemporary economic and political lexicon in the West is regarded by many as constituted by a coalition between neoliberal and neoconservative rationalities. Neoliberalism has become hegemonic as a system of political and economic organization, while neoconservatism infuses our popular morality and underpins regulatory projects both domestically and overseas (Brown 1995, 2006; Harvey 2005; Fraser 2009). Neoliberalism, which developed first in the United States and then rapidly in Western Europe (Duggan 2003: xi–xii), is premised on the absolute freedom of capitalist markets and trading relationships which was a central tenet of classical liberal thinking, but has cascaded these principles into the social realm with a central assumption that societies function best with a minimum of state intervention (Harvey 2005). The liberalization of the economy (for example, the elimination of price controls, deregulation of capital markets and removal of trade barriers) has shaped social reforms such as the privatization of state-owned services and fiscal austerity informed by the rhetoric of personal responsibility (Boas and Gans-Morse 2009).

Furthermore, as Brown (2006: 691) argues, the 'market-political' rationality of neoliberalism has entered into social discourse and begun to structure subjectivities. Indeed, she contends, it now 'governs the sayable, the intelligible and the truth criteria' of western culture (Brown 2006: 693). Through channels such as government policy, advertising and popular culture, neoliberalism has become a normative framework, based on the idea of citizens as rational and self-interested economic actors with agency and control over their own lives. Within its architecture political and social problems are converted into market terms, becoming individual issues with consumption-based solutions (Brown 2006: 704). The body is a key site at which this process occurs, a vehicle for the 'appropriate' consumption practices which are put forward as a panacea for contemporary social problems (Evans and Riley 2012: 3). Success is measured by individuals' capacity for self-care via the market, and those who do not achieve their potential are viewed as failures rather than as victims of oppressive social structures. For example, obesity in a neoliberal context is recast as an issue of individual responsibility and lifestyle choice rather than class- and resource-based inequality (Evans and Riley 2012: 11). This, for Brown (2006: 704), is 'depoliticization on an unprecedented level: the economy is tailored to it, citizenship is organized by it, the media are dominated by it, and the political rationality of neoliberalism frames and endorses it.'

In contrast, neoconservatism is an interventionist political discourse which nevertheless has entered into a productive coalition (or unholy alliance) with its free-market partner. Brown (2006: 691) terms neoconservatism a 'moral–political rationality' which is based on traditional gender roles and family structures, the centrality of the church to social life, state-led patriotism including stringent immigration controls, and the defence of national and cultural borders (Brown 2006: 699) which involves a strong and interventionist military state (Norton 2004). This is the product of converging social and political groups and interests: 'evangelical Christians, Jewish Straussians, avowedly secular Cold Warriors who have made a fetish of the West, conservative feminists[1] and other family moralists . . . random imperialists, and converted liberals and socialists' (Brown 2006: 696). In neoliberalism and neoconservatism, business and theological models of state power have come together, and the two frameworks are at once hostile and complementary (Brown 2006: 698). They conflict over issues such as state spending, and neoconservative moralism is set against neoliberal nihilism and self-interest. However, they have hidden similarities in their regulation of the social sphere, which neoconservatism approaches directly via morality and policy while neoliberalism belies its free-market rhetoric by attempting to incentivize towards the 'right' choices (Brown 2006: 700). The influence of this coalition underpins all the issues covered in this book, and its interactions with feminism and the political left are of particular interest to my analysis. Indeed, its contemporary hegemony sometimes suggests that one cannot reject one element without embracing another: for example, neoconservative engagements with radical feminism over issues such as the sex industry and violence against women have led other feminists and left-wingers to take defensive positions which involve playing into neoliberal preoccupations with individual freedom and personal choice.

Individualization and the postmodern condition

Neoliberalism in particular operates with an individualized model of the self which can be seen as both reflecting and producing changed models of social organization and self-identity. As Beck and Beck-Gernsheim (2002: xxi) argue, contemporary society is set upon a form of 'institutionalized individualism' whereby institutions, employment structures and basic civil, political and social rights are geared to the individual rather than to the group. This works alongside what they term a 'disembedding' of identities, also informed by the decreasing stability of collective categories such as class, gender and family and the collapse of traditional social norms. Contemporary challenges, demands and constraints, 'from pension rights to insurance protection, from educational grants to tax rates', constitute an individualist paradigm within which our thinking, planning and acting now takes place (Beck and Beck-Gernsheim 2002: 2). Giddens (1991) also explores the relationship between self-identity and the institutions of modernity and proposes that we are now engaged in reflexive projects of the self, characterized by introspection, evaluation and alteration, within narratives of actualization and mastery. This shapes the context in which everyone is responsible for constituting themselves as an individual, and in which failure is one's own fault rather than the result of social inequality and disadvantage (Beck and Beck-Gernsheim 2002: 3–4): this politics of personal responsibility can be observed in many of the debates in this book.

Beck and Beck-Gernsheim argue that individualization is characteristic of 'second modernity', while Giddens terms the contemporary period 'high modernity'. However, a number of other thinkers claim that we are living in an age of postmodernity, marked by the decline of Enlightenment notions such as truth and freedom and a proliferation of difference in terms of values and identities (Callinicos 1989). For Lyotard (1979: xxiii), postmodernity refers primarily to the condition of knowledge in what he calls 'the most highly developed societies', and he interprets it as an incredulity towards 'metanarratives' such as Marxism and feminism which purported to explain the truth of social organization and incorporated ideals about how to progress to a more equitable social plane. This has been seen as a reaction to the exclusionary and Othering universalisms of modernist thought (Harvey 1990: 42), and postmodern forms of knowledge incorporate in contrast pluralistic ideas around multiple truths and forms of society, and the principle that 'all groups have a right to speak for themselves, in their own voice, and have that voice accepted as authentic and legitimate' (Harvey 1990: 48). Postmodern thinking contains a view of power as shifting and nomadic, and as productive rather than repressive (Foucault 1976, 1977). This perspective has informed my analysis as I attempt to explore the relationships between power and knowledge in contemporary debates around the body. However, postmodern ideas are also frequently articulated in the political sphere, often in problematic ways, with academic postmodernism dovetailing with an emphasis on difference, 'voice' and 'authenticity' in activist fields.

The politics of the Other

In a postmodern and neoliberal context, the dominant form of politics is focused on difference (Duggan 2003): what Nancy Fraser (1995, 2000) has termed the 'politics of recognition'. This describes the emphasis on identity which dominates post-industrial capitalist societies, with cultural recognition (defined in broad terms) supplanting socio-economic redistribution. The goal of this politics is 'a difference friendly world, where assimilation to majority or dominant cultural norms is no longer the price of equal respect' (Fraser and Honneth 2003: 1). It involves appeals for the validation of the distinctive values and perspectives of different groups, for instance on the grounds of ethnicity, culture or sexual orientation, within legal, political, economic, occupational and institutional settings. An example is the contemporary campaign for same-sex marriage in the United States, the United Kingdom and other western countries, defined by Fraser as a form of recognition politics because it is about incorporating sexual diversity into the existing institutional and legal frameworks of society (Fraser and Honneth 2003: 39). The evolution of a politics of recognition is the result of a number of related developments: neoliberal attacks on social egalitarianism, the dramatic failures of the communist bloc, and fears about the viability of state socialism in a globalized world (Fraser 2000). These shape its focus away from the structural, but it has been critiqued for creating a 'prison of identity politics' (Shakespeare 2006: 82) which promotes conformism within cultural groups, as well as oppressive forms of communitarianism whereby any critique of other values or cultures is viewed as discriminatory (Fraser 2000).

Such a politics has been particularly attractive within the feminist canon, and Fraser (2009) argues that feminism's historical politicization of the personal, although initially positive and visionary, has ultimately led to a loss of economic and political critique as neoliberal capitalist political culture and its focus on identity politics has conscripted aspects of feminist thinking (Fraser 1995, 2000, 2009). This reflects the broader turns to identity and 'affect' in postmodern academic feminism and 'third wave' activism (Blackman and Venn 2010). The politicization of the personal has also become common in the mainstream, influencing an emotionalist and expressivist politics in which social and political judgements are often centred on feeling (MacIntyre 1984; Squire 2001), a result of both the decline of Enlightenment values and the phenomenon of 'tabloidization' (Paasonen, Nikunen and Saarenmaa 2007: 7), or the prioritization of the personal in popular culture. This can be seen in self-development and counselling culture, increasing demands for political figures to show emotion, the saturation of popular media with feelings (soap melodrama, reality TV and talk-show theatre), and the way in which social, cultural and political issues are played out through celebrities' lives. As well as being a new market commodity in neoliberal capitalism (Hochschild 1983, 2000), feelings have become a new political commodity, leading to an 'expressivism' (Edwards 2004) which can be seen in debates in which hurt feelings are used as currency. Squire (2001) argues that this can have positive aspects, for instance, in inserting new issues and experiences into culture and creating a move away from individualism in *shared* experience. However, it can also close down the possibilities for critical intellectual analysis as it reduces debate to a matter of feeling, with structural analysis supplanted by the experience of being a member of an oppressed cultural or social group.

Western engagement with 'Other' cultures is often viewed through the lens of Orientalism, which refers to how 'traditional' (usually eastern) cultures have been narrated, commodified and appropriated by historical and contemporary forms of colonialism (Said 1978). This is evident in a number of different settings: the academic, which means anyone who teaches, writes about or researches the Orient; the political/artistic, meaning the ontological and epistemological distinction made between 'the Orient' and 'the Occident' in theories, novels, poems and policies; and the discursive, which refers to a discourse which has benefited European culture by 'setting itself off against the Orient as a sort of surrogate and even underground self' (Said 1978: 2–3). Orientalism, for Said (1978: 3), is 'the corporate institution for dealing with the Orient – dealing with it by making statements about it, authorizing views of it, describing it, by teaching it, settling it, ruling over it: in short, Orientalism [is] a western style for dominating, restructuring, and having authority over the Orient.'

Understood in a broad sense, forms of Orientalism can be seen in many of the debates in this book, in which neoliberal and neoconservative mentalities and powerful groups and institutions have been able to construct knowledge about social and cultural Others which shapes the formation of subjectivities and produces feelings of failure among the structurally disadvantaged. Paradoxically, also, manifestations of Orientalism can be seen informing much of the answering recognition politics which is currently in circulation, which often romanticizes and homogenizes the Other as part of its focus on difference. In this way contemporary progressive identity politics can become conservative in its effects, showing the influence of neoliberal ideas of difference, apolitically defined, and also sharing characteristics with the neoconservative focus on social Others which either creates homogeneous groups of victims for the purposes of social control or uses the notion of the dangerous Other in the service of regulation. This can be seen in debates around sex work and also gender and Islam, for example, in which essentialized constructions of identity are observed across ideological and political divides.

Feminism as subject matter and analytical resource

In all the debates in this book, the politics of gender intersects with other frameworks, for instance around class, ethnicity, 'culture' and sexual orientation. In much of my analysis I have identified a key role for the operation of privilege, in relation to whose voices are heard and who is able to set agendas pertaining to particular issues. I have also raised questions about the potential impact of including alternative voices, often from more disadvantaged social positions, in discussions. I take feminism as my theoretical and political standpoint, but I also acknowledge how mainstream feminism is itself a politics of privilege and explore how it has been used (and misused) in the debates in question. The first key theme is the influence of the neoconservative backlash against feminism and, paradoxically, how aspects of radical feminism have simultaneously been co-opted by neoconservative 'law and order' agendas. The second is how neoliberal individualism has stripped the radical and Marxist structural analysis of gender relations of its credibility, while making links with the more individualistic aspects of 'third wave', postmodern and postcolonial feminisms. At present, these latter three are the dominant strands of feminism in the political field around women's bodies, while the gains of liberal feminism are broadly thought to have been made, socialist/Marxist feminisms have gone out of fashion and radical feminism enjoys influence only in spheres which bring it into agreement with the neoconservative establishment.

The marriage between postmodernism and feminism has been a particularly fruitful one, allowing the movement both to challenge claims to 'objectivity' in mainstream social science, research and policy focused only on men's issues and needs (Haraway 1989; Fausto-Sterling 1992; Martin 2001) and to examine its own limitations in terms of the use of fixed, universalist identity categories such as 'woman' and claims on this basis to speak for all women (Butler 1999). Feminists have also been particularly attracted to postmodern accounts of agency, which is produced by the subject's situation inside a matrix of discourses which, through the performative nature of identity, they are capable of beginning to rework from within (Butler 1988, 1999, 2004). Much contemporary feminist theory situates agency in the body and in resistant and radical forms of 'body work' (Butler 2004). This includes postcolonial feminism, which has an especial focus on practices of bodily resistance, often reclaiming cultural norms and traditions previously defined as shaped by oppression (Bilge 2010). The ideas of agency and 'choice' are important in all the debates covered in this book: however, while acknowledging that there is much to be gained from these concepts, I also draw on critiques of this contemporary orthodoxy as having become, in interaction with neoliberalism, rather voluntarist and individualist (Livia and Hall 1997: 8; Webster 2000: 8), and abstracted from structural determinants (Abu-Lughod 1990; Brickell 2005; Boucher 2006). Furthermore, I attempt to highlight important, if unintentional, convergences between such feminist mainstays and the neoliberal emphasis on 'personal choice' and self-invention, which can very quickly turn into a more repressive politics of personal responsibility.

A variety of different strands of feminism, as well as the other theoretical frameworks I have introduced here, has shaped the analysis presented in this book. I contextualize my interpretation of gender within the macro-structures of global capitalism, but while I wish to retain a strong structural critique, I am also indebted to postmodern and postcolonial perspectives for highlighting the weaknesses of over-universalizing frameworks. My analysis is inspired by the work of Yuval-Davis (2006) and others (see also Phoenix 2006), in its attempt to examine the intersectionality of gender with a variety of other aspects of identity and social and economic positionalities, without slipping into an endless variety of apolitical differences. It also attempts to pay attention to the latter half of the binary between recognition and redistribution (Fraser 1995), to acknowledge the value of commonality and solidarity and to allow that there may be issues over which bonds between women may be forged while simultaneously addressing particularities which arise at various intersections (see, for example, Mohanty 2002; Walby, Armstrong and Strid 2012). This book essentially presents a discourse analysis of debates in the political, social and cultural field: as a result, there will be an inevitable loss of complexity in relation to the specificities of personal experience. However, I hope it might provide a broad framework which could inform more micro-level analyses.

The rest of this book will show how the contemporary alliance between neoliberalism and neoconservatism, with its attendant themes, has shaped a variety of issues in the politics of the body. In chapter 2, an analysis of sexual violence politics reveals how the association between radical feminism and neoconservative agendas around crime control has produced a retreat from emphasizing victimhood on the political and academic left, which often draws on strains of neoliberalism. Chapter 3 explores similar trends in relation to gender and Islam, a debate in which the 'progressive' focus on cultural difference, agency and resistance can be seen as partially responding to neoconservative Orientalisms which have settled upon women in Muslim-majority societies and communities, but also as reflecting neoliberal individualisms and constructions of 'rational choice'. In chapter 4, the current dominant sex-radical perspective on the sex industry is shown to manifest similar notions, and it is argued that, in its rejection of the radical feminist convergence with neoconservative agendas, it fails to problematize contemporary sexualized consumer culture and thereby blunts its own radicalism. Chapter 5 tackles the extant orthodoxy around 'natural' childbirth and breastfeeding, revealing its resonances with both neoconservative gender essentialism and the neoliberal politics of personal responsibility and, in the process, also questioning its 'alternative' appearance. In all four chapters, I trace the relation between the exercise of agency and the operation of privilege and explore how those with economic, social and cultural resources are able to dominate debates in problematic and potentially damaging ways. This broadly constitutes my political sociology of the body.

2

Sexual Violence and the Politics of Victimhood

The DSK case and the Assange case have brought to the fore the true ugliness of sex negative feminism and man hatred, and the extent to which they made inroads into our culture and society just as insidious as the right-wing propaganda of the Murdochs. They have also shown how those right wing forces can so easily hijack stupid blinkered man haters to the right-wing agenda.

(Craig Murray 2011)

The fact that powerful men sometimes exploit and abuse women and girls is not particularly shocking. As I write this book, the media brims with such stories, ranging from the continual speculation over the on–off and physically violent relationship between American pop stars Rihanna and Chris Brown, to the recent revelations about extensive and systematic abuse of teenage girls in 1970s Britain by DJ and television presenter Jimmy Savile and others associated with the BBC. There is a narrative of outrage in contemporary western tabloid media and popular culture around such cases, particularly those which involve the sexualization and abuse of girls. The three cases I cover in this chapter, however, are antithetical to this, characterized by contention and debate, censure and defence. I discuss WikiLeaks founder Julian Assange and politician Dominique Strauss-Kahn, both accused of sexual assault, and film-maker Roman Polanski, convicted of unlawful sex with a minor. I do not wish to rehearse the rights and wrongs of these matters: instead, my focus is encapsulated by the chapter's opening quote, taken from the blog of left-wing dissident and human rights campaigner Craig Murray. For Murray, Assange was the victim of feminist misandry, allied with a right-wing witch-hunt; Strauss-Kahn and Polanski were similarly positioned by their supporters within broader conspiratorial narratives which often eclipsed discussion of the cases themselves. I examine the support given to all three men, drawing out common themes and contextualizing these within the dominant neoliberal/neoconservative framework and prevailing political positionings and sensitivities, such as the backlash against feminism and the leftist critique of US neo-imperialist projects. I argue that these conditions of possibility framed the politicking around these cases, producing rape apologism and victim-blaming from a variety of quarters. Throughout the chapter, these case studies are used to raise questions about the constraints on sexual violence activism created by the contemporary lexicon.

WikiLeaks, founded in 2006, is an organization and website publishing secret information, news leaks and classified information from anonymous news sources and whistle-blowers. Following a number of releases of information pertaining to the US-led 'war on terror', in 2010 the organization collaborated with major global media outlets to release a large collection of diplomatic cables. Soon afterwards, its Australian founder Julian Assange was arrested in the United Kingdom in relation to allegations of rape and sexual assault made by two women in Sweden. Since he had previously had consensual sex with both women, their complaints were immediately positioned within the sometimes controversial paradigm of 'date rape', a term which has been criticized for minimizing the experiences of women who are attacked by someone they know (the majority of sexual violence cases) (McColgan 1996). The substance of the allegations was this: the first plaintiff claimed that during one act of intercourse Assange had used his body weight to hold her down and, despite being asked to, had not used a condom, and that on another occasion he had molested her by pressing his erect penis against her body. The second claimed that he had engaged in intercourse with her while she was asleep, again without using any protection. After a prolonged legal battle, in 2012 Assange lost his appeal against extradition to Sweden to face questioning. He immediately fled to the Ecuadorean Embassy in London, where he was granted asylum on humanitarian grounds. He was backed by a broad coalition of journalists, political figures, activists and celebrities, many located on the Left and almost all inspired by the belief that the matter was part of a larger neoconservative persecution of a prominent dissident and a plot to eventually extradite him to the United States to face charges relating to WikiLeaks.[1] These supporters used a variety of strategies including questioning the seriousness of the charges, naming the complainants and undermining their integrity by suggesting that they were politically or emotionally motivated and had made false or exaggerated statements.

The broad left-wing support for Assange brought to mind the earlier case of Roman Polanski, a Polish-French producer, writer, director and actor who has made a string of internationally acclaimed films. Polanski was similarly widely defended after being arrested in 2009 in Switzerland at the request of US authorities, en route to accept a lifetime achievement award at the Zurich Film Festival. However, unlike Assange, Polanski had actually been convicted of a sexual offence. In 1977, he had been arrested in the United States for the sexual abuse of a 13-year-old girl, Samantha Gailey (now Geimer), who alleged that he had provided her with champagne and a sedative and performed oral, vaginal and anal sex upon her without her consent. Polanski insisted that the acts had been consensual, and as part of a plea bargain (designed to protect Gailey from a trial) in which five of six counts of criminal behaviour were dismissed, pleaded guilty to the charge of unlawful sex with a minor. However, before being sentenced, he fled to his home in London and eventually settled in France with the case still unresolved. Arrested again more than thirty years later, Polanski was incarcerated near Zurich for two months, then placed under house arrest at his home in Gstaad while, like Assange, he fought extradition (in this case to the United States). In summer 2010, the Swiss government rejected the extradition request and declared Polanski a free man. Although there are important differences between this case and that of Assange (most importantly the fact that Polanski had been convicted of a sex crime), there were striking similarities in the arguments used to support him. A group of film industry figures and others rallied around the director, positioning him as the victim of a vengeful US criminal justice system and questioning the gravity of his crime. There were also suggestions (implicit too in the case of Assange), that his status as a revered icon should entitle him to leniency.

Requests for special treatment, among other themes, link these two men with French Socialist Party politician Dominique Strauss-Kahn, arrested in 2011 for the attempted rape of a housekeeping worker in a Manhattan hotel. Like the others, Strauss-Kahn maintained that he had engaged in consensual sexual relations with the complainant: however, he subsequently resigned his position as head of the International Monetary Fund after a string of similar allegations from women in France and overseas (BBC News 2011b; Cochrane 2011). Although Strauss-Kahn was not as widely defended as Assange or Polanski, he nevertheless enjoyed a great deal of support from the French left-wing political elite, especially after doubts emerged about his accuser's credibility (BBC News 2011a). The charges against him were eventually dismissed, although his complainant, alongside a French journalist who had alleged an attempted rape in 2003, subsequently initiated a civil case which was settled out of court (Fine 2012; Moynihan 2012). In 2012, Strauss-Kahn was investigated in France in relation to involvement in a prostitution ring (Moynihan 2012). At the time of his 2011 arrest, he was tipped to be the next Socialist Party president of France: advocates argued that due to this elevated status, he should not be treated as a subject of justice like any other. Like the other two cases, there were also attempts to smear his accusers through raising questions about their sexual histories, honesty and motivations.

The discussion in this chapter is not about the guilt or innocence of Julian Assange, Dominique Strauss-Kahn or Roman

Polanski. Indeed, many of their supporters did not debate this, instead arguing that, regardless of any wrongdoing, they should be entitled to particular consideration. I raise questions here about who supported them and why, what discourses and rhetorics were employed, and what this reveals about contemporary politics and the possibilities for feminism and sexual violence activism. I attempt to illuminate several elements of what I see as a new orthodoxy: a suspicion of victimhood and a reluctance to moralize which merge well with neoliberal individualism, produced at least partly in response to the focus on pathological predators and criminal justice solutions which speaks to the power of neoconservative 'law and order' mentalities. The various sections of this chapter deal with a number of common themes in the three case studies: the neoliberal 'meritocracy' which has augmented the rights of powerful men to act with impunity and attendant politics of personal responsibility which has exacerbated victim-blaming, and the rather uncomfortable association between neoconservative morality and radical feminism which has shaped an answering left-wing discomfort in relation to the politics of victimhood and morality. Underpinning all this is the postmodern turn in academia and cultural commentary and two related backlashes: the first against feminism and the second against the United States. Together, I argue, these factors have produced a dismissal of the experience of sexual violence and a gender-blindness and rape apologism which can be extant on the Left as well as on the Right.

Contemporary 'meritocracy': neoliberalism and celebrity culture

The most obvious factor uniting all three of these cases in this chapter is the suggestion from supporters that such successful and powerful men had earned the right to be treated differently from everyone else. For example, after Polanski's arrest, a transnational group of more than a hundred film-makers, actors and producers signed a petition urging his release. This list included luminaries and recognized left-wingers such as Woody Allen, Martin Scorcese,

David Lynch, Milan Kundera, Tilda Swinton, Wes Anderson, Natalie Portman, Harrison Ford, Isabelle Huppert, Jeremy Irons, Bernard-Henri Lévy, Salman Rushdie, Diane von Furstenberg, Isabelle Adjani and Pedro Almodovar. A number of organizations also endorsed the petition, including ABC distribution, the Cannes Film Festival and Pathé. It was coordinated from France by the SACD, an organization which represents performance and visual artists (Knegt 2009). The demand for Polanski's release was based on one key argument: that his artistry was evidence of his irreproachability and had earned him the right to clemency (Bennett 2010). The text began as follows:

> We have learned the astonishing news of Roman Polanski's arrest by the Swiss police on September 26, upon arrival in Zurich while on his way to a film festival where he was due to receive an award for his career in film-making. His arrest follows an American arrest warrant dating from 1977 against the film-maker, in a case of morals. Roman Polanski is a French citizen, a renowned and international artist now facing extradition. This extradition, if it takes place, will be heavy in consequences and will take away his freedom. Film-makers, actors, producers and technicians – everyone involved in international film-making – want him to know that he has their support and friendship. (Soares 2013)

The opening sentence established that it was 'astonishing' for a person of Polanski's consequence to be arrested: 'apprehended like a common terrorist', wrote French philosopher Bernard-Henri Lévy (Bennett 2010). The subsequent reference to the case as one of 'morals' suggested that a man such as this ought to be considered above parochial concerns. The significance of Polanski's artistic contribution appeared to dwarf his crime: in his 2009 memoir, Australian author and broadcaster Clive James mused, 'I couldn't help feeling that we were all better off if a man like that was living in comfort near the Avenue Montaigne rather than bouncing off the walls in Chino prison' (Deacon 2009).

Polanski is one of a number of celebrities who have generated publicity for violating statutory rape laws. Others include R&B

singers R Kelly (who topped the charts in 2003 while on bail for 21 counts of statutory rape and child pornography) and Akon, and actors Woody Allen, Kelsey Grammer and Rob Lowe (Koon-Magnin 2008: 2; Malkin 2003). None of these men has served a custodial sentence. Morton (2005: 365) writes, 'sometimes it must seem to the layman that the ordinary rules of law and evidence do not apply when a celebrity . . . is the defendant in a criminal trial.' Instead, it appears that celebrity mitigates an offence or diminishes the need for justice. In Polanski's case, his behaviour was constructed as part of a broader artistic nonconformism (see, for example, Porton 2012). Lévy opined that writers and artists 'often have bad reputations . . . it's not important for them to look good' (Bennett 2010). Interpreting the case in this way, as a mere matter of *perceived* impropriety, served to invisibilize the experience of the victim. Similarly, in the case of Assange, American sex worker activist and writer Tracy Quan (2010) stated that 'subversive guys with cavalier notions about female consent are nothing new', arguing that, in the 1960s, rape was seen by some on the Left as 'insurrectionary'.

Although Dominique Strauss-Kahn is not an artist, much of the support expressed for him was also underpinned by the belief that such a celebrated figure, this time in politics, was entitled to allowances under the law. Polanski supporter Lévy (2011) was again a prominent voice, condemning the American justice system for taking Strauss-Kahn for 'a subject of justice like any other'. Likewise, Nixon speechwriter-turned-actor Ben Stein (2011) argued that a man with such a distinguished record of public service should not have been incarcerated in the notoriously tough penitentiary on Rikers Island. The BBC ran the headline: 'IMF chief sent to tough NY jail' (Napier 2011) and a CNN banner read 'Dominique Strauss-Kahn: A brilliant career, a stunning accusation' (Silverleib 2011). Again, the connotation was that the 'brilliant' do not lower themselves to commit sex crimes, and that, if they do, they nevertheless ought to be set apart when they are dealt with. There was much critique in France of how the case was conducted in the days after Strauss-Kahn's arrest, with a widespread view that he should have been exempt from the customary 'perp walk' past the assembled press and the obligatory insulting headlines in the tabloids. In response to the fact that the New York City Police Department and media did not give him such special treatment, some French supporters presented Strauss-Kahn as a hero and martyr (Fraser 2011).

Finally, Julian Assange's attempts to circumvent due process and the broad support he received for these can be seen as evidence that both he and his supporters felt he should enjoy particular privileges due to his status within the anti-American Left (Green 2012). Upon arrest, Assange refused to be photographed, fingerprinted or to give a DNA sample, as is normally routine in such cases (Davies, Jones and Hirsch 2010). He also engaged, with high-profile backing from supporters such as left-wing journalists Michael Moore and John Pilger, socialist politicians George Galloway and Tony Benn (although Benn later retracted his support – see Liberal Conspiracy 2012), socialite and writer Jemima Khan, film directors Oliver Stone and Ken Loach, academics Tariq Ali and Noam Chomsky, and feminist Naomi Wolf, in a prolonged legal battle to fight extradition. In an interview published during his period of house arrest, Assange had elevated himself to the same status as acclaimed civil rights activist Reverend Dr Martin Luther King Jr, and maintained that his WikiLeaks work was too important to answer to 'random prosecutors around the world who simply want to have a chat' (Burns and Somaiya 2010). In fact, however, he was required for the purpose of conducting criminal proceedings: the arrest warrant had been issued with probable cause, but in Swedish law an indictment cannot be made until after interrogation has taken place (England and Wales High Court 2011). Nevertheless, and in an apparent misunderstanding of this, Assange and his supporters (a group which also included the campaigning organization Women Against Rape) advocated for him to be informally questioned by telephone or Skype (see, for example, Axelsson and Longstaff 2012).

The idea that the male elite should be able to act with impunity is by no means a new one: the persistence of this into the twenty-first century in democratic states can perhaps be attributed to the rise of celebrity culture and veneration of those who have achieved a certain level of fame and notoriety (Cashmore 2006).

We have seen this recently in the United Kingdom in the case
of Jimmy Savile, who used his fame and power to serially abuse
children, but this equally applies to the three cases covered in this
chapter. This is partly due to a general trend in which the spheres
of the media, the entertainment industry and the political have
come to intersect (Marsh, Hart and Tindall 2010), creating a new
aristocracy in the public gaze and imagination. As Choi and Berger
(2010) contend, the apex of the social hierarchy is now reserved
for celebrities: it could be argued that fame itself has now become
a form of cultural capital and a marker of distinction (Bourdieu
1984 [1979]), seen in the popularity of 'star search' television shows
such as *American Idol* and *The X Factor*. The reach of celebrities has
extended beyond the entertainment industry into arenas such as
politics, health, philanthropy and religion: Choi and Berger (2010:
213) use the example of American actor Richard Gere, in a broadcast during the Palestinian presidential elections, stating, 'Hi, I'm
Richard Gere, and I'm speaking for the entire world.' There are
numerous illustrations of celebrity politicking in this chapter, and
Assange in particular can be seen as a product of the corresponding
trend for career politicians to become 'brands' (Marsh, Hart and
Tindall 2010; Thebes 2012). This cult of stardom, together with
the persistence of gendered 'rape myths' and a general failure to
take violence against women as seriously as other crimes, connects
Assange, Strauss-Kahn and Polanski with others who have similarly
evaded justice for acts of gendered violence or have been feted
despite them (Chris Brown, Charlie Sheen and Mike Tyson are
good examples).

Celebrity culture is also perpetuated by a rather facile notion of
meritocracy offering a free-market version of success and individualizing failure. This sits within a broader milieu in which neoliberal
values such as competition, consumption and deregulation have
moved out of the market and into our 'common sense' beliefs and
subjectivities (Harvey 2005; Brown 2006). Applied to individual
biographies, this brings a focus on personal responsibility, choice
and agency. The neoliberal subject is autonomous, rational, risk
managing and responsible for their own destiny (Giddens 1991;
Beck and Beck-Gernsheim 2002). This means that society's

'successes' are lauded for making the most of their opportunities: however, it also denotes that 'failures' are characterized as at best diffident and at worst lazy, and ultimately responsible for their fate (Harris 2003; Smart 2012). This market-political rationality (Brown 2006) marries well with the contemporary retreat from welfare provision in economic and social policy (Baker 2009). The influence of individualistic constructions is reflected in an extant popular and political distaste for social 'failures' who complain about their lot in life (markedly welfare recipients), framed by an 'anti-victim' politics and slew of cultural commentary. This will be discussed in more detail in the next sections of this chapter since, in all three of the case studies covered, it arguably intensified the victim-blaming which in any case continues to be rife in relation to incidents of sexual violence (Ullman 2010).

Blame the victim: rape myths persist

It is notable that support for all three men, from both ends of the political spectrum, was frequently expressed via questioning the complainants' stories and integrity (Harding 2010; McEwan 2010). Often this drew on now-familiar rape myths and victim-blaming tropes. In the case of Polanski, American actress Whoopi Goldberg asserted that his crime was not 'rape-rape' because alcohol and drugs had been involved; other allies pointed to the 13-year-old victim's previous sexual activity as a factor mitigating the crime (Chaudhry 2010; Clarke 2010). Assange complained that one of his accusers had been wearing a 'revealing pink sweater' (Miriam 2010). Together with his lawyers and other defenders, he made use of the term 'sex by surprise', incorrectly arguing that sex with someone who was sleeping was an act within the boundaries of normalcy which had been defined as rape by Sweden's over-stringent laws (Zeisler 2010). Perhaps most shocking were the opinions expressed by Assange advocate and American feminist Naomi Wolf, who not only opined that sex with a sleeping partner was not rape, but also ventured that an incident in which a woman

did not fight back against her assailant did not merit this definition. Furthermore, she claimed that the first complainant could
not truly have been raped, as she continued to share Assange's
bed after the alleged assault (Democracy Now 2010). These statements (for which she later apologized and appeared partially at
least to retract – see Edinburgh Eye 2012) were incredible in their
ignorance of the body of feminist research on 'rape myths', or fal-
lacious beliefs which function to justify sexual violence and abuse
(see, for example, Suarez and Gadalla 2010; Turchik and Edwards
2012). The myth that victims of sexual violence will either resist
assault or immediately extricate themselves from an abusive situation is an enduring and particularly dangerous one since it relies on
misunderstandings of the experience of sexual violence and the fear
it instils, even in assaults which do not threaten or cause physical
injury, and demonstrates a failure to appreciate the dynamics of
abusive relationships.

Writing in the *Huffington Post*, Wolf had minimized the accusations against Assange, declaring Interpol, which had issued a 'red
notice', or international wanted persons alert, to be nothing more
than the 'dating police'. She also suggested that both complainants
were simply attempting to deal with feelings of rejection caused
by Assange's dissolute approach to relationships (Wolf 2010). This
'false accusation' trope, common in sexual violence cases, was
also drawn upon by other supporters (Pollitt 2010). American
left-wing activist Daniel Ellsberg (who had leaked classified documents relating to the Vietnam War in 1971) called the allegations
'false and slanderous', while British right-wing journalist Richard
Pendlebury (2010) made much of the women's 'personal aggrieved
feelings'. Some advocates went further, launching personal attacks
upon the women in question and suggesting that they were
pawns of the CIA or other neoconservative forces (Penny 2010;
Rawlinson 2013). Libby Brooks, writing in the UK *Guardian*,
commented that this focus on the women's integrity had united
Assange's left-wing supporters with:

> a motley assemblage of conspiracy theorists and internet attack dogs
> that has been mauling the characters of Assange's accusers since their

complaints were first lodged in August. Barely established online niceties regarding the discussion of sexual assault cases were over-turned: the women's personal photographs, CVs and blogposts have been dredged for evidence of sexual deviance, mental instability and vengeful intent. (Brooks 2010)

The myth that women are highly likely to make false reports of sexual violence, persistent despite the evidence that this happens no more frequently than in any other type of crime (Saunders 2012), relies on reactionary gender stereotypes about the vindictive woman and the victimized man, as well as resting on the assumption that 'real rape' involves a pathological stranger and a virginal victim (Belknap 2012; Kelly 2012). It was remarkable to see, in the case of Assange, the perpetuation of this myth by those on the political Left.

In the case of Dominique Strauss-Kahn, such ideas were extremely pronounced, perhaps partly because the incident was intertwined with the politics of class and 'race'. Three months after the New York accusations emerged, prosecutors filed a recom-mendation for dismissal of the charges, due to inconsistencies in the complainant's story and other suggestions of untruthfulness, for instance on statements related to her tax records and, critically, her asylum application. As the case fell apart, a media frenzy began, with vilification proceeding from various quarters. For Ben Stein (2011), her occupation itself appeared to be a strike against her integrity: in a statement beginning rather incongruously, 'I love and admire hotel maids', he went on to say, 'I have had hotel maids that were complete lunatics, stealing airline tickets from me, stealing money from me, throwing away important papers, [and] stealing medications from me.' In the French left-wing press, where Strauss-Kahn was especially staunchly defended, the com-plainant's identity was leaked before she chose to reveal it herself. Lévy spoke of a noble man who had been the victim of a 'spiral of horror and calumny', and also attacked the French journalist who had accused Strauss-Kahn of attempted rape in 2003: in his words, she 'pretends to have been the victim of the same kind of attempted rape, [and] has shut up for eight years but, sensing the golden opportunity, whips out her old dossier and comes to flog it on television.' American left-wing civil liberties lawyer Alan Dershowitz (2011) opined that the anonymity traditionally given to rape complainants should be withheld in order to make it possible to investigate their characters, seemingly in ignorance of the fact that 'rape shield laws' were originally instituted in order to protect plaintiffs from just this type of intrusive stigma (Call, Nice and Talarico 1991; Temkin 1995).

The attacks levelled at Strauss-Kahn's accuser also acquired a sexual nature, with the *New York Post* and other sources suggesting that she was a sex worker as well as a hotel housekeeper (Italiano 2011); an attempt to cast doubt upon her character which tapped into prevailing stigma surrounding sex workers and the common myth that, because they trade sex for money, they consent to all sexual acts (Phipps 2009). Beforehand, there had been suggestions in the press that Strauss-Kahn could be forgiven for mistaking the woman cleaning his room for a sex worker and therefore for assaulting her (Gira Grant 2011), which also drew upon class prejudice. An interview with a New York taxi driver was published in which he stated that she had 'big boobs and beautiful buttocks' (Cochrane 2011) as though this spoke to her sexual availability. Conversely, *Paris Match* ran quotes which negatively assessed her allure, and Strauss-Kahn's lawyers called her 'not very seductive' (Cochrane 2011), perpetuating the myth that only attractive women could be raped. There was a clear 'race' angle informing much of the reactionary politics: in *Le Parisien*, Lévy declared that Strauss-Kahn had been 'lynched' by the 'friends of [US] minorities', mobilizing neoconservative ideas of reverse discrimination and arguing that the poor, immigrant victim had been presumed innocent and the powerful politician had been assumed to be guilty (Chrisafis 2011a).

However, these elements of the case also appeared to inspire more left-wing support for Strauss-Kahn's complainant than either Assange's or Polanski's, especially in the United States. Her advocates highlighted a history of oppression and victimization, claiming that she had endured genital cutting and had been a child bride, and speculating that this had also been in a polygamous marriage (Ellison 2011). They contended that any falsehoods told in relation to her asylum application and other affairs were merely a product of her disadvantaged social position and certainly did not cast doubt upon her credibility in the sexual assault case (Ensler 2011; Fine 2012). Taina Bien-Aimé, director of international human rights organization Equality Now, decried the way in which Strauss-Kahn's complainant had been put on trial by the world's media as though both parties in the case were equals. The matter became a metaphor for the global politics of oppression and privilege, discussed in relation to the plight of domestic workers in general (Romero 2012) and also as an emblem of whole populations and regions of the world which found themselves at a disadvantage: 'Strauss-Kahn and the maid [*sic*] have become archetypes – the oppressor versus the oppressed, players in a morality play that has riveted people on both sides of the Atlantic' (Ellison 2011). The positioning of Strauss-Kahn's accuser as oppressed and victimized by her ethnic background as well as the sexual assault is particularly interesting, given contemporary left-wing reluctance to emphasize victimhood in relation to cultural issues. However, the precedence of 'race' over gender in the left-wing reaction to the case is perhaps easier to understand, given that the backlash against feminism has touched the Left as well as the Right, whereas in contrast, contemporary left-wing multiculturalism and anti-racism have been strengthened by the neoconservative challenge.

Don't be a victim: the politics of personal responsibility

In all three cases, customary rape myths were augmented by a critique of the very notion of women's victimization, even from left-wing commentators. Writing on Strauss-Kahn, British journalist Deborah Orr (2011a) contended that viewing women as 'victims' of powerful men 'characterizes women as blank and passive, every bit as much as the pre-feminism credo that insisted that women did not really like sex at all. It must surely be acknowledged that even women, we paragons of virtue, are capable of finding power, esteem and wealth to be sexually attractive.'

European sex radical Laura Agustin (2010), who was called as an expert witness in the Assange hearings, similarly argued that Swedish rape law positioned women as helpless victims and termed everything disagreeable rape and abuse. Naomi Wolf claimed that rape shield laws were Victorian relics which did not treat women as moral adults (Naomi Wolf 2011), associating the protection offered by anonymity with archaic notions of feminine helplessness rather than seeing it as a response to the stigma and risk that sexual violence complainants face. Comments such as this equated claiming victimization with abrogating one's agency, and set it against women's empowerment and sexual liberation. They can be seen as both reflecting recent developments in feminist thinking and shaped by a neoliberal individualism in which victimhood is seen as either an identity or a psychological state.

As Beck and Beck-Gernsheim (2002) and others have argued, the contemporary self is a 'do-it-yourself' project: it can be made or unmade at will in a free market of endless opportunities. This 'meritocracy' produces disapproval of social 'failures' who are seen as lacking in entrepreneurial instinct and personal responsibility, and judged harshly if they complain. This rests upon a rather rudimentary transformation of ideas about agency into the concept of 'choice': one can choose to be a victim, and can also refuse this designation and make the best of one's lot in life. The ideal neoliberal subject, then, is one who faces adversity and makes the best of all situations. This contemporary 'positive thinking' can be criticized for its lack of attention to structural inequalities and the fact that the socially privileged may have more resources to deal with life's challenges. The pressures it creates to evade victimhood have been highlighted in empirical research: for instance, Baker (2010) conducted interviews with 55 young women in Australia who went to great lengths to avoid the 'victim' label, associating it with a lack of personal responsibility and control. This was particularly pronounced amongst the more disadvantaged in the sample. Negative experiences – including sexual and domestic violence – were presented as ultimately strengthening: this compares with McCaffrey's (1998) study of sexual violence survivors in the United States, who also emphasized taking responsibility for themselves. These themes were echoed recently in the international One Billion Rising initiative, created by American *Vagina Monologues* author Eve Ensler as a means for women to come together and (literally) dance to 'rise above' experiences of sexual violence. Although it undoubtedly had positive aspects and effects, Ensler's project also corresponded well with the neoliberal lexicon, and was criticized by women in the global South and elsewhere as being individualistic, patronizing and neocolonial (Gyte 2013).

There is psychological work involved in living up to the strictures of neoliberal individualism, and this can have punitive social and psychological consequences for those who fail to evade victimhood or 'choose' not to rise above their misfortune (Gruber 2009; Baker 2010). Indeed, the self-responsibility of the women in Baker's (2010) sample translated into a lack of sympathy for others, especially those they perceived as careless. This also needs to be seen in the context of declining social safety nets in western countries which is scaffolded by the demonization of dependency in social policy and popular culture (Baker 2010). Individualization is part of a lengthy process of depoliticizing the postmodern and neoliberal subject: inner transformation has taken the place of social change (Foucault 1988a, b; Mardorossian 2002: 756). Furthermore, this is reflected in the 'turn to interiority' in social and cultural theory, which has had two major effects in relation to sexual violence scholarship: a dominance of models that emphasize individual subjectivities while de-emphasizing the social and structural (Mardorossian 2002), and a preponderance of postmodern/post-structural work in which 'victim' is juxtaposed with agency, and in which sexual violence itself is framed and even produced by discourse. The latter has emerged directly from theoretical challenges to the politics of 'experience', most prominently Brown's (1995) critique of the feminist movement for writing sexual subordination into politics and law and inscribing femaleness as violability. Feminism, Brown argues, has fixed women's identities as 'wounded' and solidified the state in the category of 'protector', creating dependent subjects who are then easier to regulate.

Seen in this light, the comments of Wolf and others can be better understood. Indeed, the neoliberal politics of personal responsibility has developed alongside debates within the feminist movement, with radical feminists in particular seen as responsible for emphasizing women's experiences of subordination and constructing them as helpless and passive. Postmodern suspicion of the term 'victim' and politics grounded in the idea of a universal and unified women's experience has shaped the direction of contemporary feminist thought and action: recent approaches to sexual violence in particular have tended to emphasize women's resistance and agency, with victimhood seen as an unhelpful second-wave relic which has problematic links with neoconservatism (Marcus 1992; Gavey 1999; Convery 2006). There has also been a shift away from mechanisms of state support, conceptualizing these as paternalistic and expressing suspicion at how feminist anti-rape politics has, often unwittingly, been co-opted by 'law and order' agendas (Bumiller 2008). Critiques of the 'politics of pity' (Aradau 2004) have analysed how this can fit well with neoconservative criminal justice and moral projects, and uses victims' voices as a tool of state regulation (there are links here with trafficking politics). There have also been particular sensitivities around not objectifying women in 'developing' countries by positioning them as passive victims of practices considered by the West to be barbaric, and thereby strengthening neo-imperial agendas.

For some postmodern feminists, naming victims or oppressions articulates victim psychology (Convery 2006): this has been echoed in therapeutic parlance, in which the term 'survivor' has become common currency, with victimization seen as a state it is important to overcome. Recent western psychological literature has positioned victimhood as underdevelopment in the journey towards self-actualization (Convery 2006), partly in reaction to the gradual pathologization of the 'victim' which, it is argued, has meant that being one has become analogous to having a long-term illness. It is felt that these discourses have shaped victims' own conceptualizations of their experience and limited their agency

(Lamb 1999). There been similar criminological critiques of the concept, in which it is positioned as an identity and even a 'career' in relation to the criminal justice system and 'helping' professions (Walklate 2011: 183). The dominant focus now is upon the journey of personal empowerment and choice to move from 'victim' to 'survivor', seen through the lens of resilience, which helps to illuminate 'how it is that some people do well in their lives, despite being exposed to adverse life chances, while others exposed to those same adverse conditions, do not' (Walklate 2011: 180).[2]

Such debates have also been echoed by more populist arguments, which began to emanate in the 1990s from the margins of the feminist movement or from disillusioned former activists, many based in the United States. Christina Hoff-Sommers (1994) lamented what she saw as a shift within feminism from liberal demands for equal rights to seeing women as victims of patriarchy. Terming this latter 'gender feminism', she set it against 'equality feminism' which, she argued, correctly sought answers to social problems not in structural change but in women's individual self-fulfilment. Similarly, Wolf (1994) in the 1990s compared 'victim feminism' to 'power feminism', contending that the former was analogous to the Victorian invalid who relished the power over others that her illness brought (it is not difficult to see here the seeds of her defence of Assange). Journalist Katie Roiphe and maverick academic Camille Paglia both targeted feminist sexual violence politics, arguing that this reinforced women's vulnerability by celebrating their victimhood (McCaffrey 1998). Roiphe (1994) explicitly combined postmodern and neoconservative ideas in her analysis of campus feminist anti-rape campaigns as *producing* victims and potential victims through the developing 'date rape' narrative, which positioned women as weak, fragile creatures without any sexual desire. Such analyses tapped into the broader western backlash against feminism which constructed it as paranoid, grasping, anti-sex and anti-men (Faludi 1992).

Aspects of these arguments were also taken up by right-wing commentators, informing their impatience towards certain 'victims', such as welfare claimants, single mothers and asylum-seekers. This took postmodern ideas around the discursive shaping of experience and distorted them to a point at which 'constructed' became 'made up'. In relation to sexual violence, customary right-wing incredulities were strengthened: for instance, when the term 'date rape' was created in the 1990s, neoconservative critics in the United States suggested that, previously, the experience itself did not exist (Gilbert 1991, 1995). Set within these narratives, social justice advocacy was constructed as oppressive and controlling 'victimology' and 'political correctness', and neoconservatives were positioned as champions of free speech. It was argued that claims of victimization were fabricated or exaggerated, and that the 'cult of victimhood' had been manipulated to obtain special treatment or public sympathy (Cole 1999; Convery 2006). Groups pleaded 'victimhood' to evade personal responsibility, it was contended, and this set in train a cycle of dependency (Convery 2006). Ironically, however, these same conservatives often positioned themselves as 'victims' of 'special interests' (Coulter 2009) – there are links here with Lévy's defence of Dominique Strauss-Kahn, even though it came from the political Left.

Where 'victimhood' is concerned, then, the contemporary context sees a strong message emanating from a variety of different quarters and political persuasions. Neoliberal ideas about personal responsibility and neoconservative anti-victim rhetoric commingle with postmodern critiques of 'victim' subjectivity as a form of governance to create a politics in which victimhood is either a state of laziness or dependence or a sign of psychological underdevelopment and a disciplinary regime. Postmodern ideas about agency are transmuted by both neoliberal and neoconservative discourses into a rather facile formulation of 'choice', although there is little discussion of perpetrators' agency or choices. In terms of sexual violence, the old dichotomy between 'madonna' and 'whore' which defined 'undeserving' and 'deserving' victims (Phipps 2009) may now have been augmented by a new one based on ideas about personal responsibility. This individualistic politics is very western (Woodhead and Wessley 2010) and needs to be contextualized in relation to cuts to statutory services and violence against women funding. It is also, I contend, both produced by and productive of the backlash against feminism.

Feminism, neoconservatism and sexual violence

It is often illuminating to examine the silences in political debates: in the three case studies covered in this chapter, there was very little gender commentary and a certain amount of gender essentialism mobilized on the Left as well as the Right. Supporters of all three men attempted to excuse their actions via the construction of male sexuality as somehow inevitable, reflecting neoconservative gender traditionalism as well as tapping into the neoliberal sexualization of consumer culture and possibly even the resurgence of evolutionary theory. The message was clear: powerful men have powerful urges (McRobie 2011), and, once set in train, their sexual desires are difficult if not impossible to check. Assange, it was claimed, was a man of 'strong sexual appetites' (Pendlebury 2010), and the status of both Strauss-Kahn and Polanski as infamous womanizers was thought to make their actions understandable, if not unavoidable (Evans 2005; McRobie 2011). Strauss-Kahn's wife described him as a 'seducer', informing the press that the weekend of the alleged assault in Manhattan he had already had sexual relations with three other women in preparation for his presidential bid (NewsCore 2011, cited in Fine 2012), as though promiscuity self-evidently went hand-in-hand with power. Similarly, Tracy Quan (2010) speculated that the allegations against Assange might actually contribute to his popularity and status as a 'sex symbol'.

These representations framed the idea of sexual assault as merely seduction gone awry, an assiduous myth which has been refuted repeatedly by years of feminist research and theorizing of rape as a product of gendered power relations (Cahill 2001). George Galloway, ex-leader of the UK socialist party Respect, argued that Assange's actions amounted to 'bad sexual etiquette' rather than a crime, stating, 'not everybody needs to be asked prior to each insertion' (BBC News 2012b). His comments were widely

criticized and led to the departure of his successive Respect leader
Salma Yaqoob (Quinn 2012), but Galloway also received a great
deal of support, including from far-left network Socialist Unity
(Socialist Unity 2012). In influential left-wing political newsletter
Counterpunch, American economist and prominent 'war on terror'
opponent Paul Craig Roberts (2010) also asked: 'Think about this
for a minute. Other than male porn stars who are bored with it all,
how many men can stop at the point of orgasm or when approach-
ing orgasm? How does anyone know where Assange was in the
process of the sex act?' This is an example of what Adrienne Rich
in 1980 (645) termed the 'penis with a life of its own' argument;
taking as given the patriarchal rights of men over women's bodies
and mobilizing an adolescent model of a male sex drive which
'once triggered cannot take responsibility for itself or take no for
an answer' (Rich 1980: 646).

Given such regressive arguments from his advocates, it is
perhaps fitting that liberal hero Assange styled himself as the victim
of vengeful radical feminists. Calling the prosecutor a 'man-hating
lesbian' and Sweden a 'man-hating matriarchy' (Norman 2012a),
he claimed that he had fallen into a 'hornet's nest of revolutionary
feminists', and that Sweden was like Saudi Arabia for men (Miriam
2010). His supporters followed suit, with Pendlebury (2010)
terming one of the complainants a 'well-known radical feminist'
and stating that she had been 'the protégée of a militant feminist
academic', as if this somehow damaged her credibility. The prosecution lawyer was termed a 'gender lawyer', and 'malicious radical
feminist' who was 'biased against men', by retired senior Swedish
judge Brita Sundberg-Weitman (Addley 2011). In *Counterpunch*,
the other complainant was described as a 'vengeful radical feminist'
and Sweden as a 'female kingdom' (Shamir and Bennett 2010)
while, on the website Justice for Assange, it was incorrectly
claimed that in Sweden women had more rights than men. Tracy
Quan (2010) wondered whether living in egalitarian Sweden had
made Assange's accusers hungry for the 'insensitivity' he could
provide. This characterization of feminism as biased, vindictive and
anti-men is emblematic of the neoconservative backlash (Faludi
1992), but in this case was used by an anti-establishment figure and

his supporters, perhaps indicating the relatively precarious position of feminism at both ends of the political spectrum.

Similarly, in relation to Strauss-Kahn, Dershowitz (2011) argued that sex crimes prosecutors were agenda-driven zealots. Human rights campaigner and former diplomat Craig Murray went further to contend:

> The DSK case and the Assange case have brought to the fore the true ugliness of sex negative feminism and man hatred, and the extent to which they made inroads into our culture and society just as insidious as the right-wing propaganda of the Murdochs. They have also shown how those right-wing forces can so easily hijack stupid blinkered man haters to the right-wing agenda. (Murray 2011)

While pejorative, this quote cites a legitimate set of concerns which has materialized around the links between radical feminism and right-wing agendas. Alongside the neoconservative backlash against feminism, there has been a rather contradictory enmeshment of some forms of feminist activism, particularly in the sexual violence arena, with crime control and the incarceration of certain groups of underprivileged men (Daly 2006). Radical feminists have advocated a host of reforms to punish gender-based crimes which have often had the unintended effect of strengthening the state's coercive power (Gruber 2009). Sexual violence is now couched almost exclusively in the language of crime, with very little attempt at more sophisticated analyses. This also informs international activism on violence against women, which is often co-opted by neoconservative rhetorics constructing other cultures as inherently violent and dysfunctional and using women's victimization as a rhetorical device to justify culturally, politically and economically imperialist projects. This has a long history, cited by Women Against Rape in their defence of Assange:

> There is a long tradition of the use of rape and sexual assault for political agendas that have nothing to do with women's safety. In the south of the US, the lynching of black men was often justified on grounds that they had raped or even looked at a white woman.

Women don't take kindly to our demand for safety being misused.
(Axelsson 2010)

This marriage of radical feminist and neoconservative agendas
has largely been one of convenience, and voluntary sector groups
and services, in the battle to survive, frequently lack the luxury
of reflecting upon their bedfellows (Bumiller 2008). However,
many feminists who have instinctually seen their role as fighting
against the patriarchal state have lamented the fact that feminism
is now publicly and politically associated with crime control
(Bumiller 2008; Gruber 2009). There are also differences between
and among white and racialized women in the degree to which
the state and the criminal justice system are viewed as trustwor-
thy and effective sites for responding to violence against women
(Daly 2006). The strongest critiques have come from those of the
postmodern persuasion, although it could be argued that postmodern and 'third wave' preoccupations with sexual identities
and empowerment, often defined in neoliberal terms, have left
contemporary radical feminists with few allies (this can also be seen
in anti-trafficking politics). The convergence of feminist concerns
with women's victimization with neoconservative projects of
social control partially explains left-wing ambivalence in relation
to feminist sexual violence politics. However, this can also be seen
to have produced the various forms of rape apologism seen in the
three cases discussed here.

The uneasy relationship between feminism and the Left, then,
is inextricably linked to the fight against neoconservatism. In
the three case studies in this chapter, this was particularly apparent, with all the men positioned as victims of an overzealous US
criminal justice system and their supporters styling themselves as
the forces of progressiveness and freedom. This was particularly
manifest in the case of Assange: his status as an anti-American hero
situated him, for some of his supporters, as incapable of perpetrating
sexual violence. Instead, it was claimed that he had been the victim
of a CIA sting and a project to eventually extradite him to the
United States to answer charges related to WikiLeaks. Supporters
such as Michael Moore, Naomi Klein, Naomi Wolf, Guantanamo

survivor David Hicks and the European group Women Against Rape all made statements questioning the nature and purpose of the prosecution. Moore called the case 'a bunch of hooey', while American left-wing political commentator Mark Crispin Miller claimed that one of Assange's accusers had CIA and anti-Castro ties, a rumour repeated by a number of others (Harding 2010; Miriam 2010; Pollitt 2010). In *Counterpunch*, Roberts wrote:

> If reports are correct, two women, who possibly could be CIA or Mossad assets, have brought sex charges against Assange. Would a real government that had any integrity and commitment to truth try to blacken the name of the prime truth teller of our time on the basis of such flimsy charges? Obviously, Sweden has become another two-bit punk puppet government of the United States. (Roberts 2010)

This framing of the case as a matter of anti-imperial struggle eventually led to Assange being granted asylum by Ecuador on the grounds of human rights (Hughes 2012): the irony of this when set against the charges against him, as well as Ecuador's own record on human rights and free speech, was not lost on some commentators (Braiker 2012). Following this, Assange was also offered (and accepted by proxy) an Aboriginal Nations passport in a ceremony in Sydney, with Indigenous Social Justice Association president Ray Jackson stating that the Australian government had not given the WikiLeaks founder sufficient aid (World News Australia 2012).

Polanski was also positioned as the victim of an overzealous US legal system intent on sentencing him for an ancient crime. Many of his champions stressed the arbitrariness of the attempted extradition, after 31 years of official indifference (Bennett 2010). Others went further, placing Polanski as a hero and freedom fighter against a vengeful US state (Poirier 2010). Similarly, the US legal system was interpreted as malicious and fanatical in relation to Strauss-Kahn (Ellison 2011). French commentators were particularly aggrieved at how he was treated in New York, and French media were threatened with legal action for publishing photos of him in handcuffs, with the handcuffing itself characterized by some as 'hyper-violent' (Willsher 2011). Former French justice minister

Elisabeth Guigou said she found the photos of Strauss-Kahn on the front page of newspapers and magazines a sign of 'brutality and incredible cruelty', and expressed relief that the French justice system was not as 'accusatory' as that of the United States (Boot 2012: 96). Christine Boutin, head of France's Christian Democratic Party, was quoted as saying Strauss-Kahn had been trapped (Hallett 2011). A poll of the French public found that 57 per cent thought he had been framed (White 2011) by the Germans, President Sarkozy or the United States (Zoe Williams 2011a).

What is particularly interesting here is not the point that allegations against the three men had been made at politically convenient times for the United States or that, because of extraneous factors, they had been treated in a more heavy-handed way than others accused of similar crimes; it is the attendant demand that, because of this, they should be allowed to evade justice, or the assumption that, due to the surrounding politics, the accusations could not be true. As a result of this dualistic framework, three men accused of sex crimes were able to emerge as heroes for some on the western Left (Haines 2011: 28). Following the allegations against Assange, he was invited to speak at the major anti-capitalist gathering Occupy LSX (London Stock Exchange), despite the fact that many women (and more than a few men) in the Occupy movement expressed discomfort (Willitts 2011), and during his time in the Ecuadorean Embassy was invited to give video addresses to both the Oxford and Cambridge Unions, although the latter was cancelled due to technical difficulties (Chan 2013). In 2012, Strauss-Kahn was also invited to address the Cambridge Union (Eden 2012), and, though more than 750 students subsequently signed a petition asking for this decision to be reconsidered (Levy 2012), the talk went ahead (BBC News 2012a).

The assumption that left-wing men are above misogyny is contradicted by a mass of evidence, relating to the 'old' socialist labour movement and also to more contemporary punk and anarchist communities (Clarke 2004). Furthermore, there have recently been stories concerning sexual harassment and assault being perpetrated and swept under the carpet in various Occupy camps on both sides of the Atlantic (Forty Shades of Grey 2011;

Miles 2011; *The Scotsman* 2011). There is some evidence that, in addition to positioning gender issues as secondary to movement unity, left-wingers may tolerate sexual transgressions under the banner of 'progressiveness' (Sere 2004; Wu 2004), a trend which could be observed especially in the positioning of Polanski as the victim of neoconservative prudes, or, as French writer Agnès Poirier (2010) put it, a 'rampant moral McCarthyism'. In this case, as Bennett (2010) commented, a question of individual justice was transformed into a more general stand-off between Europeans and rednecks, sophisticates and puritans. Similarly, Naomi Wolf (2011) compared Assange to Oscar Wilde and the 'case of morals' around him, and Strauss-Kahn complained that the 'prudish' press objected to his 'libertine lifestyle', with some of his supporters suggesting that the progressive French would tolerate sexual transgressions which other women did not (Alcoff 2011; Fassin 2011). The position of morality in the contemporary political lexicon is a fascinating one, appearing to have become a right-wing preserve while left-wingers attempt to distance themselves. Unfortunately feminism, particularly the radical strand, has also become caught up in this politics as a form of sexual morality, and at times the fight against neoconservative moralism and imperialism appears to justify misogyny.

Conclusion

The discussion in this chapter has used the cases of Julian Assange, Dominique Strauss-Kahn and Roman Polanski to explore the contemporary terrain of sexual violence politics. There has been no attempt to decide on the relative guilt or innocence of the three men: instead, I have examined the debates around the cases and attempted to link these to the broader political and discursive context of neoliberalism and neoconservatism. I have illuminated several aspects of what I see as a new matrix in sexual violence politics: a suspicion of victimhood and reluctance to moralize which fits well with neoliberal individualism, which has emerged partly in response to the association of radical feminist activism with neoconservative 'law and order' mentalities of social control. This is framed by two related backlashes: first, the right-wing backlash against feminism, which positions it as anti-men and concerned with 'political correctness' and 'victimology', themes which can also be seen in postmodern and 'third wave' critiques of other feminisms as prudish and insufficiently focused on women's agency; second, the left-wing backlash against the United States which situates it as the driver of current neoconservative projects and also shapes a discomfort with feminist 'victimology' as being implicated in these. This informs a left-wing ambivalence towards feminist sexual violence politics which can be seen in all three cases discussed here. This contemporary field inevitably presents difficulties of positioning for feminist thought and action, particularly in terms of how to honour the experience of sexual violence victims and survivors without playing into judgemental forms of morality or punitive forms of regulation.

A key current feminist attempt to navigate these waters is Slutwalk, a 'third wave' feminist initiative focused on women's rights to look and act as they please, without risk of or blame for sexual violence. Emerging in Canada in 2011 in response to a police officer's comment that in order to remain safe, women should 'avoid dressing like sluts', these marches and rallies subsequently spread throughout North America and worldwide to seventy-five cities in countries such as India, Poland, Argentina, Sweden, Australia, Brazil, the Netherlands and the United Kingdom (Valenti 2011; Ringrose and Renold 2012). Underpinning the protests was an attempt on the part of young women (and men supporting them) to reclaim the word 'slut' in positive ways as denoting a female sexual agency which nevertheless was not an incitement to violence. Many of the women (and some of the men) involved in the marches dressed in sexually provocative ways, but also carried banners (or wrote on their bodies) slogans such as 'my short skirt is not the problem' (Ringrose and Renold 2012: 334). The Slutwalk movement was hailed by some as a victory for the politics of resig-nification and an attempt to make feminism 'sexy' again, as well as a refusal of the neoconservative politics of 'slut-shaming' sexual regulation and blame and a vehicle for unity behind the shared identity of 'slut' (Ringrose and Renold 2012: 335).

However, this laudable attempt to avoid the politics of personal responsibility and neoconservative crime control can also be seen as embedded in neoliberal individualism and sexualized consumer culture, with no critical purchase on the white, western, patriarchal, capitalist, middle-class, heteronormative and ableist nature of the 'femininity' and sexuality which is being celebrated (Henry 2004: 71; O'Keefe 2004). Such feminism, which has been critiqued for being all sexual 'liberation' and no sexual politics, has generally been to the detriment of socio-economically disadvantaged women, women of colour and women from the global South (McRobie 2011) and has been criticized by black women's groups and others for embodying parochial concerns, despite its claims to universality (Crunk Feminist Collective 2011). In particular, these groups have argued that the sexual liberation offered to white, middle-class women through the reclamation of the word 'slut' is not available to women of colour, due to the strong associations of this word with historically entrenched racist ideologies and practices (Black Women's Blueprint 2011). Slutwalk London was also recently at the centre of controversy after one of its members posted an online defence of Assange, from which the group as a whole later distanced itself. This was cited by some commentators as a sign of the apolitical and contradictory nature of the Slutwalk movement as a whole (Ditum 2012; Willitts 2012). An alternative and older form of politics can be seen in Reclaim the Night (or 'Take Back the Night' in North America), which is also focused on women's rights to move through public space as they please, but roots itself in a more traditional radical feminism. However, this initiative has also been at the centre of controversy due to issues around its 'women only' policy and what this means for trans★ inclusion, which, even after clarifications of a trans★ inclusive approach,[3] has linked the movement to a broader problematic around the rather neoconservative gender essentialism which has been situated as part of some contemporary radical feminisms (Helen G 2012).

The contemporary terrain of sexual violence politics, then, is a fraught and precarious one, and it seems that the dialectic between neoliberalism and neoconservatism tends to structure feminist initiatives by propelling them towards one of these discursive frameworks, often in reaction to the other. It is also always edifying to examine the silences in contemporary political debates, and it is notable that the experiences of the complainants were either dismissed or erased by other political agendas in all three of the case studies discussed here. As Richard Adams wrote in the *Guardian* in relation to the women who had made allegations against Assange: 'Worst of all has been the suggestion that somehow their ordeal does not count, that they are an inconvenient distraction, the mad women in the attic, caught up in the clash of powerful forces involving the world's media and the US government in all its might' (Adams 2010).

This lack of focus on the experiential, even from feminist commentators, can be compared to the disproportionate attention seen in other debates covered in this book: for instance in sex work, where the politics of 'experience' and 'authenticity' has become an end in itself. This is no doubt in part due to the politically charged nature of the three case studies, which meant that each took on a life of its own: but it can also be argued that the experience of sexual violence victimization has been co-opted by the Right in such dubious ways that on the Left it has become risky to emphasize it.

3

Gender and Islam in a
Neoconservative World

In 2002, postcolonial feminist scholar Chandra Talpade Mohanty
revisited her classic article 'Under Western Eyes' (1984), in which
she had argued that western feminists had participated in a discursive
colonization of the 'Third World woman'[1] that was homogenizing in its picture of oppression. As an antidote, she had called for
grounded, particularized analyses: however, upon her return to
the text and in the context of a dwindling women's movement
(Mohanty 2002), she chose to focus more on transnational commonalities between women and the role of global economic and
political frameworks in producing disadvantage (see also Spivak
1993). Furthermore, she lamented that her original argument had
often been misunderstood, producing a concentration only upon
'situated' knowledges and a construction of 'western' and 'Third
World' feminisms in wholly oppositional terms, within contemporary postmodern and culturally relativist frameworks which she
identified as hegemonic. As a counterpoint to this, she argued that
scholars should be making use of post-positivist realist perspectives
on experience, culture and identity to establish relationality rather
than separation. She positioned the fight against globalizing capital,
rather than Enlightenment universalism, as most important in the

current context, and referred to the rise of a variety of religious fundamentalisms, 'with their deeply masculinist and often racist rhetoric' (Mohanty 2002: 508), as one of a number of political shifts to the right which posed profound challenges for feminism and required a truly transnational movement.

Many of these issues remain, and some of Mohanty's frustrations with feminist orthodoxies have been taken up, albeit within clumsier and more self-serving narratives, by the political Right. For instance, in 2007, American author Robert Spencer, who co-founded the neoconservative groups Stop Islamization of America and the American Freedom Defense Initiative, attacked feminist academics for hesitating to condemn female genital mutilation (*sic*) due to their multicultural preoccupations with difference and fears of being accused of racism. In the comments on his piece on the Jihadwatch blog, entitled 'Cultural Abdication' (Spencer 2007), emotive descriptions of women's experiences of genital cutting sat alongside racist characterizations of Muslims as sadistic 'whackos' and descriptions of feminists as 'useless graduates of Ivy universities [*sic*] who . . . are emotionally too fragile and mentally too stupid to work in the 9–5 world'. Similar themes could be seen in the comments on an article published by Sunny Hundal in left-wing periodical *The New Statesman* in 2012. Entitled 'The left cannot remain silent over "honour killings"' (Hundal 2012), it argued that political progressives should not assume that honour-based practices are an inherent part of Asian and other cultures, and remain silent out of a fear of being accused of racism or cooperating with neo-imperialist agendas. Right-wing readers commenting on the piece made remarks including declarations that 'Muslims' had low IQs due to 'forced cousin marriage', characterizations of Islam as a 'barbarically backward, infantile culture of misogyny', and the statement '[w]hen will the left continues [*sic*] to GROW UP and confront and explore the global Islamic Jihad, Islamic Jew Hatred, Islamic demonization of Israel, Islamic Gender Apartheid, Islamic Terror, Violence and Hate all inspired by the Koran.'

This positioning of Islam as threatening and diametrically opposed to western values, in particular that of gender equality, underpinned the French parliament's 2009 inquiry into the wearing of face veils, undertaken after President Nicolas Sarkozy stated they were not welcome in the secular Republic. Dalil Boubakeur, Grand Mufti of the Paris Mosque, testified that the niqab was not prescribed in Islam and was associated with radicalization and criminal behaviour, and that wearing it was inconsistent with France's concept of the secular state. A poll carried out in the period leading up to the vote indicated that 80 per cent of French voters supported the ban (Dumoulin 2010), which was passed in 2010 with overwhelming parliamentary support (Erlanger 2010). In the same year, the Belgian lower house of parliament approved a similar bill to ban facial coverings, citing public security and the emancipation of women, although this was not voted into law due to a change of government (Associated Press 2010a). Partial bans were also being discussed in the Netherlands and Spain and had been announced in some Italian localities (later declared unconstitutional), and public and political debates on the issue had been raging in Austria, Germany, Switzerland and the United Kingdom for some time, with UK schools given the authority to ban face veils in 2007 (BBC News 2007; Jamet 2010). After the French ban there were protests, with opponents arguing that it was a violation of civil liberties driven by Islamophobia (Chrisafis 2011b). It was also condemned by Amnesty International as a violation of freedom of expression and religion (Amnesty International News 2010).

The French ban was supported by Egyptian-American activist Mona Eltahawy, who called the niqab representative of 'an ideology which does not believe in Muslim women's rights to do anything but choose to cover her face [sic]', and stated that she would like to see similar laws passed in other countries (CNN 2011). In the May/June 2012 issue of *Foreign Policy*, Eltahawy published an article entitled 'Why Do They Hate Us?' (Eltahawy 2012), which argued that the real war on women was being waged by men in the Middle East. The piece provoked a great deal of controversy, with critics contending that it was lazy and full of generalizations (Malik 2012) and arguing that Eltahawy had manipulated statistics in the service of her argument (El-Hameed 2012). It was also suggested that she was being manipulated by the American neoconservative Right, as a 'cultural insider' who could provide a mouthpiece for their neo-imperial and Orientalist sentiments (El-Hameed 2012). Adele Wilde-Blatavsky (2012), an editorial collective member of the news site The Feminist Wire, published a statement in support of Eltahawy which revealed that a similar article she herself had written previously, focused mainly on the hijab and burqa, had been denounced in comparable ways. She had been attacked for being racist and imperialist, she wrote, as well as being subject to abuse due to her skin colour (white) and religious background (non-Muslim). Following the publication of her piece, Wilde-Blatavksy was expelled by the Feminist Wire collective and her content on their site (along with comments made in support of her) was deleted.

All these examples are intended to show the complex and oftentimes confusing nature of contemporary debates about gender, 'culture'[2] and the politics of women's bodies in relation to Islam in particular. We can observe here some rather peculiar rhetorics and political alliances which seem astonishing until they are located in the present macro-political context. As I will argue in this chapter, neoconservative imperialist projects, such as the 'war on terror', shape and produce concerns in the West for women's rights in Muslim-majority countries and communities. Furthermore, the current predominance of neoconservative constructions of Islam and the symbiotic relationship this has with popular anti-Muslim prejudice frame defensive strategies on the Left which include the prioritizing of 'cultural difference' over transnational commonalities, interpreted in some quarters as 'looking the other way', even when faced with evidence of gender-based oppression. This combines with an extant academic orthodoxy around the postmodern, the postcolonial and the multicultural which tends to focus on agency, multiplicity and pluralism, and sometimes privileges 'race' above gender in ways which risk playing into the backlash against feminism. As a result, it often appears that there is a gender-blindness in the broader field, except when 'women's issues' intersect with neoconservative projects. The two sides of the debate about 'Muslim women' and their bodies may appear completely incommensurable: however, in my analysis of this contemporary arena, I highlight a number of common themes which are, in my opinion, shaped by the influence of the overarching neoliberal consensus in politics, society and culture.

Setting the scene

There are two main frameworks at play, then, in the contemporary debate around Islam and women's bodies; the first glosses over complexities and nuance while the second is often caught up within them. On the Right, and dominant in policy and mainstream public opinion, is an Orientalist construction of 'Muslim women'[3] as victims in relation to issues such as veiling, honour killings, forced marriage and female genital cutting (termed 'mutilation' in this framework). This idea has often been deployed in the service of colonial and neocolonial aims and objectives, with gender issues being used as part of the justification for the historical colonization of Africa and the Middle East, and more recently underpinning contemporary neoconservative projects such as the 'war on terror'. On the Left, and increasingly dominant in academia and anti-war/anti-capitalist activism, is a focus on Muslim women's agency and resistance (often set against the encroachment of western values, markets and militaries), and a critique of the liberal notions of freedom and autonomy which position women in Muslim-majority countries and communities as oppressed.

A large number of feminists and others have highlighted how the 'war on terror', which commenced after the September 11th attacks on the World Trade Center and the Pentagon and is currently ongoing in Afghanistan, Pakistan and elsewhere, has mobilized women's bodies in the service of military intervention (see, for example, Ayotte and Husain 2005; Bhattacharyya 2008; Fernandez 2009; Bilge 2010). The burqa in particular is thought to have become the primary symbol in a new 'clash of civilizations' (Huntington 1993) which situates the major fault line between Islam and the West not as democracy but as gender and sexual freedom (Bilge 2010). After 9/11 and as anti-Muslim prejudice reached new heights in the West, Fernandez (2009: 270) argues, Islamophobia was increasingly hidden behind or legitimated by a concern for women. Western liberal democracy, with its attendant ideals of freedom and equality, was set against an Islam which was constructed as barbaric, savage and oppressive. These polarizations were then mapped on to the burqa and other issues such as honour killings, female genital cutting and forced marriage (see also Tissot 2011). This is an example of what Ahmed in 1992 termed 'colonial feminism', referring to the historical co-optation of feminist ideas of gender equality by right-wing imperial states and agendas.[4] However, in its contemporary form it is more intense, and incorporates a merging between 'women's issues' and other areas such as LGBTQ rights, with Islam positioned as reactionary and regressive in relation to an expansively sexually liberated West (Bhattacharyya 2008).

Such 'colonial feminism' is clearly homogenizing in its construction of the 'Muslim woman' and compounding of what are often diverse sets of practices representing multiple cultural and ethnic groups. It also erases the voices and subjectivities of women in Muslim-majority countries and communities in the West, being largely concerned with 'speaking for' rather than 'speaking with' or allowing women to speak for themselves. Spivak (1988) and other critics have gone so far as to term this a form of 'epistemic violence' since these narratives have a deep impact on the subjectivities of those they interpellate and reduce them to eternal victimhood in the face of a maniacal agency which is attributed to Muslim men, and the Taliban and al-Qaeda in particular (Ayotte and Husain 2005: 113, 121). This can be compared to the domestic 'politics of pity', through which women's sexual victimization is used as a rhetorical device by neoconservative states intent on social control. It also both creates and masks the conditions for material harms done to women in Muslim-majority and western countries by hiding the root causes of violence and structural issues such as health care, education and poverty, while at the same time detracting attention from gender oppression in the dominant culture.

These Orientalist ideas have recently met and been intensified by the populist and policy backlash in the West against multiculturalism and immigration and the move towards 'social cohesion', in which minority and immigrant rights are conceptualized as threatening women's rights (Saharso 2003; Bilge 2010; Gill and Mitra-Kahn 2012). Mullally (2011) traces how European controversies around the niqab and burqa coincided with concerns about immigration and a new politics of citizenship which encompassed a retreat from multiculturalism. In some states, there was an explicit 'gender turn' in citizenship testing in which immigrants were required to demonstrate their commitment to gender equality and in which practices defined as 'Islamic', in particular veiling, were directly or implicitly positioned as a failure to comply with western values. Ideas about gender equality have also often been combined with secularist concerns in arguments against the extension of rights to non-citizens. We can see, then, how contemporary western national identity and belonging is being at least partially formed in opposition to 'Muslims', and in particular the body of the 'Muslim woman'. Indeed, the withdrawal from multiculturalism has largely been expressed via a growing preoccupation with abuses of women in minority cultural groups, especially forced marriage, honour killings, female genital cutting and forms of dress perceived to be oppressive (Dustin and Phillips 2008).

This entanglement of women's protection with the politics of anti-immigration has, according to Dustin and Phillips (2008), made it difficult to address abuses of women without simultaneously promoting stereotypes of culture. Many western feminists have found their allies on the Right in this context, which can at least partially be seen as a form of *realpolitik* in difficult times. These feminists have joined LGBTQ groups and activists (see, for example, Tatchell 2009) in arguing for the importance of universal human rights and contending that anti-racism should not take precedence over equality for women or LGBTQ people. However, this politics has sometimes led to clashes between these groups and anti-racist activists who have argued that discourses of liberation have been co-opted in the service of power. There is a 'homonationalism' evident in campaigns against abuses of LGBTQ people in Muslim-majority societies, in which it is assumed that LGBTQ people the world over share the same experiences, sexual practices, needs, desires and identities. It is argued that this feeds the idea of western queerness as a symbol of 'freedom' which is used to rationalize projects such as the 'war on terror' (Puar 2007).

In contrast to neoconservative initiatives such as the 'war on terror' (and often formulated in direct opposition to them) is a focus on the agency and resistance of women in Muslim-majority countries and communities, set within a broader rejection of Orientalist constructions of women in 'developing' countries and a critique of western modernist-liberal versions of autonomy. This politics of difference refuses to situate Islam as a monolith, instead arguing that it can be a cultural toolkit of practices with an endless variety of meanings for diverse individuals, and that women can express agency through observance (see, for example, Bartowski and Read 2003; Avishai 2008). Religious and cultural forms of dress in particular are often seen as an act of resistance to capitalist sexualized femininity or colonial legacies (Guindi 1999; El-Hamel 2002; Parvez 2011), although there are also discussions of women's agency in relation to practices such as female genital cutting, with motivations cited such as increasing sexual pleasure or following group fashions (Leonard 2000; Meyers 2000).

This perspective has become dominant in academic discussions of gender and Islam (especially among postmodern and postcolonial scholars) and left-wing politics and activism, but has been critiqued by some as being overly romantic and culturally relativist (Abu-Lughod 1990; Davis 2004). In addition, it is argued, such multicultural perspectives often position 'race' above gender, which invisibilizes gender-oppressive cultural practices (Beckett and Macey 2001). This can be just as homogenizing as the 'colonial feminism' described above since it reifies culture and ignores intra-cultural power relations. It also erases the voices and subjectivities of women who are critical of their cultures, who are often positioned as western dupes (Abu-Lughod 1990). More strongly, it has been argued that left-wing multiculturalism has directly contributed to a contemporary legitimation of religious fundamentalism, which has led to a rather problematic justification of gender oppression in the name of cultural or political liberation and concealed the operation of radical Islam as a form of neoconservatism comparable to the US-led incarnation which is informed by fundamentalist Christianity (Winter 2001: 25).

This politics has coincided with the revival of radical Islam in the Middle East, Africa and Asia and amongst immigrant communities in the West, and also intersects with anti-imperialism on the activist Left, and the growth of a movement of anti-American resistance. The marriage of these various developments and perspectives has led to some rather contradictory positions, often due to the dissonance between the largely conservative gender values which characterize radical Islam and policy in Islamic states (Mahmood 2001; Stivens 2006) and the western Left's attempt to maintain a progressive approach to women's issues. A good example of this is the British Socialist Workers' Party's simultaneous support of Slutwalk and conservative groups such as Egypt's Muslim Brotherhood (Bassiouny 2012), which has a chequered history on women's rights (Danahar 2012), for instance recently claiming that a UN declaration calling for an end to violence against women would lead to the 'complete disintegration of society' (Kingsley 2013). The postcolonial and anti-imperialist politics of difference and resistance is often explicitly set against the colonial feminism of neoconservative projects of empire as though the two were completely incompatible. However, in this chapter I will argue that these two discourses share a number of common themes, many drawn from the dominant neoliberal lexicon. These include a focus on culture and identity often at the expense of structural analysis, rather individualistic formulations of empowerment and 'choice', and a tendency to essentialize which is apolitical, ahistorical and serves to inhibit constructive engagement.

Recognition, 'voice' and male privilege

First, on both sides of this debate we can identify a politics of recognition (or anti-recognition) around culture and identity, which has come to predominate over issues of structural oppression and social justice. This can be observed in right-wing 'ethnicization', whereby the actions of minority ethnic people are seen solely as expressions of their culture rather than as products of global power relations (Dustin and Phillips 2008) or as historically situated and temporally mediated. Indeed, 'culture' is routinely invoked to explain forms of violence against the 'developing' world or immigrant women where it is not similarly indicated in discussions of violence in the mainstream of the West (Volpp 2001; Gill and Mitra-Kahn 2012). However, a politics of recognition can also be read into left-wing silences, underneath which is a more generalized belief that it is oppressive to criticize other cultures, or disloyal for members of marginalized cultural groups to criticize their own (see Fraser 1995, 2000). In Hundal's (2012) article on honour killings, he tells the story of a poster reading 'Forced Marriage is Abuse, not Cultural', which was put up in an East London school at the request of the charity Karma Nirvana, but subsequently taken down by the head teacher due to concerns that it would upset Muslim parents. These concerns about being accused of cultural insensitivity or Orientalizing (Moghissi 1999) or playing into neoconservative imperialism or Islamophobia (Tadros 2009) have real material impacts: Meetoo and Mirza (2007) highlight how minority ethnic women can lack protection because governments and organizations are fearful of being seen as racist when taking a positive stance in relation to problems attributed to culture. In 2012, the UK debate on female genital cutting resurfaced with campaigners from groups such as Equality Now and MPs in the All-Party Parliamentary Group on Female Genital Mutilation (*sic*) arguing that the government had previously failed to push for prosecutions on the issue because it was afraid of being branded racist, and that police, health workers, teachers and other professionals shared those fears (Batha 2012).

Right-wing ethnicization and a responding tendency to 'walk on eggshells' on the Left have been identified in recent political discussions, for instance in the United Kingdom in relation to multiple linked cases of sexual abuse perpetrated by Asian men in Rochdale in 2012. A group of nine men was convicted of offences including sex trafficking, rape, and conspiracy to engage in sexual activity with a child. Forty-seven white girls were identified as victims during the investigation; eight of the men convicted were of British-Pakistani origin and one was an asylum-seeker from Afghanistan. During the case, it was claimed that one of the victims had reported her abuser in 2008, but he was not charged due to police fears of being labelled racist (Norman 2012b). In a radio interview, ex-head of Barnardo's children's charity Martin Narey highlighted what he called a 'disproportionate number' of men of Pakistani origin involved in such crimes. Around the same time, extreme-right British National Party leader Nick Griffin took to Twitter to hold forth about 'Muslim paedophile rapists'. Countering statements such as this, Labour MP Keith Vaz warned about the perils of 'stigmatizing a whole community' and produced statistics showing that more young people were abused by white men than those of Pakistani origin (White 2012).[5] Some commentators noted a silence in the press about the connections of the cases with culture and 'race', thought to be rooted in a fear of giving ammunition to far-right groups (Norman 2012b; White 2012). Similar discussions were heard in 2013 in relation to an analogous case which occurred in Oxford (Vallely 2013), and silences on the part of the western Left, and feminists in particular, were also highlighted in relation to a spate of brutal sexual assaults on girls and women in India (Parashar 2012).

This politics of recognition (and anti-recognition) relies on a construction of Islam as an identity or a culture; interesting in light of the parallel growth in fundamentalist Christianity in the United States, which is not seen in the same terms. Malik (2007), writing about the history of multicultural policy in Bradford, charts a shift from political issues such as policing and immigration to cultural ones such as Muslim schools and separate education for girls, a campaign for *halal* meat to be served in schools, and confrontations over offence caused by Salman Rushdie's novel *The Satanic Verses*. Similar processes of 'ethnicization' have also been observed elsewhere in Europe and in the United States (Kurien 2003; Modood 2003). It has been argued that culture and ethnicity are now seen as a means of pursuing social and political ends (Anthias 2002), whether these are characterized as anti-western terror or anti-colonial liberation. Neither side of the debate around gender and

Islam very often features more nuanced distinctions between Islam as a religion and Islam as a (conservative or radical, depending on your viewpoint) political or state project. Within these rather homogenizing discourses of cultural condemnation or celebration, Islam is all-fundamentalist or all-progressive and differences within it, its different forms, incarnations and, most importantly, uses, are erased. There has been a failure to note the dynamic character of culture (Davis 2004), with ethnic identities defined as 'possessive properties rather than fluid and processual social relations' and no attempt to deconstruct the hierarchies *within* cultures (Anthias 2002: 280). This, says Anthias (2002: 276), amounts to a 'museumizing' of culture which can become rather idealistic.

Within left-wing identity politics, emotional and personal vocabularies are now often substituted for political ones, an 'expressivist' model (see Edwards 2004) which is not socio-economic but rooted in matters of difference. In some quarters, sensitivity has replaced justice: this can be seen in the use of the term 'Islamophobia' to denote anti-Muslim prejudice. Although this term, like 'homophobia', has been useful in highlighting the often irrational hatred which underpins discrimination (Davids 2009; Strudwick 2012), it also risks turning discussions about structural inequality and issues of justice into issues of personal feeling. For instance, after US retailer Lowe's pulled its advertising from the reality TV show *All-American Muslim* in 2011 in response to complaints from an anti-Muslim organization (CNN Wire Staff 2011), an article in *Psychology Today* discussing the case presented Islamophobia as a 'cognitive distortion' associated with negative and emotional thinking (Saedi 2011). Within this framework, issues of social and political oppression can be recast solely as matters of personal prejudice, with bigotry opposed but not properly understood, because it is not contextualized or historicized within power relations which function at broader levels. This lack of attention to the contextual and historical also makes it possible for critiques of oppressive practices situated within Muslim-majority societies or communities to be labelled 'Islamophobic' if they are heard at personal or cultural, rather than structural, levels. This serves to close down debate, for instance in relation to academic feminist engagements with the problematics of practices such as veiling or forced marriage (see, for example, Hasan 2012) and activist protests such as those staged by the (admittedly dubious) topless feminist group FEMEN against Sharia law in European cities and at the London Olympics (Badcock 2012).

The personal nature of this politics also shapes an emphasis on 'voice' on both sides, with experiential accounts used as evidence of culture-based oppression or liberation often in the absence of a more expansive analytical framework. Furthermore, because very few Muslim voices are heard in the West (Wing and Smith 2005), those which are audible become increasingly loaded and are likely to represent those with educational and social privilege. Jacobsen and Stenvoll (2010) point to the proliferation of personal accounts within 'victim discourse' around Muslim women, with 'experts' or 'native informants' (such as Mona Eltahawy or Ayaan Hirsi Ali) brought forward to testify to the oppressive nature of various cultural practices (see also Majid 1998; Bilge 2010). These 'internal feminist Orientalists', as Bilge (2010: 16) terms them, are part of a broader group of 'native' critics of Islam who have been criticized in some quarters for seeking notoriety and being entrapped in mainstream western perceptions and values (Majid 1998; Meyers 2000; Tadros 2009). This characterization, often put forward in academic circles, echoes those propounded in the political sphere by Muslim groups and Islamic governments which condemn opponents as individuals who have sold out to the West and its values (Tadros 2009).

In opposition to this, the left-wing politics of 'voice' mobilizes the notion of authenticity, with practices seen as being of value if they are 'authentic' to a community and alternative native informants being used to attest to their empowerment via religion and culture. This politics meets the postmodern academic celebration of 'authentic', 'local' and 'situated' practices, as well as its hostility to western modernity (Moghissi 1999). Islam in particular is seen as 'the most authentic voice of the South in its struggle against the western-inspired and racially informed hegemonic aims of transnational capital' (Majid 1998: 341). However, this politics also has much *in common* with recent developments in global capitalism; namely, the marketing of culturally 'authentic' products, such as clothing, music and foods, and experiences such as package tours which allow travellers to meet 'natives' (see, for example, AuthentiCity 2012). This focus on authenticity is now also informing international development practice, with experts attempting to harness the power of religion as an identity in order to reach eastern and southern hearts and minds, and as a politics in order to create social change (Sholkamy 2009). In the arena of women's rights specifically, this is seen as the ideal means of winning gains for equality in indigenous, authentic, participatory and culturally appropriate ways, although it often excludes 'native' feminists who wish to use frameworks other than cultural or religious ones, terming them disloyal (Tadros 2009). Furthermore, in this current pursuit of the 'authentic' and 'native', questions need to be asked about who represents these terms.

As Anthias (2002) points out, it is often the traditional male voices who represent the 'cultures' of groups, and it is possible to argue that Muslim cultures, like western ones, are dominated by socially advantaged men (Winter 2001). For example, the '500 most influential Muslims' list, published yearly at Georgetown University in the United States, contains so few women that they have their own small section separate from the main categories: in the first edition in 2009, forty-three of the five hundred were women and only one woman appeared in the top fifty, which was headed by King Abdullah of Saudi Arabia, the Ayatollah Khomeini and King Mohammed of Morocco (Royal Islamic Strategic Studies Centre 2009). There have been a number of critiques emanating from academics and community groups, of 'multiculturalism' as being in part a contract between patriarchal states and conservative religious leaders in which dominant cultural norms, often patriarchal ones, are taken to be the values and practices of a whole group (Dustin and Phillips 2008). Multicultural policy, Reddy (2008) argues, often serves to strengthen such dominant groups and individuals and means that dissenters are less likely to be able to take an active part in defining 'culture'. It is interesting to note here that the pro-hijab protests in Washington DC, in reaction to a 2004 law banning conspicuous religious symbols in schools, were organized almost entirely by men and some women involved reported that they felt pressured to participate (Wing and Smith 2005).

Individualism, empowerment and 'choice'

In some debates, particularly those relating to women's dress, the idea of Islam as an identity and notions of 'authenticity' in relation to particular cultural practices sit uncomfortably alongside a rational-individualist conception of 'choice'. Veiling in its various different forms, but especially the niqab and burqa, has come under intense media and political scrutiny in recent years, with two competing extant interpretations. The first centres on veiling as a symbol of patriarchal force and an oppressive culture. The second has emerged partly in response to this, and asserts that covering is a choice which symbolizes women's empowerment and resistance to western hegemony and capitalist sexualized femininity (Hussein 2007; Bilge 2010; Rana 2011). In discussions of veiling-as-oppression, neoconservative cultural imperialism meets the concerns of some feminists, mainly of the liberal and radical persuasion. In veiling-as-resistance, neoliberal ideas of individual agency and self-invention can be observed at work alongside postmodern and postcolonial feminisms and some neo-Marxist frameworks. Both narratives are simplistic and do not reflect the body of ethnographic research revealing the complexity of contemporary headscarf/veil cultures and the numerous reasons why women might choose to cover their hair, bodies and faces (Bilge 2010: 14). As Bilge (2010) argues for example, postcolonial accounts which focus on anti-capitalist resistance often fail to address the reasons of piety, morality, modesty, virtue and divinity more frequently given by veiled women.

The veiling-as-resistance narrative has become a common refrain among Muslim women in the West and can be seen as partly produced by the dichotomous nature of contemporary politics and efforts to avoid making alliances with neoconservative projects or inflaming anti-Muslim prejudice, discrimination and harassment (Hussein 2007; Mustafa 2011). Debating Eltahawy on the French face-veil ban, Egyptian-American MuslimMatters blogger Hebah Ahmed defined her own choice to adopt the niqab as a form of empowerment and protest against sexual objectification, and stated 'I have never met a single Muslim woman in all of my travels around the world that is being forced to wear it' (CNN 2011). However, Hussein argues that although 'choice' is an easily digestible message in media terms, it tends to erase other rationales and motivations, and glosses over complexities. It is a meaningless concept, she contends, when it involves 'negotiating racist prejudice and harassment on the one hand, and/or family and community conflict and pressure on the other' (Hussein 2007: 8). This double bind between patriarchy and racism which structures women's choices to cover or not is also felt by Muslim activists and scholars as they attempt to negotiate the choppy political waters around Islam and women's dress, as Hussein further explains:

> By seeking to complicate the discourse of hijab-as-choice, I risk giving aid and comfort to those who attack hijabis in the national parliament, in the media, and on the street. By challenging the notion of hijab-as-force, I risk appearing to defend regimes and social forces that impose mandatory covering and/or hold Hilali-esque attitudes to non-veiling. In [the] face of this dilemma, the temptation to stay silent is almost overwhelming. (Hussein 2007: 4)

'Choice', then, must be socially situated: but in many contemporary accounts it is decontextualized, with the process of deciding in itself seen as empowering (Meyers 2000), regardless of the circumstances, content or effect. This formulation of choice can be seen in other debates in this book, for instance that around sex work, and it is only in relation to such abstracted single-issue politics that some contemporary positions can be understood, for example the Socialist Workers' Party's simultaneous support for Slutwalk and the Muslim Brotherhood, which rapidly becomes incoherent if one situates these groups within their broader political and social milieu. This framework around choice is cognizant with the neoliberal idea of the individual as rational, calculating, entrepreneurial and self-regulating. It also casts aside the most relevant elements of postmodern and post-structural theory and psychoanalysis, which focus on the formation of the subject within networks of discourse and the importance of unconscious investments and contradictory positionings (Gill 2007). Indeed, as Gill (2007: 76) argues, the autonomous, freely choosing subject is 'apparently not governed by any forces other than those she could fully articulate if asked to do so by an academic interviewer'.

This narrative is also easily mobilized by the more libertarian right: for instance, it can be seen in statements made about women's individual 'freedom of choice' in relation to how they dress by Conservative Environment Secretary Caroline Spelman during the UK debates about the niqab and burqa: 'We are a free country, we attach importance to people being free and for a woman it is empowering to be able to choose each morning when you wake up what you wear' (Indo Asian News Service 2010). However, the contrasting right–wing perspective, that of the veil as fundamentally oppressive, can also be seen as neoliberal in its equation of sexuality with agency, contradicting the neoconservative moral sentiments which generally hold sway within right-wing frameworks and exposing the *realpolitik* underpinnings of these concerns for the rights of Muslim women. More recently there has also been a shift of anti-veil rhetoric away from discussions of patriarchal control, and towards the idea of veiling as a symbol of religious separatism, chosen by women themselves as an act of defiance against the West (Hussein 2007: 14). The idea of 'choice' here has been co-opted by racist ideologies in a way similar to the 'gay gene' debate, in which Christian evangelicals have positioned homosexuality as a choice in order to make it a target of moralizing and normalizing judgement.

All these positions serve to mask the structural and material histories of particular cultural practices, with attention directed away from issues such as colonialism (in its various different forms, both historical and contemporary), economic restructuring, global societal inequalities and western border and immigration regimes (Jacobsen and Stenvoll 2010: 280). As Abu-Lughod (2002) reminds us, structure *shapes* culture: many 'authentic' Muslim rituals are a product of history and a variety of social and economic influences and interactions, some of which may have been less-than-positive (Winter 2001; El-Hamel 2002). The role of global capitalism and economic imperialism in shaping particular cultural practices is largely ignored (Mohanty 2002; Bilge 2010), and instead 'Islam' is set against the capitalist West as either a force of cultural authenticity and resistance on the Left, or a premodern jihad culture on the Right (El-Hamel 2002). However, contemporary political Islam can instead be positioned as a quintessentially modern political and identity project tied to nationalist, economic, social and cultural struggles, as is its answering 'Islamophobia' (Winter 2001; Scott 2007). The false distinction between the 'West' and the 'rest' in much of the debate also erases the influence (for better or worse) of western states in shaping Muslim forms of society and politics, and the history of indigenous groups informing the liberal western notions of freedom and empowerment which are now critiqued by post-colonial and postmodern scholars as being essentially western and therefore exclusionary (Mohanty 2002).

Contemporary radical and political Islam has been interpreted by some as a form of political neoconservatism which is related to the rise of extreme-right and Christian fundamentalist movements in the West (El Saadawi 1997; Moghadam 2001; Winter 2001; Mohanty 2002). However, by others it is situated as a radical reaction to neoconservatism, due to its shared positioning with the western Left in opposition to western imperialism and in particular to America (Moghissi 1999). Political Islam is implicitly positioned as a liberatory socio-political project on the Left due to its contemporary geopolitical framings: in previous historical moments with different conditions it has been situated very differently, for instance when Islamic governments or Muslim opposition movements have been backed by western powers (Moghissi 1999). This current interpretation of radical and political Islam is also informed by flows of migration and the links between religion, culture and belonging, as it has shifted away from being a symbol of repressive state power and become instead a focus for nostalgia and social and political struggle in western immigrant communities who may be located in hostile host societies (El-Hamel 2002). This is reflected in the increasing adoption of religious identities and practices among second-generation immigrants in western countries (see, for example, Crul and Vermeulen 2003), which is often taken out of context on the Right to fuel fears around the radicalization of these populations, intensified by the fact that 'home-grown' terrorists have perpetrated attacks carried out in Europe since 9/11 (Murshed and Pavan 2009).

Orientalisms and straw (wo)men

On both sides of the debate, and in accordance with the politics of recognition and relative invisibility of the structural, there is an assumption of essential difference rather than a search for commonality and solidarity, which is apposite to the depoliticizing and atomizing logic of late capitalism and neoliberalism (Mohanty 2002). On the Right, dichotomies are drawn between 'us' and 'them' in the service of neoconservative political projects, and left-wing perspectives often collapse into a proliferation of difference without politics, in the context of a postmodernist discourse which positions systematic thinking as 'totalizing' (Mohanty 2002: 504) and focuses only on the local, shifting and performative. This latter has been accused of fostering cultural relativism (Moghissi 1999: 52–3), an answer to right-wing imperialist constructions which nevertheless carries comparable remnants of historical Orientalisms (Ayotte and Husain 2005). For instance, Moghissi (1999) argues that the 'Muslim woman' who emerges in many contemporary postcolonial academic writings is romantically presented as dignified, spiritually empowered and immune from the toxic influence of the West, and Bilge (2010) and Mahmood (2005) have made similar arguments in relation to the romanticization of Muslim women's 'resistance' (see Hoodfar 2003; Jouili and Amir-Moazami

2006; and Haddad 2007 for examples). This can be seen as at least partially produced by feminist efforts to avoid gender essentialism in positioning Muslim women as the downtrodden counterparts of their liberated western sisters within a narrative in which all women want, and are oppressed by, the same things. However, it can also create cultural essentialisms in homogenizing the 'Muslim woman' and constructing her as essentially different from her western counterpart in unhelpful ways (Narayan 1998).

The veil in particular has become a totem of essential difference, with the niqab and burqa invested with almost animate powers and seen as essentially oppressive – or essentially empowering – outside the structural conditions under which they are either adopted or imposed (Ayotte and Husain 2005: 119). Now in many ways a racialized characteristic, the burqa has on the neoconservative Right become emblematic of women's suffering and representative of a collection of acts and practices such as forced marriage, female genital cutting and honour killings (Guindi 1999; Abu-Lughod 2002; Ayotte and Husain 2005; Martino and Rezai-Rashti 2008). These symbolics have been used to great political effect by right-wing politicians such as Nicolas Sarkozy, who have situated the veil itself as a threat to western values while, conversely, left-wingers such as US President Barack Obama have chosen to emphasize individual personal choice but have been critiqued for ignoring the broader problems faced by women in Muslim-majority societies (Power 2009). Both forms of politics homogenize a diverse set of populations, values and practices across the Middle East and parts of Africa and Asia. They also ignore the fact that covering has been utilized in very different ways depending on the context: it has been forced upon women by Islamic governments, for instance in Iran and Saudi Arabia, has been adopted as an expression of agency against secular governments in Turkey, Egypt and Algeria, and has been used strategically by the Revolutionary Association of the Women of Afghanistan (RAWA) for smuggling books and supplies, filming abuses and to help women flee persecution (Ayotte and Husain 2005: 117). There has also been a disproportionate emphasis on the veil as compared to other major issues of significance (Power 2009).

In contrast to the melodramas which have played out around the veil, cultural essentialisms have produced minimization of or justification for other practices on both sides of the political field. For instance, honour killings and forced marriages have been incorrectly dismissed as 'Muslim phenomena' on the Right, which has shaped a rather laissez-faire attitude and an unwillingness to engage with parallel forms of violence in western society, and an interpretation of western 'crimes of passion' as aberrations rather than emblematic of western culture (Volpp 2000; Gill 2006; Reddy 2008; Fernandez 2009; Meetoo and Mirza 2007).[6] For instance, the label of 'honour-based' violence was not applied to the white mother and father in the United Kingdom who in 2012 attacked their daughter for bringing 'shame' on the family by going out with a black man (*Daily Telegraph* 2012). The epithet 'passion' was used in the case of former Palm Beach County employee Lance McLellan who, in an act strikingly similar to many 'honour killings', murdered his wife in 2012 after he caught her being unfaithful (Palm Beach Post 2012). This dismissal of only some crimes as 'cultural' in nature has been identified as a factor in the lesser protection of the rights of minority women in western states as immigrant and minority communities are left to deal with their own problems (Gill 2006; Reddy 2008). 'Culture-based' crimes are often also denied or minimized by progressive groups due to fears of racism and a reluctance to create universalizing gender-based analyses, when these crimes should in fact be positioned as cross-cultural forms of violence against women (Gill 2006; see, for example, Geller 2011; Orr 2011b). As a result, Beckett and Macey (2001) write, multiculturalism has frequently produced a conspiracy of silence between minority ethnic men, male academics, professionals and the state. 'Cultural' evidence has often been presented as mitigation in cases of violence against women in both the United States and the United Kingdom (Coleman 1996; Dustin and Phillips 2008; Gill 2009; Okin 2011).

In addition to cultural essentialisms, on both sides of the debate there has also been a pseudo–psychological interpretation of intentions and motivations, on the Right focused on the 'dangerous Other' and on the Left on 'western feminists'. This production of 'straw' men and women can be seen in right-wing characterizations of 'angry Muslims' which pathologize rather than engage at political and structural levels, or which diagnose Muslim men in particular with an inherent sexism and sexual hang-ups that produce the contemporary 'clash of civilizations' (Bhattacharyya 2008). It can also be seen in left-wing suggestions that feminists and other 'helpers' are motivated by a desire for superiority (Abu-Lughod 2002: 787). The term 'white saviour industrial complex' (Cole 2012) has recently been used to express the idea that 'saving victims' plays an important role in the construction of some western identities, feminist ones in particular (Doezema 2000). This can be compared to the critiques of 'victim feminism' and of 'social helpers' within discussions of trafficking. There have also been suggestions that empathy is patronizing (Pedwell 2007) and a practice of consumption in relation to the Other (Lather 2009). These arguments partly reflect the lamentable convergence of 'colonial feminism' with other forms (Davis 2004), and the smugness of many western feminist 'interventions' in developing countries, often without sufficient background knowledge or consultation with local activists. In a recent article on radical blog Kafila, American Professor Carole Vance (2013) pointed to legions of gender and women's studies students in the United States who wanted to 'change the world' and 'save women', and described a curriculum project at Harvard wherein a group of such students were asked to design a policy working paper with recommendations to India and other South Asian countries in the wake of the 2012 New Delhi gang rape and murder. In recent years, there have also been a number of similarly inept or at times flippant celebrity forays into such issues (Hirschkind and Mahmood 2002). However, the attribution of individual psychological and identitarian motives to such 'helpers' can be homogenizing and also illustrates the contemporary replacement of political vocabularies with personal and emotional ones (Mardorossian 2002) and psychologizing of political critique which is characteristic of neo-liberal individualism. On both Left and Right, such constructions of straw men and women serve to close down debate and any search for solidarity or commonality which would need to inform a truly transnational and effective feminist movement (Davis 2004; Mohanty 2002).

Much of this on the Left is framed by the anti-imperial critique, which understandably tends to oppose anything which might play into the neoconservative project. However, Moghissi (1999) argues that, in the name of anti-imperialism and in the current climate of Islamophobia, some western groups and thinkers have become apologists for Muslim fundamentalism, a destructive defensiveness which denies the more punishing aspects of Islamic regimes. It also, she argues, draws simplistic parallels between disadvantaged Muslim minorities or opposition movements in western countries and powerful Islamic governments and political Islam in the Middle East and North Africa (Moghissi 1999: 4). This dynamic is evident in many recent contradictory engagements between the radical Left and radical Islam (Cohen 2012). For instance, it can be observed in the support given to Saddam Hussein and Colonel Gaddafi by the UK Workers Revolutionary Party and US left-wing journalists, revolutionaries and politicians, under the banner of anti-imperialism (Baker 2008; Jones 2011; Curtis 2012), and the exclusion of the political group Hands Off the People of Iran from the UK Stop the War Coalition, due to its statements about abuses of women's and LGBTQ rights by Islamic governments (Williams 2012). It can also be seen in UK socialist politician Ken Livingstone's links with Yusuf al-Qaradawi, an Egyptian televangelist who has supported practices such as wife-beating and female genital cutting and has said that LGBTQ people should be executed by stoning, but who was described by Livingstone as 'progressive', a position subsequently defended in the left-wing press (Readings 2010). In the wake of the Taliban shooting of 14-year-old Pakistani gender activist Malala Yousafzai, the online journal *World War 4*, which cites its mission as being to oppose both the 'war on terror' and political Islam, posted an article critiquing American extreme-left groups for not speaking out against the Taliban and highlighting conspiracy theories which had been circulating amongst some individuals and groups about the shooting being staged as part of ongoing neoconservative projects (Weinberg 2012).

Conclusion

In this chapter, I have explored the two main frameworks in the contemporary debate around gender and 'culture' in relation to Muslim women in particular. On the Right, I have examined the Orientalist construction of the 'Muslim woman' as an eternal and passive victim, which has often been produced by neoconservative governments and which has used the idea of Muslim cultures as gender-oppressive as justification for racist domination and to feed populist anti-Muslim prejudice. Answering this on the Left, I have explored the ascendant view in academia and left-wing activism, which focuses on uncovering the agency and resistance of women in Islamic states and Muslim-majority cultures and communities, and bases itself in a celebration of cultural difference. Although these frameworks often appear and position themselves as completely opposed to one another, I have argued that both have a tendency towards dogma and essentialisms, and that, furthermore, they share a number of themes which are drawn from the contemporary neoliberal context.

The first of these is the deployment of a politics of recognition around culture and identity, which can be seen in a right-wing ethnicization and vilification of practices identified with Islam and a left-wing reluctance to criticize the same. On both sides, a politics of 'voice' has also emerged in which personal narratives are used as the main evidence of cultural oppression or empowerment, and there is also a celebration of the 'traditional' and 'authentic' among some left-wing political groups and postcolonial academics and a reduction of structural oppressions to issues of personal feeling, which echoes some of the other debates in this book. This ignores the broader framings of cultural and religious practices and the fact that cultures do not exist in a vacuum: instead they reflect a variety of different influences and inputs which constitute a range between positive and negative. It also elides the differences between Islam as a religion and as a state or political project and avoids important questions about the uses to which radical Islam, much like its counterpart fundamentalist Christianity, has been put. Within such cultural essentialisms, Islam is either wholly liberating or entirely oppressive, with little attention paid to hierarchies within religious and cultural communities and in particular the possibility that these communities, like many in the West, may be dominated by socially advantaged men.

Notions of cultural authenticity and tradition also sit rather uncomfortably with the rational-economistic formulation of 'choice' which has been deployed in some quarters, particularly in relation to practices of veiling. Again, there is dichotomous and simplistic thinking in evidence, and gender and cultural essentialisms which serve to limit debate. On the Right, 'the veil' (often meaning the niqab and burqa) is emblematic of gender-oppressive Muslim cultures. On the Left, practices of veiling are often understood as symbolic of women's empowerment and resistance to western capitalist sexualized femininity. These binaries have historical antecedents: the niqab and burqa have been central to right-wing neocolonial discourses around Islam as a reactionary religious framework and Muslim-majority states and communities as gender-oppressive, which has produced a defensive left-wing and progressive formulation of covering as an empowering personal choice. However, such perspectives ignore the structural and contextual, with little or no discussion of the influences and conditions which frame women's choices to cover or not to cover and of the material histories of particular practices in which adopting a veil may be the result of oppression at one end of the spectrum, and a sign of liberation at the other.

Both sides of this debate are also characterized by assumptions of essential difference rather than a search for commonality and solidarity, which has led to symbolism and imagery revealing remnants of Orientalism throughout the political field. The victimized 'Muslim woman' constructed on the Right shares much with the dignified, spiritually empowered and pure 'Muslim woman' constructed on the Left. The veil in particular has become a symbol of an essential difference between 'Muslim cultures' and 'the West'. This has also led to the dismissal of other 'cultural practices', such as honour killings and forced marriages, by progressive groups anxious to foreground issues of difference and to avoid perpetuating racialized oppressions, and right-wing governments which are happy to leave Muslim communities to solve their own problems. On both sides, this has inhibited analysis of practices such as honour killings as cross-cultural forms of gender-based oppression which are also highly evident in the West, yet invisibilized by the definition of such crimes as 'Muslim phenomena'. Straw men and women are being created, either in the form of angry 'Muslim men' who are terrorists in training, or insecure 'western feminists' who seek to rescue women from Other cultures in order to underline their own superiority. This caricaturing often serves to close down constructive engagement, and, while feminists in the West undoubtedly benefit from critical reflexivity in relation to their privilege, their class and 'race' politics and the types of macro-political agendas they may have become complicit in, the setting of groups of feminists against one another as mortal enemies also undermines the possibility of a truly transnational movement (Mohanty 2002).

In a similar way to sexual violence politics, much of the contemporary Left's approach to gender issues within Muslim-majority communities and countries is framed by the anti-imperial critique and the fear of playing into deeply problematic neoconservative agendas. This is particularly relevant in a post-9/11 world which sees reactionaries of many religious persuasions, as well as rampant anti-Muslim prejudice. However, the contemporary tendency to dichotomize in reaction to neoconservative hegemony can be seen as a suspect and potentially risky strategy. The current progressive matrix situates radical and political Islam as a form of resistance and reaction against neoconservative political and cultural agendas: however, this masks the fact that in some of its values, particularly those related to gender, Islam is a conservative religious and political framework which shares much with its counterpart, fundamentalist Christianity. In similar ways to those revealed in the discussion of sexual violence debates, contemporary progressive and left-wing frameworks risk justifying gender-based oppression in the name of anti-imperial resistance. Non-western does not necessarily mean anti-imperial – there are many examples of *realpolitik*-driven collaborations between neoconservative regimes and fundamentalist states (Narayan 1998) which suggest that the current matrix is not set in stone and that the relationship between radical and political Islam and neoconservative projects is temporally and contextually bound. However, in the current debate it appears that gender has become merely a line of attack or defence in this broader battle, often interpreted via or used in the service of other political priorities. This poses challenges in terms of identifying and meeting women's needs, both within Muslim-majority countries and communities and outside them.

4

The Commodified Politics of the Sex Industry

The exchange of money for sexual services is certainly not new. Neither is it particularly novel to state that, in a globalized world, sex has become a multi-billion-dollar industry. A plethora of academic, political and media discussions of the sex industry has materialized since the 1980s, largely focused on its rights and wrongs and often characterized by extreme position-taking and binary oppositions between women and men, oppression and empowerment, coercion and choice. This chapter focuses mainly on the 'sex radicalism' which has emerged victorious in both academic and activist circles in recent years. This perspective positions sexual freedom as an essential component of women's liberation and prioritizes values such as freedom of expression, increasing sexual opportunities and embracing diverse sexualities. It sets itself against what it terms 'sex-negative' radical feminism, which is rooted in the anti-pornography campaigns of the 1980s but which has now expanded to include issues such as sex trafficking and the sexualization of children and young people. Such critics of the sex industry are often associated with 'victim feminism' and have found their main political allies on the neoconservative right. However, I will argue here that that current sex-radical politics is

also associated with right-wing values in its neoliberal individualism, identity politics and consumerist approach to empowerment
and choice. Furthermore, the original radicalism of such politics
has been blunted by the mainstreaming and corporatizing of the
sex industry: rather than being a counter-cultural voice, contemporary sex radicalism is often now amalgamated with capitalist
principles, processes and structures.

Commodified bodies in a globalized world

During the past thirty years, there has been burgeoning demand for
commercial sexual services from a sector which is thriving, despite
efforts by governments and police forces to regulate or obliterate
it (Bernstein 2001). The sale of sex on such a scale is a product of
the shift to post-industrial economies, with its attendant techno-
logical, cultural and sexual transformations (Paasonen, Nikunen
and Saarenmaa 2007; Scoular and Sanders 2010). The economic
engine of the West is now consumption rather than production:
services are the core industries and new commodities, new forms
of consumption and new types of labour have developed (Brents
and Hausbeck 2007; Kotiswaran 2010). Sex suffuses globalizing
societies, with most major cities boasting a cosmopolitan army of
sex workers and sexualized bodies being used to market countless
products (Altman 2004; Brents and Sanders 2010). The unprecedented growth of sexual commerce in the West is supported by
neoliberal policies of economic deregulation, particularly with
regard to the internet (Paasonen, Nikunen and Saarenmaa 2007;
Brents and Sanders 2010). It is also associated with free-market
rhetoric in which the principles of freedom and choice have
become a new morality (Brents and Sanders 2010). In the developing world, the commercial sex sector has been positioned as a
factor supporting economic growth and it incorporates powerful
financial vested interests (Lim 1998).

Today's western sex industry is a child of neoliberal capitalism,
with its merging of public and private, extension of the service

sector and commodification of experiences, including sexual ones (Bernstein 2001; Brents and Hausbeck 2007). For instance, wealthy consumers are able to purchase a 'girlfriend experience' – a personalized, intimate interaction with a paid escort which may include dinner and conversation, cuddling, kissing and foreplay – marketed as being akin to a 'real' relationship. Customers at Dennis Hof's Bunny Ranch, the zenith of Nevada's legalized brothels, visit a sexual theme park open 24/7 which offers massages, lactation, vibrator shows, Viagra parties, tantric sex, BDSM (bondage and discipline, sadism and masochism), 'two and three girls' parties, overnight stays and 'the porn star experience', and employs more than 500 'Bunny Babes'. This reflects the fact that commercial sex has been subject to the general trend for market specialization, now including text, image and video pornography, live sex shows, strip and lap-dancing clubs, telephone and cyber-sex companies, escort agencies, independent sex workers and organized sex tourism (Harcourt and Donovan 2005; Phipps 2013). It is difficult to estimate the current worth of the sex industry, due to the fact that many businesses operate on the fringes of the mainstream economy: however, a 2004 European Parliament report estimated prostitution[1] to be worth US$5 billion–US$7 billion globally, higher than world military expenditure (Eriksson 2004). The sex industry is also thought to be fairly recession-resistant (Brents and Sanders 2010).

The sex industry has begun to mainstream in recent years, with businesses adopting more traditional corporate structures and advertising strategies and interacting with conventional enterprise: this is most pronounced in the urban night-time economy, which has integrated sexual services into its offerings (Brents and Hausbeck 2007; Brents and Sanders 2010; Coulmont and Hubbard 2010). There has also been a spread of adult entertainment into businesses which do not primarily sell sex, for instance adult pay-per-view videos being sold in hotels, pornography being distributed by major television networks or pole-dancing classes being marketed as mainstream forms of exercise (Paasonen, Nikunen and Saarenmaa 2007; Holland and Attwood 2009; Brents and Sanders 2010). Direct and indirect purchase of sex on the high street (or main street) has also become more visible – for instance, the British retail chain Ann Summers, which markets sex toys and pornography DVDs, and the now ubiquitous Playboy bunny logo, which graces a wide variety of products (Brents and Sanders 2010). Rather than being a 'shadow sexscape' (Penttinen 2010: 30), Brents and Hausbeck (2007) argue that the sex industry has been 'McDonaldized' – shifting from being a set of small, private and illegitimate businesses to a multi-billion-dollar corporatized sector.

In a globalized world, commerce and culture exist in a kind of symbiosis, and sex which involves some element of commercial exchange is becoming increasingly normalized (Brents and Hausbeck 2007; Scoular and Sanders 2010). With late-capitalist mass consumption comes what some term a liberalization of sexual attitudes and others call a pornified or 'raunch' culture, together with 'tabloidization' (Paasonen, Nikunen and Saarenmaa 2007: 7), meaning a prioritizing of the personal and sexual, and characterizations of relationships, like products, as fleeting and disposable if they do not provide full satisfaction (Levy 2005; Paasonen, Nikunen and Saarenmaa 2007; Brents and Sanders 2010). The 'sexing up' of contemporary culture is also linked to the decline of religion and associated forms of morality, and a growing global tourist economy which is a product of increased leisure time and the search for relaxation and pleasure (Brents and Hausbeck 2007; Brents and Sanders 2010; Kotiswaran 2010). Tourists can now purchase escapism, themed adventure, spectacle, fantasy, voyeurism and even transgression, much of which has a sexual overtone (Brents and Sanders 2010: 45). With the help of omnipresent technologies, we are witnessing what Bernstein (2001: 392) has termed an 'increasingly unbridled ethic of sexual consumption'. Alongside this comes the phenomenon of 'porno chic', or the integration of the sex industry into everyday culture (McNair 2002) and notions of 'good sex' through, for instance, the marketing of pornography as a tool with which couples can spice up their sex lives (Paasonen, Nikunen and Saarenmaa 2007). Prominent figures in the sex industry are enjoying broader celebrity – for instance, in reality TV shows or through the crossover of pornography actors into conventional films – and mainstream actors are starring in productions featuring the sex industry or drawing on its cultural milieu (Paasonen, Nikunen and Saarenmaa 2007; Attwood 2009). However, there is still considerable social ambivalence at work, and a tension between sex-as-recreation and sex-as-romance which, it is argued, reflects the friction between neoliberal and neoconservative values (Bernstein 2001; Brents and Sanders 2010).

As a result of all these developments, sexual labour has become a mainstream work option for particular groups of women and some men (Brents and Sanders 2010). Indeed, some researchers now argue that sex work and ordinary service work are becoming less distinguishable (Agustín 2007b; Brents and Sanders 2010). Workers in the sex industry are increasingly middle class, a trend which both reflects and perpetuates its growing respectability. Within a social structure characterized by high-cost urban living, relatively low wages and continued gender stratification of labour markets, lower-middle-class women in western countries may find themselves turning to sex work for a liveable income (Bernstein 2007a; Brents and Sanders 2010). Joining them are what Bernstein (2007a) identifies as a new petit bourgeoisie who seek fun, pleasure and freedom in their work and for whom, due to their relative social privilege, sex work has become a lifestyle choice (Brents and Sanders 2010). The gentrification of sex work is accompanied by a professionalization: the adoption of more 'high class' strategies and images, and increasing numbers of middle-class clients and consumers (Brents and Sanders 2010).

The 'sex work glitterati'

The British TV drama *Secret Diary of a Call Girl*, based on the blog and books of the £300 per hour call girl Belle de Jour, averaged 1,242,125 viewers per episode for its first series in 2007 (Broadcasters' Audience Research Board 2007). In 2009, the woman behind the original 'Belle' blog and books outed herself as Bristol University research scientist Dr Brooke Magnanti. Magnanti joined the swelling ranks of other high-class sex workers whose memoirs have become a cultural phenomenon across Europe and North America, located at the nexus of pornography, conspicuous consumption and confessional chick-lit. Since her 'coming out', she has also enjoyed influence as a cultural and political commentator, attested by appearances on BBC's *Newsnight*, interviews in the tabloid and broadsheet press and her more than 20,000-strong Twitter following. The sex-worker-turned-celebrity is not a new phenomenon: since the 1970s, and especially in the United States, writers and performance artists such as Annie M. Sprinkle, Carol Leigh (the 'Scarlot Harlot') and New York madam Xaviera Hollander (the 'Happy Hooker') have been on the scene. However, the centring of such figures within the Zeitgeist is a recent development which reflects the broader mainstreaming of the sex industry described above. One of the most successful recent US examples is Tracy Quan, whose novels *Diary of a Manhattan Call Girl*, *Diary of a Married Call Girl* and *Diary of a Jetsetting Call Girl* (2005, 2006, 2008) document the double life of her alter-ego Nancy Chan. Quan has written for a number of publications including *Cosmopolitan*, the *Financial Times*, the *Guardian*, the *New York Times* and the *Washington Post*, has contributed chapters to academic anthologies and guested on TV shows including *Larry King Live*, *The Montel Williams Show*, and *The Early Show* on CBS.

Magnanti and Quan and other similar writers (see for example Miss S. 2007; McLennan 2008; Moore 2008; Gee 2010; Lauren 2010) hail from the indoor sex market, which differs from street sex work in a number of ways. Indoor workers provide services in the private sphere – brothels, massage parlours, saunas, hotels or homes – settings which are less exposed than that of the street, although they do not insulate workers from violence (Phipps 2013). They are less likely to be from socially excluded backgrounds and it is common for them to have been involved in conventional work and to have professional credentials. Perhaps because of this, indoor sex workers suffer less from chronic/acute illnesses and drug and alcohol addictions than their street-based counterparts (Sanders 2007). The indoor sector is growing rapidly: in the United Kingdom, 70 per cent of sex work is now thought to be carried out indoors (Sanders 2006; Kinnell 2008), and shifts from outdoor to indoor sex work have also been observed in mainland Europe, the United States and Australia (Weitzer 2009; Indoors 2010). However, the celebrity and literary sex workers featured here constitute a privileged subgroup of this indoor market whose professional choices intersect with issues around lifestyle, identity and conspicuous consumption.

Many contemporary sex work memoirs differ from anthologies of sex work writings published in the 1980s (see, for example, Delacoste and Alexander 1988) in their univocality and largely glossy take on the industry (Sterry 2009 being a notable exception). As high-profile examples of this new paradigm, Magnanti and Quan's writings share a number of common themes. They construct the sex worker as a professional 'everywoman' with a variety of alluring and elegant personas and a ready flow of income. Quan's first novel describes Nancy Chan as follows:

> Nancy Chan appears to be just like the rest of New York's female population. Except she isn't. Nancy is an exclusive member of Manhattan's lucrative demimonde, where loyal and generous patrons keep her in designer outfits in return for the best tailor-made sex in town. Nancy has a natural gift for the erotic arts, a great apartment and a gaggle of glamorous girlfriends. (Quan 2005)

The sale of 'tailor-made sex' gives these sex workers dominion over men who are prepared to purchase their services for extremely high fees (see also Egan 2006), and the financial rewards give them access to the trappings of consumer capitalist success. The pages of the novels are littered with designer labels and high society: Belle de Jour (2005) writes that she originally became a call girl in order to be able to afford her lavish London lifestyle in a difficult job market. The choice to trade one's body on the sex market is presented as a rational response to the pressures of contemporary bourgeois life. These women enjoy high levels of cultural capital, and the literature frequently incorporates cultural 'position takings' (Bourdieu 1984) in its vocabulary and discussion of upscale products. 'The surest way to tell the prostitute walking into a hotel at Heathrow', Belle de Jour (2005: 10) writes, 'is to look for the lady in the designer suit.'

The New York City reading series 'sex worker literati' features numerous other Magnantis and Quans: 'sex workers, former sex workers, and people with stories about the sex industry who read, monologue, perform, and shimmy their ways into your hearts, minds, and naughty bits' (Sex Worker Literati 2011). Although some of the performers in this series have grittier stories to tell, the quote above illustrates the central idea of the sex industry as a seductive, glamorous alternative culture. In their autoethnographic collection *Flesh for Fantasy*, ex-exotic dancers Danielle Egan, Katherine Frank and Merri Lisa Johnson set the stage:

> We open our lockers, pull out leather whips or feather boas, racy schoolgirl costumes or floor-length white dresses that shimmer under the lights, and we ascend the stage, or hover our hips over a young man's lap, or grind against his zipper with a thin thread of spandex as a barely there barrier. We sip champagne in the fantasy rooms or VIP suites with businessmen and blind men, single men and married men, men with wandering hands but nothing to say and men who pay us to sit and chat without ever asking to see us naked. We count our money at the end of the day, awash in sweat and glitter, side by side with college students, single moms, professional women looking to augment their incomes, young girls anxious to rebel, and women who just don't know what else to do. (Egan, Frank and Johnson 2006: xii).

These writers position themselves as a radical force working against a repressive and repressed society: 'advocates of gender justice, sexual freedom, safe work environments, and the importance of erotic play' (Egan, Frank and Johnson 2006: xxxiii). Synergies and alliances between such writers, political groups and prominent academics mean that theirs is the most influential voice in the sex work debate today.

One of the most important connections to make here is between the 'sex worker literati' and sex workers' labour and advocacy groups, which are currently enjoying new levels of growth, proliferation and influence. Sex workers' union organizing dates back to the nineteenth century (Pritchard 2010), but the origins of the current movement can be traced back to the prostitutes'[2] rights activity associated with the 'feminist sex wars' of the 1970s and 1980s. The first major organization to be created was Call Off Your Old Tired Ethics (COYOTE), founded in California in 1973 by former sex worker Margo St James. In 1975, the French and English Collectives of Prostitutes, as well as the International Prostitutes' Collective, were launched. 1979 saw the formation of the New York Prostitutes' Collective, later to become the US Prostitutes Collective (US PROS). Such groups all had similar aims: the decriminalization of sex work, the improvement of the conditions under which it was performed, and protection from violence. The central notion was that of sex work as a legitimate profession which should be afforded the same rights as others, which meant that the working environment, rather than the sale of sex itself, was the source of oppression (Gall 2006). Furthermore, it was contended that sex work in conducive settings could be empowering and pleasurable (Bernstein 1999; Scoular 2004). This agenda has largely persisted into the present, although there is now a stronger human rights focus and critiques of anti-trafficking efforts as being implicated in liberal 'rescue industries' which merge with neoconservative projects. The movement has massively grown in scale and influence, with organizations becoming larger and more structured and enjoying higher levels of funding.

A small sample of the sex workers' rights groups currently in existence includes, in the United States, the Desiree Alliance and Sex Work Activists, Allies and You (SWAAY), a public outreach organization launched in 2011. SWAAY has links on its website to similar groups in thirty-three countries across the globe. There are also state and local unions and campaigning groups, and sex work outreach projects which primarily provide support but which may have advocacy functions (Phipps 2013). Some of these date back to the 1970s and 1980s – for instance, The Red Thread in the Netherlands, the Italian Committee for the Civil Rights of Prostitutes and the New Zealand Prostitutes' Collective – but the majority are more recent in inception. The field also demonstrates the entrée into activism of corporate trends for networking and strategic alliance: since 2000, a number of cross-national umbrella organizations have emerged. These include the Asia Pacific Network of Sex Workers, the African Sex Worker Alliance, the Latin American and Caribbean Network of Sex Workers, the International Committee on the Rights of Sex Workers in Europe, and the Sex Workers' Rights Advocacy Network in Central and Eastern Europe and Central Asia. The year 2000 also saw the formation of the International Union of Sex Workers (IUSW), based in the United Kingdom. In 2002, this organization established a sex workers' branch of the GMB, Britain's general union (Pritchard 2010), reflecting the mainstreaming of sex workers' politics (Gall 2006).[3]

Although their advocacy on behalf of stigmatized and marginalized workers is undeniably valuable, these organizations, much like the 'sex worker literati', tend to be populated by a class elite. Day (2007) writes that some have in fact contained few sex workers: this is likely due to issues with many sex workers having no fixed address, some not wishing to be 'outed' and the affordability of membership dues, if these are charged. Bernstein's (1999) research confirms that sex workers active in labour and advocacy organizations tend to be employed at the 'high' end of the industry – the call girls and exotic dancers who also largely constitute the sex worker literati – and that these workers are often reluctant to cross the class divide to reach out to streetwalkers. Those at the vanguard of this politics tend to have extremely high levels of cultural capital: for instance, Ana Lopes, President of the IUSW, has an MSc in anthropology from the University of London and a PhD from the University of East London. The founder of SWAAY, who goes by the name Furry Girl, describes herself as 'an overachiever kid with killer standardized test scores' and is a successful entrepreneur, owning her own pornography enterprise. The staff and board of SWEAT, a large sex workers' rights and advocacy group based in Cape Town, includes only one ex-sex worker among nine personnel, the others being a previous executive director of Women's Net and various mental health and development professionals.

These professionals are often networked with contemporary 'sex positive' academics, many of them feminists (for example,

Agustín, Bernstein, Day, Egan, Hubbard, Kinnell, McNair, Sanders, Weitzer), who mainly subscribe to a repackaged version of the 1980s' sex-radical perspective (see below). There are also a number of key recent 'popular feminist' writers and activists who are supportive of the sex industry and argue for the production of more woman-centred pornography and/or legalization of prostitution (Valenti 2007; Levenson 2009; Baumgardner and Richards 2010; Penny 2010; Moran 2011).[4] These writers are often featured in the left-wing and progressive media, alongside others such as anti-censorship activists and Chicago School economists who take up themes around freedom of expression and choice. In 2011, London saw its first sex worker film festival, featuring pieces from the United Kingdom and other European countries, as well as Australia, Brazil, Canada and the United States. This event, organized by the Sex Worker Open University (a coalition of sex workers, academics and allies), hosted the first UK screening of the 2006 Canadian film *69 Things I Love about Sex Work*, directed by Isabel Hosti. Interestingly, however, and despite the rather elite demographic of the movement as a whole, these 'sex positive' academics have recently come under fire from others in the sex workers' rights movement for being 'race-' and class-privileged (Ray 2012) 'hipster feminists with only brief involvement with sex work' who are unable to represent the reality of the industry (Furry Girl 2011).

'Sex war' and victory

The ideas articulated by the 'sex worker literati', sex workers' rights organizations and 'sex positive' academics constitute a revised form of the sex radicalism first engendered during the US-led 'feminist sex wars' of the 1970s and 1980s. This activist and academic confrontation over issues such as pornography, prostitution and sadomasochism originally came to a head around competing claims of sexist oppression and sexual repression (Chancer 2000). On one side were radical feminists such as Gloria Steinem, Catharine

MacKinnon, Andrea Dworkin and Robin Morgan, who pos-
tulated a causal link between the sex industry and violence.
Positioning sexuality as the linchpin of gender inequality, they saw
pornography and prostitution as the pinnacle of women's objectification and the power of men over women's bodies (Chancer
1996; Bernstein 1999; Barton 2002; Sutherland 2004). They were
critiqued on a number of levels: for relying on essentialist gender
divisions within which commercial sex was solely identified with
male sexuality; for working with ephemeral notions of the obscene
and deterministic ideas about oppression; for simplifying questions
of representation, desire and fantasy; and for locating patriarchal
domination solely in the personal sphere (Paasonen, Nikunen
and Saarenmaa 2007). They were also accused of themselves
objectifying the sex workers for whom they presumed to speak
and attributing false consciousness to those who claimed to have
chosen the profession (Sutherland 2004). These feminists were
seen in many left-wing circles as authoritarian and moralistic,
and found their main political allies on the neoconservative right
(Chancer 1996; Bernstein 1999).

The opposite corner was inhabited by sex-radical feminists
such as Gayle Rubin, Lisa Duggan, Pat Califia and Camille Paglia.
Resisting the radical feminists' equation of sexuality with sexism,
they saw sex and sexuality as cultural constructions which allowed
room for creativity and agency. Although it was generally con-
ceded that mainstream heterosex could be oppressive, sex-radical
feminism imbued non-normative sexualities with the potential to
challenge and change the status quo. It was also argued that having
sex for money could do the same since this removed sex from the
tacit marriage contract, making it a straightforward (rather than
an implicit) transaction (Chancer 1996; Barton 2002; Sutherland
2004). These feminists made alliances with left-wing and libertarian freedom-of-speech lobbies, equating freedom of expression
with sexual freedom and often positioning sexuality as a key
means of empowerment. It was argued that some women could
experience pornography and sex work as liberating, especially
since their sexual feelings had been suppressed and/or co-opted
by patriarchy (Chancer 2000). There was also an emphasis on sex

workers speaking for themselves, although in practice this often turned out to be the most privileged (Sutherland 2004) and these sex radicals were in danger of constructing their own theory of false consciousness in implying that women who objected to the sex industry were repressed (Chancer 1996). They were also criticized for depoliticizing the industry by ignoring structural 'push' factors in their emphasis on individual choice (Sutherland 2004; Paasonen, Nikunen and Saarenmaa 2007). However, by the end of the decade it was widely felt that they had won their battle (Miriam 2005), although radical feminist perspectives had had more impact in legislative arenas due to their resonances with neoconservative 'law and order' agendas (Sutherland 2004).

The dominant contemporary perspective on the sex industry draws much from this sex-radical paradigm, although it also differs in important ways. For example, liberal concerns about sexual freedom and freedom of expression have now been augmented with neoliberal ideas around consumer choice. The right of men to purchase women's bodies is justified by free-market principles, as is women's choice to offer their bodies for sale. Reflecting this, the politics of the sex industry now utilizes the language of late capitalist customer service: 'prostitutes' and 'punters' have become sexual service providers and clients. Echoing market differentiation, there has been a move away from monolithic definitions of the sex industry towards more sophisticated explorations of its various sectors. In today's sex-radical movement, 'sex positive' feminism meets the anarchic and libertarian Left, but also neoliberalism and occasionally the libertarian and neoconservative Right. For example, after the 2012 massacre of twenty children and six adults at an elementary school in Connecticut, high-profile American sex radicals Furry Girl and Maggie McNeil (the 'Honest Courtesan') took to Twitter apparently to echo prominent members of the extreme-right Tea Party movement in opposing gun control legislation, relating this to their struggles around freedom of speech.

The new sex radicalism has also been articulated by and around sex industry entrepreneurs: men such as Playboy's Hugh Hefner, Hustler's Larry Flynt and Dennis Hof of the Bunny Ranch. Hefner, for example, is a celebrity patron of liberal organizations such as the

American Civil Liberties Union (ACLU) and has been positioned as a sexual and political progressive in his rebellion against 1950s' puritan family values and the shame and guilt they attached to sex (Davis 2009). In a 2010 interview in the *New York Times*, he cited his role in changing dominant social and sexual values in the United States. The NBC drama *The Playboy Club* is co-branded with the Playboy empire and described by executive producer Chad Hodge as being centrally concerned with women's empowerment. In his voice-over for the 2011 pilot, Hefner affirmed that his bunny girls 'could be anything they wanted' (Holmes 2011). Similarly, Larry Flynt has positioned himself as a crusader for free speech and sexual rights (Flynt and Eisenbach 2011) and, despite the graphically violent and misogynist nature of much of his product (Chancellor 2012), has become revered in some circles as a defender of America's first amendment (Hari 2011), immortalized in the 1996 film *The People vs. Larry Flynt*.

Contemporary sex-radical discourse also interpellates men who purchase commercial sex, positioned in two recent studies as sexual nonconformists for whom conventional relationships are not enough. Sanders's (2008a) UK study found that 'push' factors for clients were dissatisfaction with dating etiquette and the failure of traditional heterosexual marriage to provide fulfilment. Paying for sex, for her respondents, was seen as either the route to erotic adventure or a more straightforward alternative to relational normativity. Bernstein's (2007b) US study led her similarly to conclude that such men are in search of 'bounded authenticity', an alternative to normative heterosexual relationships. She commends the 'disembedding of the (male) individual from the sex–romance nexus of the privatized nuclear family' (Bernstein 2007b: 121), and positions the purchase of sex as more honest than the illicit affair or the romantic fib in the service of a one-night stand. Bernstein argues that erotic expression and the ethos of the market are not antithetical for some men. Sanders (2008a) similarly constructs the decision to buy sex as a rational response to an overly repressed or moralistic society, seeing online commercial sex communities in particular as being at the vanguard of a new sexual morality.

The new sex radicalism, then, is a discourse which appears to circulate between high-end sex workers, the leaders of sex workers' rights organizations, contemporary 'sex positive' academics, sex industry entrepreneurs and populations of clients. This group constitutes a class and ethnic elite and may represent sectors of the middle class which have gained most from neoliberalism and late consumer capitalism. Debates with radical feminists and other sex industry critics continue but are mainly concentrated in discussions around trafficking[5] (Ciclitira 2004; Miriam 2005), where radical feminist perspectives' compatibility with neoconservative concerns about crime and immigration have given them the upper hand and led sex radicals to argue both that official statistics grossly overestimate and dramatize the problem and that 'trafficked women' are more often opportunistic entrepreneurs (Doezema 1999, 2000; Agustín 2007b; Rothschild 2009; Magnanti 2012). Furthermore, they have contended that a new 'war on sex workers' is being conducted by feminists, whose 'victim politics' and 'rescue' efforts have brought them into alliance with social conservatives and law enforcement (Penny 2012; Gira Grant 2013). Feminist critics of the sex industry are often positioned as 'anti-sex', 'anti-male' and sometimes 'anti-fun', and jealous of sex workers' sexual freedoms (Lamb 2010; Snyder-Hall 2010; see also *Daily Mail* 2011a).

There is no doubt that contemporary sex industry critics are problematically located due to resonances between their views and neoconservative agendas and the retrograde nature of some of the associated contemporary radical feminist politics, particularly around trans* issues (F Word 2012). There is also a growing critique of high-profile celebrities who (often rather clumsily) attempt to piggyback upon sex industry critiques, the most widely opposed of whom is *New York Times* columnist Nicholas Kristof, whose 'rescues' of trafficked women, profiled in the documentary *Half the Sky*, have been denounced for being underpinned by suspect *noblesse oblige* sentiments and the idea of the 'white man's burden' (Agustín 2007b; DasGupta 2012; North 2012). However, the setting up of feminism as a monolithic straw man and personalization and psychologization of political analysis is similar to that observed in other debates and has the effect of detracting from the structural conditions and power relations which oppress sex workers, both within the industry and without. Furthermore, in their 'anti-victim' politics, sex radicals frequently position themselves as victims of 'sex negativity and radical feminist bullying' (Sarah M 2012). Most importantly, in their opposition to radical feminist and neoconservative projects, contemporary sex radicals have constructed themselves as an unequivocally progressive force, which renders invisible key synergies between their ideas and the neoliberal political lexicon.

Recognition, emotionalism and voice – the politics of 'whorephobia'

A major theme in the Belle de Jour series of novels is the main protagonist's love of sex. She also gives her readers insights into a passion for 'kink' and various BDSM practices (Belle de Jour 2005: 2, 2006: vii), and suggests that her erotic proclivities, alongside the financial demands of her high-end London lifestyle, motivated her choice of profession. She describes the more unusual demands of her clients with relish, suggesting that repeated requests for 'vanilla' interactions can get a little boring (Belle de Jour 2006: 6). Belle constructs herself as a deviant sexual subject whose profession allows her to express and explore her identity: the opening line of her book series states 'the first thing you should know is that I'm a whore' (Belle de Jour 2005: 1). This exemplifies one of the most important components of sex radicalism: the notion of 'sex worker' as an identity (which contradicts other ideas about sex work as just a job). Within this discourse, sex workers embody a transgressive commercial sexual self which divorces the erotic from the domestic and traditionally feminine. Echoing themes in some strands of LGBTQ politics, sexuality is seen as central to identity and even a pre-social form of deviance (Scoular 2004; Vogel 2011). 'Whores', American sex educator and former sex worker Annie Sprinkle (2009: 10) argues, challenge sexual mores, help people, are creative, 'hot and hip', free spirits, healers and not afraid of sex.

These identities are positioned within a 'recreational sexual ethic' (Bernstein 2007b: 181) or ideas about 'sexual democratization' (McNair 2002) and diversity (Sanders 2008b). Sex workers' rights are also associated with other forms of identity politics through alliances with LGBTQ groups (Bernstein 1999; Maddison 2010), black women (Egan, Frank and Johnson 2006) and disabled people (Egan 2006; Sprinkle 2009).

Complementing the focus on identity is a corresponding politics of 'voice' which is rooted in historical and very legitimate sex-radical demands to allow sex workers themselves to speak on issues which primarily affect them. However, this has been synthesized with the fetishization of the personal in politics and popular culture (Paasonen, Nikunen and Saarenmaa 2007: 7) and a preoccupation with 'authenticity' in much qualitative academic research (O'Neill 2001) to create a framework which valorizes the experiential and invisibilizes the structural. Like other debates in this book, that around sex work has become characterized by first-hand accounts: the autobiographical, semi-fictional and fictional work of the literati, tales from the grassroots which are a key component of sex worker politics, and the ethnographic evidence amassed by 'sex positive' academics. This provides a rich body of stories and experiences: however, its diversity and representativeness are limited by the 'race' and class privilege of the limited samples represented (Agustín 2007a; Phipps 2009). Nevertheless, the claims to groundedness and authenticity which accompany this politics of voice (Story 2011) allow it to dominate the field. This is also evident on the other side of the debate, where alternative voices are mobilized: radical feminists have been criticized for exploiting sex workers' stories of trauma and creating what Scarlet Alliance president Elena Jeffreys has termed 'tragedy porn' (Jeffreys 2011) in their attempts to compete with the dominant paradigm around identity, empowerment and choice (Weitzer 2010).

The idea of sex work as an identity makes possible the notion of 'whorephobia', a term for sex worker stigma which is growing in popularity (Scoular 2004). This is defined as the fear or hate of sex workers, linked to the patriarchal madonna/whore dichotomy and thought to be expressed not only by moral conservatives but also by radical feminists, who are accused of resenting sex workers' erotic freedoms (Agustín 2007b; Schaffauser 2010). It is argued that this stigma is at the root of sex worker trauma and often the motivating factor for violence (Day 2007; Sanders 2008a; Sprinkle 2009). The group most often labelled as 'whorephobes' are neoconservative moralists, but this epithet has also been used to describe feminist opponents of the sex industry, and structural critiques have sometimes been reinterpreted as personal attacks (see, for example, Queen 2001: 101; Betts 2013). The idea of 'whorephobia' is a paradigmatic example of the politics of recognition, locating injustice in demeaning representations of sex workers rather than the social relations of their existence (Fraser 2000), and drawing on the emotionalism of the contemporary political field. It also reflects a neoliberal individualism and the psychologization of contemporary political debate, with discussions around sex work most commonly seen as being associated with underlying sexual ethics (Bernstein 2007b), an interpretation which homogenizes all critics of the sex industry as contemporary Victorians (Bernstein 2007b) and prudes (Sanders 2008a). This was illustrated in 2012 by Peter Stringfellow, who owns a chain of lap-dancing clubs in the United Kingdom and who made statements in the debate about exotic dancing which compounded 'moralists' and 'extreme feminists' and set their 'hardline agenda' against a characterization of the sex industry as a 'positive force in terms of our sexual attitudes' (Kelly 2012).

Under the banner of 'slut shaming', the idea of 'whorephobia' recently united the sex workers' rights lobby with 'third wave' feminists in the worldwide Slutwalk movement around sexual violence. However, these marches were challenged by some as being an uncritical celebration of the sexual 'empowerment' which is a central component of neoliberal capitalism. Positioning commercial sex as an arena of transgressive identities and sexual self-expression is a partial perspective which tends to equate sexual freedom with a choice of pre-packaged commodities and ignores the role of the capitalist system and other structures in shaping sexual discourses. Freedom of consumption comes to stand in for freedom of expression (Maddison 2010), a rather apolitical neoliberal formulation which posits liberty in individualized market terms (Paasonen, Nikunen and Saarenmaa 2007). The capitalist framings and profit motive of the sex industry are not included in this interpretation: in particular, it ignores how the market shapes the content of what is bought and sold and very often defines the 'sexy'. There is a need to engage with the fact that sex worker identities, like many other contemporary sexual identities, are frequently informed by a hypersexualized femininity positioned within a 'raunchiness' which is mainstream (rather than marginal), consumerist and has been seen as related to the backlash against feminism (Levy 2005; Walter 2010; Walby 2011). Sex worker identity politics does not often take into account that identities are socially produced within a matrix of discourses which may have both positive and negative aspects and which are inextricable from the operation of power (Foucault 1976).

The sexonomical self: sex radicalism, money and rational choice

Contradicting the focus on 'sex worker' as an identity is the idea of sex work as a job like any other, often seen as superior in its flexibility and financial rewards to service and unskilled jobs available to women in particular social positions (Holsopple 1999; Bernstein 2007a; Pritchard 2010). For instance, Belle de Jour describes her job as a customer service role (2005: 94) which is 'better than watching the clock until the next scheduled tea break in a dismal staff room' (2005: 1). Similarly, American journalist Jennifer Abel (2009), writing in the British *Guardian*, explains that her foray into exotic dancing as a college student meant that all she had to do was 'jiggle the twins a bit' and she could 'make more money in an hour than a McDonald's burger-flipper got all week'. The language of sex work has been professionalized and corporatized: prostitutes have become sex workers and 'industrial sex technicians' (Sterry 2009: 3), and punters and johns are now customers or clients (Sanders 2008a). Legitimizing sex work as labour is necessary in order to demand rights for those in the industry. Furthermore, the idea that there is no preordained meaning or morality behind the industry facilitates a focus on the conditions in which it is carried out as highly problematic (Sutherland 2004; Egan, Frank and Johnson 2006). However, this labour rights framework sits strangely alongside the essentialism of sex worker identity politics and is belied by the stories of disassociation in many sex work memoirs (Egan 2006; Manaster 2006; Sterry 2009) and evidence of trauma in sex work research (Phipps 2013), even that supportive of the industry (see, for example, Sanders 2005). It also presents a contradiction with the idea of sex as inherently empowering, as discussed above: if sex work has no intrinsic meaning, selling it, like selling any commodity, will inevitably reflect existing structures of inequality.

Furthermore, the notions of rational choice which underpin the idea of sex work as 'just a job' rely on a decontextualized, unified and rational notion of the self and do not engage with ideas about how power constructs subjectivities and choices (Foucault 1976, 1977; Gill 2007). This reflects neoliberal values and also speaks to the contemporary influence of Chicago School economics upon political debate. Contemporary sex radicalism borrows heavily from this canon, constructing sex workers as entrepreneurs and positioning agency in economic terms, granted by the conditions of a free market and the absence of physical force. This can be seen in Agustín's (2007b) account of a Latin American migrant trading sex to a German train conductor for the return of her own and her companions' passports. She narrates this as an act of resourcefulness and ingenuity on the part of the woman, and characterizes the conductor's actions as 'help' rather than coercion (Phipps 2009). Some sex radicals also channel contemporary 'anti-victim' politics (Hursh 2007) in their interpretations of power relations in the industry within a neoliberal narrative of personal responsibility. This is exemplified in an article by Jahnet de Light entitled '50 Tips for Prostitutes' on the website of the Sexual Freedom Coalition,[6] in which she opines that 'a lot of the people who live with or support a person who beats them or forces them into sexwork [. . .] have a need for that kind of relationship.' This framework creates a simplistic dichotomy between agency and victimhood and ignores the fact that the notion of 'choice' can provide a protective veneer and a means of survival in challenging circumstances (Gill 2007; Mott 2011; Ray 2012).

As Belle de Jour (2008: 15–16) states, 'Who I am and what I am doing is a rational response to the current economic and cultural climate. Deal with it.' Before becoming embroiled in a trademark dispute,[7] Magnanti had entitled her first non-fiction book (2012) *Sexonomics*, a deliberate nod to Levitt and Dubner's *Freakonomics* (2005) and *Superfreakonomics* (2009), American texts which are exemplars of the contemporary application of economic theory to the non-economic. These books have achieved huge popularity, despite an identified lack of rigour (DiNardo 2006), and outclass sex-radical texts in their influence on the Zeitgeist: nonetheless, the two literatures share a similar economistic worldview. This is based on incentives, positioning social agents as consumers with the goal of maximizing utility, and applies the theory of supply and demand to the social realm. Market values achieve almost moralistic status, despite the fact that these are essentially undemocratic (Satz 2010b). Morality itself is either downplayed or antagonized: for Levitt and Dubner, it is another incentive, while in sex-radical literature it is at best an inconvenience and at worst a foe. Satz (2010a: 74) is one of many thinkers who have challenged such application of economic analysis to non-economic problems, arguing that the economic and the social are distinct and that, as well as their own rational self-interest, people are guided by norms, including norms about what is right and just.

In *Superfreakonomics*, Levitt and Dubner tackle the sex industry directly in a chapter entitled 'How is a Street Prostitute like a Department Store Santa?' Their arguments here share much with the sex-radical literature, as they position sex work as a rational choice in response to a difficult labour market and the financial incentives for selling sex. Despite the chapter title, however, their illustrative case study is from the world of high-class escorting: the story of Allie, whose entry into commercialized sex was a result of her love of money and dislike of hard work, and who used business techniques and marketing strategies to achieve success as a sexual entrepreneur. Like contemporary sex radicals, Levitt and Dubner conceptualize the sex industry as a simple realm of supply and demand and do not situate the need for commercial sex within structural gender relations. This allows the choice to sell sex to be conceptualized solely in economic terms, for instance migrant women seeking work opportunities, bourgeois women looking for more money and flexibility, and avoidance of student debt (see, for example, Sanders 2008b). Furthermore, the emphasis on the sex worker's choice to sell rather than the client's choice to buy masks the gendered construction of demand for sexual services, as well as the profit motive and financial relationships which structure the industry as a whole, which complicates discussions around rational choice (Spelvin 2009).

Bernstein (2007b) argues that, for some sex workers, the exchange of money for sex makes their profession more empowering than other forms of heterosexual intimacy. This draws on 1980s' sex-radical and socialist-feminist ideas about ascribing value to women's affective labour, with sex workers valorized for exercising their right to charge for what other women give free (Delacoste and Alexander 1988). However, most sex radicals (see Bernstein 1999 as an exception) do not allow that the exchange of sex for money may only be empowering in a society in which women's sexuality is already appropriated and dominated and in which historically most women have exchanged their sexuality for their husband's wage. Furthermore, within the 'sex worker literati' there is evidence of a much more consumer-capitalistic and acquisitive strand of this argument, focused on the accumulation of money and consumer goods, rather than on any redress for patriarchal oppression. 'If Nancy [Chan] has any regrets', reads the tagline for Tracy Quan's blog at Salon.com, 'she's more likely to regret the free sex she had when she could have been working.' In statements such as this, ideas about revealing and disarming the implicit transaction of heterosexual marriage are replaced by the values of competitive commerce.

This perhaps reflects Bernstein's (2007b: 175–6) point that 'Those who participate most fully in the emotionally contained economy of recreational sex and bounded authenticity are also those whose psychic lives are most fully penetrated by the cultural logic of late capitalism.' Indeed, many contemporary sex radicals position consumer capitalism as a positive force in terms of articulating diverse sexual identities and practices (McNair 2002). In the world of the 'sex worker literati', much like in other commercialized spheres, money is power as is reflected in the focus on the money that sex workers are able to earn, the pleasure they take in earning it and how easy it is to do so (Barton 2002). Quan (2005: 88) writes that 'early financial – not sexual – conduct is the key to what makes a hooker tick', describing Jasmine, a character in her Nancy Chan series, as a woman who 'always had her eye on the bottom line'. In some accounts, money is positioned as more important than happiness: for instance, Manaster (2006: 18) characterizes lap dancing as 'treading water', but admits that she makes too much money seriously to consider swimming to shore. This money is used to finance a certain lifestyle, with the world of sex work being rife with conspicuous consumption (Fensterstock 2006) and ideas about economic 'necessity' reflecting the operation of social privilege. These values underline the relationship between contemporary sex-radical politics and the neoliberal context.

Conclusion

This chapter has focused on the sex radicalism which emerged victorious from the 'sex wars' of the 1980s and 1990s to become the dominant voice in the contemporary sex industry debate. This framework is currently favoured by academics, left-wing activists and journalists and 'sex positive' feminists, as well as underpinning sex workers' rights politics and the work of the newly emergent 'sex worker literati'. This 'sex work glitterati', as I have termed them, construct much of the contemporary common sense about the industry: however, they constitute a class and ethnic elite, which means that their perspectives are partial and reflect their positions of social and economic privilege. The chapter has covered a number of themes within contemporary sex radicalism and has argued that, although much of its current formulation continues the ideas and preoccupations of 1980s' and 1990s' 'sex positive' feminism, it also shows the influence of the neoliberal context, in particular in the shift from concerns about sexual freedom and freedom of expression towards ideas about commodity choice, identity and rational decision making, all positioned within a largely individualistic frame. This contemporary sex radicalism is often set against remaining strands of radical feminist thought and organizing which have resonances with neoconservative agendas, particularly in the debate around trafficking: echoing other debates, the polarization of these perspectives can be seen to have produced zealotry and dogma on both sides.

The first sex-radical theme I explored was the idea of sex worker as an identity, which is positioned within a politics of authenticity and voice that governs who is able to make valid statements about the industry. This has led to a 'war of voice' in the contemporary debate, with sex workers' experiences of empowerment or oppression used as political capital on both sides. Sex worker identity politics also underpins the new concept of 'whorephobia'. This can be seen as a useful way of naming and opposing prejudice, but also functions to psychologize and individualize political and structural critiques of the industry. This is an example of what Fraser terms the 'politics of recognition', which is focused on damaging representations of particular groups, superseding analyses which are socio-economic in emphasis. It sits within a broader turn towards the cultural and identitarian and a politicization of the personal, which has been identified in a number of the debates in this book. Sex worker identity politics can also be seen as a kind of Orientalism, or fetishization of the marginal, which again is echoed in other chapters. However, there is a need critically to examine the 'marginality' celebrated in contemporary sex radicalism since it shares much with contemporary commercialized discourses around sexuality. Furthermore, the focus on identity within sex work debates reflects the relative privilege of those who dominate the discussions, and the fact that they are less likely to be subject to the socio-economic 'push' factors which may be a significant influence on others (Women's Resource Centre 2007). An intersectional analysis, then, would complicate the idea of sex work as a radical expression of identity.

The second part of the chapter dealt with the idea of sex work as just another job, which is superior in its flexibility and financial rewards to other service-industry professions. This contradicts the focus on sex work as a radical form of self-expression and also raises the possibility, not often discussed in sex-radical literature, that the industry may be subject to the same structures of inequality which produce discrimination in other professions. Within this strand of sex radicalism, women's choices to work in the sex industry are seen in individualistic terms and as the result of rational market-based calculations. However, this economistic framework does not engage with the ways in which power may construct subjectivities and shape choices, and it is not well equipped to deal with motivations beyond the accumulation of capital and consumer goods. Furthermore, the focus on the sex worker's choice to sell rather than the client's choice to buy does not engage with debates about the gendered, classed and 'raced' shaping of the demand for commercialized sex. This theme within contemporary sex-radical politics is also marked by privilege, since those likely to be able to make a rational choice to participate in sex work are also likely to have access to a certain level of economic, social and cultural resources (Sterry 2009). This strand of the discussion is similarly, then, rendered more complex by applying an intersectional frame.

Within much contemporary sex-radical thinking, feminism has been reduced to the status of a straw man: seen as anti-sex, anti-men, anti-fun and the ideology of repressed women who are jealous of sex workers' freedoms. This caricaturing of feminist thought and activism is both homogenizing and simplistic, and also at times belies the 'anti-victim' emphasis of sex-radical politics since sex workers and their advocates and allies often position themselves as victims of radical feminists and neoconservative prudes. This fraught engagement with feminist agendas is partly of course due to the convergence of radical feminism with neo-conservative and neo-imperialist projects around sexuality, sexual violence and immigration, a problematic which can be seen in particular in debates and interventions around trafficking. This calls into question the 'radicalism' of contemporary radical feminism, which is often treated with suspicion in progressive political and activist circles. However, it is also important to question the radicalism of current sex-radical politics, since it is highly individualistic in its focus on identity and representation and based on formulations of sexual identity which draw from contemporary mainstream 'raunchy' commercialized sexuality and values which are economistic in their constructions of choice and equation of money with power. This is in many ways merely reflective of the capitalist structures of the sex industry, which, like other economic sectors, is shaped by neoliberal rationalities. However, it becomes problematic when it produces simple interpretations of sex work as a counter-cultural form of empowerment or expression of sexual freedom, characterizations which are also complicated by applying the principle of intersectionality and considering differences between sex workers in terms of motivations, identities and experiences. In reality, then, neither the figure of the victim nor that of the 'happy hooker' may be a representative one, and sex workers should not need to be happy, empowered or to have chosen their profession in order to be able to demand rights and respect.

5

The New Reproductive Regimes of Truth

Doula, home birth, water birth outside, squatted, feeling wonderful, paced house, breathed, hummed and sang through contractions, focussed on candle flame, baby came through the water as if like a magical baby. Every doubt was followed up by beautiful thoughts, actions and connections.

www.positivebirthstories.com

My son's [homebirth] was beyond painful. I really cannot come up with words to describe the horrible pain I experienced. I felt like I was screaming the whole time. My midwife called it vocalizing but it felt like screaming to me. It was horrible. It is not supposed to be this way. I thought my endorphins were supposed to kick in and help.

www.homebirthdebate.blogspot.com

Birth in the 1970s (for white, middle-class western women) was very different from both these contemporary examples. For many, it was an institutionalized experience: they were delivered in hospitals by male obstetricians, with access to a variety of anaesthetics and analgesics. Labour was often a supine process and women birthed in the lithotomy position, legs in stirrups; interventions such as forceps and vacuum extraction were commonplace, and caesarean sections were on the rise. Babies were routinely washed, dressed and taken away immediately post-partum, to be formula fed by nurses while the mother was in recovery (Palmer 1988; Lee 2008). This represented the apex of more than two hundred years of medicalization. Until the seventeenth century, childbirth and the neonatal period in most parts of the world had been firmly positioned in the domestic arena, with women attended by lay midwives, family and close friends (Henley-Einion 2009). As the medical body became the subject of analysis post-Enlightenment (Foucault 1973[1963]), reproduction in the West turned into a key site for surveillance and normalization. Pregnant women and birthing mothers were transformed into patients under the new specialisms of obstetrics and gynaecology, with symptoms which needed to be assessed, treated and monitored by doctors, consultants and an increasingly professionalized cadre of midwives.

The medicalization of childbirth was partly a constructive response to the deteriorating living and birthing conditions which accompanied industrialization, an effort to reduce rates of infant and maternal mortality from complications such as foetal injury, haemorrhage and puerperal sepsis (childbed fever) during a pre-antibiotic era (Purdy 2001; Henley-Einion 2009; Gibson 2011). This was largely achieved, and together with improvements in disease control, living standards and diet, medicalization meant that maternal mortality in the West fell rapidly during the twentieth century. However, from the 1970s onwards, a critical mass of western feminists, obstetricians, midwives and other activists, led by individuals such as British anthropologist Sheila Kitzinger (1972, 1978), American midwife Ina May Gaskin (1976), French doctor Michel Odent (1984) and British gynaecologist Wendy Savage (1986), began to form around the idea that these gains were being made at the expense of women's control over their reproductive capacities (Beckett 2005; Henley-Einion 2009).[1] Medicalization, it was claimed, had repositioned women as objects of scientific discourse rather than subjects with their own agency and knowledge (Johnson 2008). One of the negative effects of this was to override women's own expertise and ability to manage

normal bodily events, such as childbirth and breastfeeding, as
well as undermining the midwives who had historically provided
assistance (Beckett 2005). Instead, the ideology of technology
treated women's bodies as birthing machines within a system of
masculine and industrialized values of order, predictability and
control (Henley-Einion 2009). Medicalized pregnancy and hos-
pitalized birth were disembodied processes where the focus was
on managing symptoms and interventions, rather than on the
overall meaning of the experience (Johnson 2008). Furthermore,
the relocation of childbirth to institutional settings had led to a
loss of intimacy and physicality and a marginalizing of domestic
support, as well as the adoption of procedures which made labour
and delivery easier for physicians and more difficult for women
(Beckett 2005; Henley-Einion 2009). As a result, it was argued,
the inherently empowering nature of pregnancy and childbirth had
been forgotten (Henley-Einion 2009).

Moreover, it was claimed, the agenda of medicalization had
taken on a life of its own due to underlying profit-making impera-
tives and territorial battles between midwives and obstetricians, as
well as the fact that each intervention in the process of childbirth
made subsequent ones more likely (Beckett 2005). Feminists and
birth activists highlighted rising levels of unnecessary interfer-
ence in uncomplicated deliveries, for instance the routine use of
electronic foetal monitoring, epidural anaesthesia and oxytocin to
augment labour, which had led to a rise in assisted and surgical
deliveries and routine episiotomies within a 'cascade of intervention' (World Health Organization 1996: 10). It was also thought
that women were being encouraged to choose these interventions because of a lack of education about their implications and
a learned fear of the pain and 'risk' of childbirth (Henley-Einion
2009). This masculinist agenda perpetuated men's control over
women's bodies and reflected a pathologization of women's
natural reproductive capacities (Purdy 2001; Johnson 2008).
Feminists argued that doctors had used their growing political and
cultural authority to define pregnancy and childbirth as inherently
risky, to eliminate and/or regulate midwives and to fuel the perception that women (especially middle- and upper-class women)

were unable to withstand the process (Beckett 2005; Henley-Einion 2009). This also positioned the foetus as a separate patient in need of protection, on the basis of which pregnant and birthing women were controlled and regulated (Beckett 2005). There were accompanying anti-capitalist critiques of the infant formula industry (the US-led boycott of Nestlé which began in the 1970s being the most high-profile and successful resultant campaign), which was associated with its own profit-making imperative, with harm to infants in developing countries and with maintaining productivity in industrialized nations since breastfeeding was difficult to combine with paid work in the absence of structural supports for breastfeeding mothers (Palmer 1988).

In the early twentieth century, first-wave western feminists had struggled against the prevailing medical culture to overcome resistance to the use of pain relief in labour (Beckett 2005) as part of a broader fight to free women from the dominion of biology and the tyranny of their reproductive capacities (Purdy 2001). Second-wave birth and breastfeeding activists took a similarly counter-cultural stance, only the object of their opposition had dramatically shifted and, ironically, there was a subsequent convergence between feminist critiques of medicalization and conservative and religious discourses on childbirth and child rearing (Beckett 2005). These alliances gave rise to 'natural birth' and breastfeeding movements in many western countries, which remain to the present day and which, I will argue, resonate with neoliberal frameworks around health care and neoconservative gender traditionalism, and so have had substantial influence on policy in the West and elsewhere. This, however, has meant that agendas which originally started in valuable feminist efforts to empower women have begun to take different forms due to their intersections with neoliberal and neoconservative projects.

'Normal birth' and 'breast is best'

In their resistance to the language of medicalization, feminists and other activists have tended to employ the idiom of the 'normal' or the 'natural' (Beckett 2005). In the late 1980s and early 1990s, this language was institutionalized when the World Health Organization (WHO) adopted a definition of 'normal birth'. This was premised on the belief that interventions, although helpful in some cases, were unwelcome in non-complicated labour and delivery (World Health Organization 1996; Chalmers and Porter 2001). The definition of 'normal birth' was '[s]pontaneous in onset, low-risk at the start of labour and remaining so throughout labour and delivery. The infant is born spontaneously in the vertex [head first] position between 37 and 42 completed weeks of pregnancy. After birth, mother and infant are in good condition' (World Health Organization 1996: 4). In such low-risk situations, the WHO argued, women should not be subject to major interventions unnecessarily: in normal birth, there should be a valid reason to intervene in the natural process (World Health Organization 1996: 4).

By the 2000s, the concept of 'normal' or 'natural' birth had become common parlance among birth activists and health professionals in western countries. However, 'normalcy' by this point had become a target to achieve: a desired outcome rather than a designation of low-risk status implying that efforts should be made to avoid unnecessary procedures. From 2003 to 2006, 'normal delivery' rates were published annually in England by the National Health Service Information Centre (National Childbirth Trust 2010). In 2007, a report by the UK Maternity Care Working Party, which included the Royal College of Midwives, the Royal College of Obstetricians and Gynaecologists, the National Childbirth Trust, the Association of Radical Midwives and BirthChoiceUK, said that maternity services should aim to increase their 'normal birth' rates to 60 per cent by 2010. 'Normal birth' was defined as being 'Without induction, without the use of instruments, not by caesarean section and without general, spinal or epidural anaesthetic before or during delivery' (UK Maternity Care Working Party 2007: 1). This was exemplified by women whose labours began spontaneously and progressed spontaneously without drugs, and who gave birth spontaneously.[2] In all four countries of the United Kingdom, maternity policy in the 2000s was directed towards promoting 'normal birth' and reducing interventions (National Childbirth Trust 2010). The idea of 'normal birth' was also being promoted in other European countries, North America and around the world in similar ways (Hendrix 2011). In the United States, the 1989 revision of the Standard Certificate of Live Birth had introduced new items on obstetric procedures and method of delivery as a means of monitoring uses of technology during labour (Freedman et al. 1988), and the caesarean rate had been a matter of concern since the late 1970s (Menacker 2005).

A shift had occurred, from the feminist-inspired aim of protecting women from the process of medicalization to the more neoliberalized practice of using 'normal birth' as an indicator and target and promoting 'normalcy' of outcome: within this new framework, there was a clear preference for particular types of birth over others. There was also an implication that almost every woman was able to birth 'normally', so the focus should be on proactively attempting to reduce levels of intervention rather than merely ensuring that low-risk women were not interfered with. This was signalled by an overarching shift in language, for example from the WHO's 1990s' notion of 'care in normal birth' (World Health Organization 1996) to the Royal College of Midwives' 'Campaign for Normal Birth', launched in 2005, and the Canadian 'Power to Push Campaign', inaugurated in 2010. In this outcome-focused agenda, a particular birth script took centre stage, often predominant over maternal preference or the experience of the birthing mother. Indeed, in 2010 the UK National Childbirth Trust began recommending the use of the outcome of 'normal birth' as a measure of the quality of the process of care (National Childbirth Trust 2010), assuming that the latter could be read off from the former. This hypothesis was not completely supported by empirical research, suggesting that birth trauma was most often related to lack of support during labour and delivery, and that most women experiencing trauma in fact had 'normal' deliveries (Ayers and Ford 2009; Ford and Ayers 2009). Nevertheless, the outcome-focused model coincided with neoliberal health service frameworks and cost-cutting agendas: in a 2010 document detailing frontline UK health service staff suggestions for cost-effective care, increasing the 'normal birth' rate and reducing unnecessary caesareans was positioned as a way to save millions of pounds (National Health Service 2010), and in 2013 US think tank the Center for Healthcare Quality and Payment Reform reported that reducing the caesarean rate to the WHO-recommended 15 per cent would save the government US$5 billion in healthcare spending.

In the United Kingdom, alongside the promotion of 'normal birth', the National Health Service also adopted the slogan 'breast is best' in the 2000s in a drive to encourage all new mothers to breastfeed and to persuade fathers and the wider population to support breastfeeding (Smyth 2012). This evoked broader trends towards grassroots breastfeeding promotion which had begun in the 1970s and 1980s in western countries, and also built upon WHO recommendations that there should be immediate skin-to-skin contact post-partum and that suckling/breastfeeding should be encouraged in the first hour after birth (World Health Organization/UNICEF 1989; World Health Organization 1996: 33). The United Nations Children's Fund (UNICEF) and WHO Baby Friendly Hospital Initiative was established in 1991 to encourage maternity hospitals to promote breastfeeding and act in accordance with the 1981 WHO International Code of Marketing of Breast-milk Substitutes, which stated that health facilities should not sell, give away or display materials related to infant formula (World Health Organization and UNICEF 2009). This fed into a growing political movement around breastfeeding which was underpinned by a burgeoning 'science' in which breast milk and suckling were associated with a host of health benefits – protection from allergies, infection and disease and high IQ scores for infants and children, as well as health benefits for the mother and superior mother/child bonding (Smyth 2012; Joan Wolf 2011). Formula feeding was correspondingly associated with a large number of dangers to infants, such as asthma, allergies, reduced cognitive development, acute respiratory and cardiovascular disease, diabetes, infection, nutritional deficiencies, obesity and death, and risks to mothers such as breast, ovarian and endometrial cancer, osteoporosis, arthritis, diabetes, stress and obesity (InFact Canada

2006). However, these claims were often based on patchy evidence or studies which confused cause and effect, failed to control for socio-economic differences or parental behaviour, used very small or unrepresentative samples, such as premature infants, or extrapolated evidence from developing countries to those in the West (Goldin, Smyth and Foulkes 2006; Joan Wolf 2007, 2011; Hoddinott, Tappin and Wright 2008; Fewtrell et al. 2011).

Much like the initiatives on 'normal birth', promoting breastfeeding cohered with broader neoliberal health service trends: in particular, preventative agendas around risk which aimed to create behavioural change through target-setting and monitoring and which emphasized individual responsibility rather than structural constraints (there were similarities, for example, with initiatives around obesity and smoking). In the United Kingdom, targets were set to increase the number of mothers who started breastfeeding and continued exclusive breastfeeding for up to six months (Crossley 2009; Fewtrell et al. 2011). This was supported by legislation, with discrimination against breastfeeding mothers outlawed by the Breastfeeding etc. (Scotland) Act in 2005 and the Equality Act 2010 in England and Wales, and the Workplace Regulations and Approved Code of Practice requiring employers to provide suitable facilities for pregnant and breastfeeding women to rest (National Health Service 2008).[3] In the United States, breastfeeding had also become a target: from 2006, following a two-year National Breastfeeding Awareness Campaign (Kukla 2006; Wolf 2007), the Centers for Disease Control and Prevention began to produce a 'breastfeeding report card', providing information on state and national trends. There were stronger attempts here to legislate behaviour: as of 2011, every state except West Virginia had some law related to breastfeeding, whether these concerned the right to breastfeed in public or employers making space and time for breastfeeding and educational initiatives to promote it, and in 2010 the federal Fair Labor Standards Act was amended to mandate employers to provide time for mothers to express breast milk (National Conference of State Legislatures 2011). In 2012, a statement issued by the American Academy of Pediatrics positioned breastfeeding as a public health issue and not a lifestyle choice (American Academy of Pediatrics 2012). A study published in Pediatrics in 2010 (Bartick and Reinhold 2010) indicated that exclusive breastfeeding for six months could save the US economy US$13 billion annually, mostly related to infant mortality and morbidity.

Other countries also either debated or adopted legislative frameworks around breastfeeding, for instance, South Africa (Motsoaledi 2011), Armenia (Mkrtchyan 2011), Indonesia (Vaswani 2010) and Venezuela (Reuters 2013), and still more were engaged in breastfeeding awareness initiatives (see, for example, Wall 2001). Breastfeeding laws generally banned the advertising of formula milk or its free distribution in health facilities, although the Indonesian legislation specified that anyone standing in the way of six months' exclusive breastfeeding could face a fine and up to a year in prison. By 2009, 20,000 maternity facilities in 156 countries had been awarded the WHO/UNICEF 'baby-friendly' designation for their promotion of breastfeeding (World Health Organization and UNICEF 2009). Like 'normal birth', the promotion of breastfeeding had by this point begun to shift from a positive and productive grassroots resistance to medicalization to a normalized imperative. Issues around maternal preference and women's bodily autonomy were superseded by prescribed practices, often regardless of circumstances, with the implication being that all women could and should breastfeed (Wall 2001). Breastfeeding interventions were targeted at large-scale behavioural change, often using mechanisms of fear-production relating to the proposed dangers of formula feeding (see Wolf 2007 for a full discussion of this) and using the rhetoric of risk which had initially been the focus of critique for anti-medicalization activists (Joan Wolf 2011).

As it grew out of the grassroots movement of the 1960s and 1970s, the arena of activism around 'normal birth' and breast-feeding in the 2000s and after began to morph into a more institutionalized coalition of national and international health and policy organizations, non-profit and profit-making companies, health professionals' groups, community and religious groups, and individuals. At times, wildly divergent agendas were brought together. The contemporary field includes key international actors such as the WHO, UNICEF and similar bodies (Smyth 2012). There is also a general academic consensus (Schmied and Lupton 2001), with journals such as *Birth*, the *Journal of Perinatal Education*, the *International Breastfeeding Journal* and the *Journal of Obstetric, Gynecologic and Neonatal Nursing* important sites for the dissemination of these agendas. Midwives remain a key group of advocates, and midwifery has grown into a powerful profession with independent and 'radical' midwives' groups, as well as professional organizations for midwives, some state-sponsored and some of which have the ability to license or certify practitioners (Beckett and Hoffman 2005). The International Confederation of Midwives, with more than a hundred member associations in countries worldwide, acts as an umbrella for the various national efforts. The history of midwifery as a social movement informs this new professional politics, which is concerned with promoting and helping midwives as well as helping women (Daviss 2001; MacDonald 2011), especially in the United States where battles over the legitimacy of midwifery remain (Beckett and Hoffman 2005).

There is also an arena of non-profit-making companies, offering ante- and postnatal education to those who can afford to pay for their services, and web-based and helpline assistance which is often provided at no cost. In the United Kingdom, the National Childbirth Trust was founded in 1956 by a middle-class mother who wished to promote the teachings of obstetrician and natural childbirth advocate Grantly Dick-Read. At the time of writing, the Trust had grown into a major organization, operating at local and national levels with a membership of around 100,000 and with a key role in policy (Roberts, Satchwell and Tyler 2011). Four years after the genesis of the NCT, US-based Lamaze International was set up by a group of parents, childbirth educators and health professionals in order to teach the natural childbirth method developed by Dr Fernand Lamaze. By the end of 2010, the association had 2,355 members, and 13,300 subscribers to its Building Confidence Week By Week antenatal mails (Lamaze 2011). The La Leche League, also formed in 1956, was initially a small mother-to-mother breastfeeding support group founded by a number of Catholic women in the United States. At the time of writing, it had developed into a broader (and non-religious) organization with over 3000 groups in more than 60 countries, offering support to breastfeeding mothers and promoting exclusive breastfeeding for six months and continued breastfeeding after that (La Leche League 2012). The contemporary non-profit sector also includes international organizations and initiatives such as One World Birth, the global Breastfeeding Initiative for Child Survival, the World Breastfeeding Trends Initiative, the World Alliance for Breastfeeding Action and the International Baby Food Action Network.

At the grassroots level, a plethora of birth, breastfeeding and 'holistic parenting' support groups has emerged, as well as Christian and spiritual groups (Smyth 2012). Many of these make use of the internet and social media, and this also provides a platform for individual advocates and activists, mainly drawn from the burgeoning cadre of largely white and middle-class 'Mummy/ Mommy bloggers' (Lopez 2009). There are also any number of local 'alternative birth' and breastfeeding and 'holistic parenting' support groups, communities and helplines, whether local chapters of larger organizations or more grassroots initiatives (see, for example, Beckett and Hoffman 2005; Shaw and Kitzinger 2005; Abbott, Renfrew and McFadden 2006). All this provides a framework in which (predominantly white and middle-class) women are able to educate themselves about birth and breastfeeding choices and use their lay knowledge to demand less childbirth intervention and more breastfeeding support (Johnson 2008). High-profile role models are provided in the form of public figures who are celebrated within activist communities for their positive choices to birth naturally and breastfeed and who represent a fascinating union of agendas around natural and alternative health and competitive commercialized celebrity culture. For example, model Gisele Bündchen, actresses Nicole Richie, Jessica Alba and Halle Berry, and TV presenter Ricki Lake have all been praised for choosing natural childbirth (Babble 2012), while fashion designer and singer Victoria Beckham was widely criticized as being 'too posh to push' for opting for caesarean section for all four of her children (*Daily*

Telegraph 2011). Singer Jennifer Lopez and TV personality Katie Price (Jordan) have both come under fire for formula feeding, and there has been widespread speculation about and monitoring of actress Angelina Jolie's infant feeding choices (*Daily Mail* 2011b; Babyworld 2012; Breastfeeding.com 2012; Rochman 2012).

'Part of me': the new intensive motherhood

It is my contention that the new reproductive 'regimes of truth' around 'normal birth' and breastfeeding have gained immense sociocultural power, partly due to their resonance with contemporary neoliberal and neoconservative agendas, for instance the resurgent gender essentialism and pronatalism which characterizes the moral-political rationality of the New Right (Snitow 1992; Brown 2006). Western commentators (Cameron 2010; Walter 2010) have identified a growing populist biological determinism in increasingly gender-differentiated consumer goods for children, media rhetoric about women's 'emotional intelligence' and a celebration of choices in favour of stay-at-home motherhood, which has been echoed by some academics (notably Hakim 2000, 2003). There are similar themes in the 'self-help' literature which is key to the construction of the neoliberal DIY biography, which makes use of popular and evolutionary psychology and pseudo-neuroscience to claim that 'men are from Mars and women are from Venus' (Gray 1992). These developments have fused with the backlash against feminism and high-achieving women, economic pressures which have intensified competition in labour markets and a general return to biologism in popular science and culture (Cameron 2010). The emergence of evolutionary psychology as a discipline is key: this largely unfalsifiable form of biological constructionism both fixes and romanticizes particular gendered characteristics (Dupré 2010), with no place for the productive role of power and oppression.

The history of the anti-medicalization movement yields similar gender essentialisms in its appeals to women's innate abilities and desires to birth and nurture: as a result, it has been suggested that it was in part a conservative response to women's emancipation (Mosucci 2003). For example, Grantly Dick-Read, author of *Childbirth Without Fear* (originally published in 1933) and widely regarded as the father of natural childbirth, was a gender conservative who believed that motherhood was a woman's ultimate source of fulfilment, argued that privileged women should drop their claims to emancipation and return to the home (Mosucci 2003), and found one of his first major supporters in the Pope (Caton 1996). Ina May Gaskin, a leading US exponent of natural childbirth, was famous for her spiritual approach to midwifery but also for her residence in New Age community The Farm, set up in 1971 and still operating today with 175 members. Some contemporaneous analysts described this commune as a gender-equal utopia (Conover 1975), but others saw it as a fanatical personality cult centred on Gaskin's husband, whose word was law (Kinkade 1974). Contemporary reproductive politics continues to base itself around biological motherhood, albeit with enduring conflicts between feminist and maternalist ideals (Beckett and Hoffman 2005). Gender essentialisms, together with the neoliberal values of personal achievement and individual responsibility, frame the new politics of 'intensive motherhood' (Lee 2008; Faircloth 2013), 'total motherhood' (Wolf 2007) or 'exclusive motherhood' (Wall 2001), in which mothering is entirely the preserve of women, a journey of self-fulfilment which is absorbing, completely child-centred and in which the mother becomes solely responsible for her child's development and protection from risk (Joan Wolf 2011).

Within this discourse, 'normal' or 'natural' birth is positioned as a defining moment of womanhood, a positive, life-changing and even spiritual experience (see, for example, Humenick 2006). Achieving 'normal birth' is equated with women's empowerment (Beckett 2005), deploying a Cartesian idea of 'mind over matter'. For instance, 'hypnobirthing' mothers are recommended to use the word 'surge' instead of 'contraction' and refer to the waters 'releasing' rather than 'breaking' (Mottershead 2006). Some activists go further to argue that childbirth can (and should) be painless and even erotic, linking women's sexual fulfilment with the mothering role (see, for example, Hotelling 2009b). This is exemplified by the growing fascination with orgasmic childbirth in the United States and elsewhere, with some proponents positioning this as the only authentic birthing experience, an attainment of physical and emotional ecstasy, rather than merely a successful avoidance of pain medication (see, for example, Hotelling 2009a). However, these ideas are problematized by empirical evidence that painless labour is a reality for a very small minority of women (Melzack 1984; Johnson 2008), and as a result there is a corresponding formulation of motherhood as an experience which allows women to find and fulfil themselves through self-sacrifice. In this narrative, withstanding the ordeal of childbirth is the route to authentic motherhood: in 2009, leading UK midwife Denis Walsh exemplified this view in an interview in the *Observer*, in which he argued that more women should experience painful contractions since they were a 'rite of passage' which facilitated bonding with the infant. These comments were welcomed by the National Childbirth Trust (Campbell 2009). Ideas about women's self-fulfilment through pain tap into long-standing stereotypes about feminine masochism (Baker 2010), and it is worth remembering here that the principle of women's rights to relieve suffering and gain control of the birthing process fuelled first-wave feminist calls for the use of the drug scopolamine in labour (Beckett 2005). In 2011, a survey distributed by the UK Birth Trauma Association revealed that many labouring women had been denied the pain relief they required.

Breastfeeding is similarly positioned as an inherently rewarding, pleasurable and even erotic[4] process facilitated by maternal instinct and love, and has been celebrated by feminists and others as a means by which to reclaim feminine values and the value of nurturing (Schmied and Lupton 2001; Bartlett 2005). During discussions about the Venezuelan bottle-feeding ban, socialist minister Odalis Monzon stated that it was being considered as a way to 'increase the love (between mother and child) because this [had] been lost by these transnational companies selling formula' (Reuters 2013). Again, this is not fully supported by the empirical evidence which shows that many women find nursing both physically and emotionally exhausting (Lee 2008; Schmied et al.

2011): however, these women are generally positioned as immature, disengaged or selfish or as having a false consciousness (Kukla 2006). As Illinois-based lactation consultant Beth Seidel writes, some mothers 'give up at the first hint of a challenge' (Seidel 2012). There is also a corresponding construction of breastfeeding as a heroic act of self-sacrifice, often applied when it is painful or difficult (Wall 2001; Smyth 2012). Many of these messages come together in the following quote from another US lactation consultant, Glenda Dickerson:

> I have felt for years that many mothers wean because they thought they were supposed to love and/or enjoy breastfeeding 24 hours a day. Some of the mothers I have admired the most are mothers that breastfed in spite of not being in love with the act of breastfeeding. They breastfed because they knew it was the right choice for their babies. (from kellymom.com)

These narratives share much with right-wing pronatalism as well as maternalist feminism (see, for example, Gilligan 1982; Ruddick 1989). The idea of maternality as a route to liberation also needs to be set alongside the fact that despite almost fifty years of second-wave activism and some important political gains, the ability to combine motherhood with other social roles does not yet fully exist in many parts of the West and worldwide (Yerkes 2010; Misra, Budig and Boeckmann 2011).

The biological mother/baby relationship underpins breastfeeding politics and advocacy, with fathers and non-biological parents reduced to a supporting role, if any at all (Wall 2001; Schmied and Lupton 2001), and an erasure of others who might be able/wish to conceive, birth and breastfeed a child, for instance some trans men. Materials promoting breastfeeding describe the biological mother and her infant as a 'dyad' (Lauwers and Swisher 2011) or a 'continuum' (Romano and Lothian 2008: 102), indicating a single biological unit (Wolf 2007). Exclusive breastfeeding is seen as essential to this mother/infant symbiosis (Schmied and Lupton 2001), with the primary need of the infant being the breast, and other sources of comfort or sustenance coming second or even being seen as a threat. The La Leche League's advice to partners states, 'your first job is to *support* breastfeeding, not *compete* with it. A "relief bottle" may seem helpful, but it's more likely to cause breastfeeding problems and health risks for your baby' (La Leche League 2010: 467). Some feminists have argued that this conceptualization of the mother–child continuum is a key element of motherhood as a political project, since it challenges the western neoliberal idea of the autonomous individual (Davis-Floyd 1999; Hausman 2004). However, its effects can also be seen as problematic in that issues around women's sense of self are ignored (Wall 2001), and their needs (for instance, to work, control their bodies or sustain an identity independent of their children) become subsumed by those of the infant or seen as weaknesses to be corrected through educational messages (Kukla 2006: 175). This assumes that women can and should find fulfilment in merging with another, an idea which is not supported by all the empirical evidence (Schmied and Lupton 2001). It also ignores the needs of fathers and partners (both men and women) to establish a meaningful bond, and the fact that infants might benefit from these relationships. Conceptualizations of the breast as essential to bonding have caused some mothers who formula-feed to engage in onerous 'identity work' in order to ease their guilt and shame and preserve a sense of themselves as good mothers (Lee 2008; Crossley 2009; Barston 2012).

Such 'attachment parenting' models originally emerged as part of the post-war agenda around domesticity and gender traditionalism, with ideas about infants needing continual contact with their mothers seen in some quarters as a means of putting women back in their place since they were based on very shaky scientific evidence (Wall 2001; Lee 2008).[5] These connections can be observed in the present day, with the more zealous contemporary breastfeeding advice relying on and perpetuating traditional gender roles in its recommendations for constant mother/infant skin-to-skin contact or 'kangaroo care' (initially used for premature infants – see World Health Organization 2003) and proscribing the use of dummies/pacifiers and artificial feeding devices, even if used to feed breast milk. Exclusive breastfeeding need not mean gender traditionalism in theory, but in practice this is often the case due to a lack of support for breastfeeding at work or in public (Palmer 1988). This is obviously an argument for structural change rather than a case against breastfeeding, but it is also inevitable that current breastfeeding advocacy should be associated to some extent with stay-at-home motherhood. Commentators such as French feminist Elisabeth Badinter (2010) and American author Erica Jong (2010) have highlighted the pressure that such attachment parenting models place upon mothers, particularly those who lack the resources necessary to engage in intensive parenting practices, and have linked this to rising postnatal depression (see also Zoe Williams 2011b; Pollitt 2012).

A maternalist view of parenting is also echoed in some contemporary models of childbirth which conceptualize it as a women-only experience (and again, exclude the trans man as potential birther of an infant). These have their roots in feminist critiques of masculinist medicine, with valid arguments for preserving women-only space if this is desired and required (Draper 1997). However, such frameworks can also be reactionary in terms of privileging the mother–infant bond and perpetuating essentialisms about women's innate abilities to support and nurture and men's propensities to be controlling and lack emotional intelligence.[6] The most famous proponent of this view is celebrated French obstetrician and 'natural childbirth' activist Michel Odent, who feels that men should never be at the birth of their children, since they tend to keep their partners in the rational world and stop them accessing the primitive, instinctive parts of their brains. In a 2008 article in UK tabloid the *Daily Mail*, Odent also suggested that men who are present at births are often unable to feel attracted to their wives afterwards, mobilizing a construction of male sexuality as being aroused by physical perfection and ignoring other, more plausible causes of a decline in sexual activity after the arrival of a child (Ahlborg, Dahlöf and Hallberg 2005). The idea that men cannot cope with the experience of childbirth or add anything of value to this event is both essentialist and challenged by some of the empirical evidence (Erlandsson and Lindgren 2011). It is partly rooted in the branch of anti-medicalization activism in which midwifery has often been infused with feminine mystique in order to produce particular narratives around the benefits of this type of care, in the context of threats to the profession. Midwifery has been conceptualized as holistic, in contrast to the objectified and technologized environment of the hospital; midwives are presented as empathic and intuitive, and able to communicate with women in a way that male doctors cannot (Carolan 2010). This is currently magnified in relation to the doula, the privileged West's version of the 'traditional' birth attendant: these women, who are usually untrained, are advertised as kind, caring, supportive, wise and motherly (from britishdoulas.co.uk).

'Nature' and 'culture' commodified

While the gender essentialisms of the new reproductive politics provide a link with neoconservative agendas, there are also a number of key elements which tap into neoliberal rationalities. One of the most obvious is the way in which 'normal birth' and breastfeeding movements are underpinned by western middle-class 'healthism'. This refers to the increasing preoccupation with health issues on the part of privileged social groups and an accompanying politics of patients' rights which draws on neoliberal ideas of consumer choice. It is also characterized by a sceptical engagement with the medical profession and technology, and an allegiance to 'natural' health practices, self-help and eastern medicine (Greenhalgh and Wessley 2004). Like alternative health, the politics of birth and breastfeeding relies very much on lay expertise, with activists assuming their own authority in relation to these and related health issues. The doula exemplifies this trend and is also an embodiment of the movement's opposition to medicalization and embrace of alternative values to do with nature, home and spirituality. It is perhaps partly this connection with the alternative health arena which allows birth and breastfeeding activists to position themselves as avant-garde, counter-cultural and discriminated against (see, for example, Cheyney 2008; Evans 2010), despite the contemporary hegemony of their ideas (Beckett and Hoffman 2005). However, and perhaps paradoxically, they often also make appeals to science in order to stress the benefits of their preferred practices (Beckett and Hoffman 2005).

Achieving 'normal birth' and successful breastfeeding can also be conceptualized as a 'body project', reflecting the emphasis on bodily maintenance, modification and performance which characterizes contemporary neoliberal societies due to the decline of religious formations of identity, the growth of consumer culture, the performative nature of postmodern identities and the emphasis on individual responsibility. This has produced heightened levels of narcissism and increased levels of surveillance of our own and others' bodies (Foucault 1977; Featherstone 1991; Giddens 1991; Shilling 1993). The new reproductive politics resonates with this model in its individualism, focus on achievement and increasing commodification. Breastfeeding, for example, is often constructed as something which needs to be worked on and attained, creating pressure on women to perform appropriately (Lee 2008; Crossley 2009; Thomson et al. 2011). Similarly, MacDonald (2006) argues that achieving a 'natural' delivery has now become an important accomplishment. Reflecting this and also illustrating the confessional nature of contemporary culture (Foucault 1976), activists who make use of social media often present evidence of their reproductive triumphs on their blogs and websites, and there is a variety of YouTube channels dedicated to women's videos of their birthing events (Longhurst 2009). The accompanying narratives of self-actualization belie the fact that the majority of women reporting post-traumatic stress disorder after childbirth have had obstetrically 'normal' vaginal deliveries (Ford and Ayers 2009). They also conceal the fact that in order for 'natural' birth to be positioned as a romanticized ideal, some women are required to 'fail' (MacDonald 2006; Frost et al. 2006). The 'birth plan', originally envisaged as a way for women to avoid escalating interventions (Lothian 2006), has become in some quarters a template for women to 'design their ideal birth' (from birthingnaturally.net) or 'envision [their] perfect divine birth' (from birthsong.com.au) in consumerist terms. Frost et al. (2006) argue that this is implicated in embedding natural birth into women's psyches and prohibits any discussion of, or preparation for, operative delivery: this makes it likely that women will experience trauma if they do not achieve their objectives.

It is perhaps notable here that in recent years veteran activist Sheila Kitzinger has expressed dismay at the mutation of 'natural birth' into a goal-oriented agenda (Donnelly 2009; Saner 2013). Kitzinger, however, was a key figure in the healthist framings of the new reproductive politics, particularly in terms of its fetishization of the 'natural' and also its associated appropriation of 'traditional' cultures. Her 'psychosexual approach' to childbirth, positioning it as a powerfully erotic experience, was partly the result of anthropological research (Kitzinger 2011 [1980]), and as MacDonald (2006: 239) states, '[p]art of Kitzinger's message was to rest on the claim that natural female bodies and natural births had been rediscovered, as it were, dwelling in traditional societies throughout the globe, proving the existence of a prediscursive nature uncorrupted by scientific culture.' Contemporary reproductive politics similarly takes the 'natural' for granted and conflates it with 'normal' and with a positive and easy experience of birth (Righard 2001; Maternity Care Working Party 2007). As MacDonald (2006) argues, the discourse of 'natural birth' can be seen as positive in its construction of women as strong and powerful in their abilities to deliver by themselves: however, this can also be disempowering for women who are unable to achieve the ideal. Together with the positioning of breast milk as 'nature's perfect food' (Wolf 2007), these ideas also assume that nature is always good and natural substances are always pure. This provides a link with right-wing discourses such as social Darwinism, in which the idea of 'letting nature take its course' has justified eugenic principles and laissez-faire social policies in order to let the most superior individuals flourish while the inferior eventually die out. Unimpeded nature, then, is deeply marked by privilege, and in rejecting a medicalized birth, middle-class activists confirm their elevated social position since only women who know they are able to give birth safely are able to reject the trappings of technology (MacDonald 2011).

Complementing this focus on the 'natural', there is a tendency to search for authenticity and origins in the discussion of alternative birth practices (MacDonald 2006). This positions women as instinctive and closer to nature (Frost et al. 2006), and often involves the Orientalizing of 'traditional' cultures, whether prehistoric or from developing countries (Shuval and Gross 2008). American childbirth educator Judith Lothian (2007: 45) describes her Lamaze class as modelling 'traditional ways of passing information about birth from generation to generation', and advice to mothers to pursue on-demand or extended breastfeeding often makes reference to the fact that these practices are common outside the West, but without highlighting pertinent differences in culture and lifestyle (see, for example, Bumgarner 2000; Kamnitzer 2009; Niala 2012). Grantly Dick-Read's ideas about natural childbirth were partly based on his conviction that 'primitive women' were not troubled by the process. Furthermore, he argued that 'primitives' who died in childbirth did so without sadness, realizing they were not competent to produce children and be members of their tribe. Like the claims of many contemporary activists, however, Dick-Read's points were made despite the fact that he had not spent extensive time in non-western countries (Caton 1996). The lack of an evidence base to corroborate such assertions is particularly problematic when non-western birthing practices are appropriated in the service of authenticity rather than effectiveness. For instance, the 'traditional' birth attendants on which the doula is modelled have not been shown to reduce maternal mortality in developing countries (Kvåle et al. 2005). Indeed, 99% of all maternal deaths worldwide occur in developing countries, often from preventable complications which could be treated with interventions such as assisted or surgical delivery (Dogba and Fournier 2009). Post-partum depression is also more common, especially among rural women (Villegas et al. 2011), and 98% of all neonatal deaths and 97% of all stillbirths occur in these countries, largely due to preventable complications before and during delivery (Zupan 2005). The professionalization of midwifery/provision of other forms of skilled care has been shown to reduce mortality in such cases (Zupan 2005; Dogba and Fournier 2009).

Due to their largely unregulated status, there are no figures for perinatal mortality rates relating to doula-attended births in the West: however, Symon et al. (2010) found a significantly higher rate for births booked under an independent midwife than births in health service units in the United Kingdom. The Birthplace in England study, a national prospective cohort study of almost 65,000 women with low-risk pregnancies (Birthplace in England Collaborative Group 2011), found that there was a threefold increase in poor outcomes for first-time mothers planning a home birth, as opposed to those in midwifery and obstetric units, although the risks were still very small (Newburn 2011). Worldwide, the WHO has estimated that 15 per cent of all women giving birth develop complications serious enough to require rapid and skilled intervention if they are to survive without lifelong disabilities. The 'Trends in Maternal Mortality' joint report by the UN estimated that providing timely interventions to such women, alongside trained midwifery care, had been instrumental in reducing maternal mortality rates by 47 per cent between 1990 and 2010 (UNFPA, UNICEF, WHO, World Bank 2012). It is interesting that in western countries those most likely to choose birth interventions (and also those less likely to breastfeed) are our own social Others, such as working-class and minority ethnic women (Kukla 2006; Brubaker 2007; Hildingsson, Radestad and Lindgren 2010; MacDorman, Declerq and Menacker 2010; Cammu, Martens and Keirse 2011), who may be stigmatized by natural birth and breast-feeding discourses while global Others are romanticized (see, for example, Millner 2012).

This fetishization of the 'natural' and non-western cultures also masks the fact that reproduction and parenting activism are highly commodified arenas. There is a variety of products in circulation, including birthing pools, balls, dresses and wraps, cooling sprays and moisturizers, TENS (transcutaneous electrical nerve stimulation) machines, breast pumps, nipple shields, pregnancy and breastfeeding pillows, slings, nipple creams, herbs to increase milk production, nursing bras and a huge range of books. Many activists receive revenue via their blogs and publications from placement and reviews of these products, as well as direct advertising. This sits uncomfortably with their critiques of women requesting birth interventions as being conditioned by consumerist values (Glantz 2011), and their otherwise understandable opposition to aggressive formula marketing (see, for example, the Alpha Parent 2011; PhD in Parenting 2011). The growing industry of 'mommy bloggers', generally well-educated women in their thirties, is estimated to control around US$2 trillion worth of purchasing power in the United States (Basen 2012). In the United Kingdom, these bloggers have their own annual conference sponsored by corporations including Hewlett Packard, Disney, Lego, Twentieth Century Fox, Pampers, Johnsons Baby and Hyundai. In the United States, the Mom 2.0 Summit in 2012 was sponsored by corporations including Honda, Aldi, Dove, Intel and LG. Furthermore, many childbirth and breastfeeding support services are commercial (a doula can cost up to £1,000 for a birth and a private midwife up to £4,000 in the United Kingdom – see Donnelly 2011), even though they are often recommended as though there is no profit motive.

Identity politics and the privatization of responsibility

'Natural birth' and breastfeeding, then, are increasingly positioned within the domain of individualized consumer choice, and breast-feeding advocacy in particular often shies away from targeting the gendered structures which make women solely responsible for parenting and caring, and in fact can even emphasize these with the principle that nutrition and comfort should only come from the breast. It is relevant here that Nordic states with high rates of breastfeeding tend to have family-friendly policies in place (Gupta, Smith and Verner 2008), compared to the efforts to facilitate change in the United Kingdom, the United States and other countries through the behavioural rhetoric of 'breast is best'. This also points to broader policy contradictions: promoting breastfeeding without providing structural supports is not necessarily compatible with the welfare-to-work policies which have become popular in the United Kingdom, the United States and elsewhere. The lack of acknowledgement of this is an insight into the privilege of breast-feeding activists, reflected in advice to let chores wait, sleep when the baby sleeps, or take a 'babymoon', which involves going to bed with the infant for several days. Lone mothers and women from disadvantaged social groups may face a variety of issues that are not compatible with such activities (Wolf 2007). Individualistic breast-feeding advice also ignores structural factors affecting child health such as inadequate pre- and antenatal care, poverty and shrinking welfare states (Wolf 2007), which are perhaps more important than the knowledge and attitudes prioritized within the contemporary politics of reproduction (see, for example, Schmied and Lupton 2001). This can be linked to the neoliberal privatization of respon-sibility: it is now a woman's duty to build a better baby through breastfeeding and her fault if her child develops allergies, infections or other conditions such as obesity (Wall 2001). Questions need to be raised about the complicity of reproduction activists in per-petuating such doctrines: indeed, in 1986 Adrienne Rich returned to her 1976 maternalist feminist classic *Of Woman Born* to critique the movement 'narrowly concerned with pregnancy and birth which does not ask questions and demand answers about the lives of children, the priorities of government; a movement in which individual families rely on consumerism and educational privilege to supply their own children with nutrition, schooling, healthcare' (1986 [1976]).

The new reproductive politics is largely concerned with rep-resentations of birth and breastfeeding and attitudes towards them rather than how they are structurally framed. A key element of breastfeeding activism, or 'lactivism', is the general public's reac-tion, with initiatives such as 'nurse-ins', 'flashmobs' where groups of mothers congregate and feed in public places, and campaigns to prevent social media sites such as Facebook from deleting pictures of mothers with their nurslings under obscenity rules. Nationally and internationally, there are breastfeeding awareness initiatives: World Breastfeeding Week (launched in 1992 and sponsored by a variety of organizations including UNICEF, the La Leche League and the WHO) is celebrated in more than 170 countries. In the

United Kingdom, National Breastfeeding Awareness Week began in 1993, and the withdrawal of central government funding in 2011 sparked a wave of protest (Boseley 2011). Indeed, news of a fall in breastfeeding rates during 2012–13 was attributed to the cutting of funding for this campaign (Boffey 2013a), with a lack of effort to counter public prejudice blamed for breastfeeding going 'out of fashion' (Turner 2013) or being deemed 'unnatural and abnormal' (Boffey 2013b) in some areas of the country. Such campaigns are an example of the politics of recognition (Fraser 1995, 2000), the identity-based activism in which issues around representation supplant those of structure and socio-economic redistribution (it is worth noting here that the largest declines in breastfeeding rates in the above example were in some of the most deprived areas of the United Kingdom). 'Natural' birth and breastfeeding have become part of an identity package around organic or holistic parenting (McDaniel 2009; Faircloth 2013), while formula feeding and birth interventions (and in particular, caesarean sections) form aspects of a negative Other associated with other practices such as 'cry-it-out', vaccination and corporal punishment. The names of some of the individuals and groups within the activist arena give an insight into the types of identities being constructed: for instance, Peaceful Parenting, Primitive Mommy, and The Natural Mummy Files. Primitive Mommy (www.primitivemommy.com) draws on a number of different themes as she describes herself as 'a devoted peaceful attachment mother of three, alternative medicine advocate, raw food loving, juicing enthusiast, Intactivist, babywearing, Earth loving hippy, Lactivist, altruistically trying to save the world from itself'.

Privilege, risk and the coercion of 'informed choice'

Similar to the shift from redistribution to recognition, Salecl (2010) has identified a shift from rights to choices in the reproductive arena. This is partly characterized by an understandable call to allow women to make informed and evidence-based choices about what happens to them and their infants (see, for example, Romano and Lothian 2008). However, it is not clear whose evidence counts and studies are often cherry-picked, depending on their findings (Keirse 2010). Due to ethical issues, there are no randomized controlled clinical trials on normal birth or breastfeeding, so research is observational and highly prone to confounding (Joan Wolf 2007, 2011; Hoddinott, Tappin and Wright 2008; Donna 2011; Barston 2012), and the studies which are used are rather out of date (see, for example, Humenick 2006). Research on breastfeeding often also comes from developing countries where there are clear benefits to show, and it is questionable whether these persist at the same levels in western contexts where there are much higher vaccination rates and fewer issues with malnutrition and contaminated water (see, for example, Hoddinott, Tappin and Wright 2008). Furthermore, studies citing the benefits of breastfeeding to infants often ignore the fact that it may have detrimental effects on a women's physical, emotional or financial health (Barston 2012). It seems, then, that 'informed choice' is only as good as those doing the informing.

'Informed choice' can also be seen to have a coercive element if it involves women being educated about risk specifically in relation to birth interventions and formula feeding (see, for example, Goer 1999; Kennedy and Shannon 2004; InFact Canada 2006), and campaigns can be shaming and characterized by hyperbole (Joan Wolf 2011), for instance the comparison of formula feeding to tobacco use (Kukla 2006; Wolf 2007), or, in one Australian Breastfeeding Association class, to AIDS (Murray 2012). The construction of one 'right' choice is underpinned by national policies such as targets for reducing caesareans and international guidance such as the WHO Code of Marketing of Breastmilk Substitutes (World Health Organization 1981), which restricts the marketing of formula milks.[7] There is also a certain amount of frustration evident amongst activists at the failure to shape all women's choices in a particular direction. Lamaze educator Judith Lothian (2007), for example, argues that her organization needs to develop better marketing strategies, largely involving presenting the method as a means by which to make childbirth easier for women. Similarly,

Boyd (2006) contends that 'normal birth' advocates should take inspiration from campaigns such as Mothers Against Drunk Driving, an American initiative which has been widely critiqued for its emotive strategies and zealotry (Balko 2002). In discussions of approaches such as 'advocacy labour support', there is an implication that midwives and antenatal educators should control what women are allowed to know in order to shape their choices (see, for example, Lothian 2007: 46). The curator of the US-based Leaky Boob activist website (2011) argues that women should not be told 'stories of breastfeeding doom and gloom' in an attempt at positive marketing. More dramatically, a 2013 report by UK charity Save the Children recommended that there should be cigarette-style warnings on boxes of formula milk. These examples all raise broader questions about how health promotion can be shot through with normalizing judgement (Gastaldo 1997) and sit uneasily with the movement's claims to be empowering to women, especially if this ultimately relies on misinformation and intimidatory tactics.

Within this framework of compulsory empowerment through 'informed choice', deviant behaviours are positioned as being a product of ignorance or weak-mindedness, rather than affirmative choices in favour of an alternative. This is clear in Lothian's (2007: 44) question: 'why are women seemingly uninterested in choosing normal birth, in spite of our best efforts?' There is an idea of false consciousness at work here: when women do not make the right choices, this is interpreted as proof that they are not getting the message (Kukla 2006). However, as Kukla (2006: 163) argues, many women who do not breastfeed are well aware of the risks: to explain away their choices is therefore to deny their agency. There are a number of legitimate factors here, such as a woman's physical health and the health of her baby, the needs of other children and family members, family living conditions and other demands on a woman's time and energy such as paid work (Schmied and Lupton 2001). Many of these factors are structural, and they challenge the formulation of birth and breastfeeding decisions as individual ones which can be shaped by behavioural interventions. There is a convolution here of popular western 'rational choice' arguments, in which 'normal' birth and breast-feeding are the outcome of sensible cost/benefit decision making, while electing alternatives is either irrationally driven or a product of rampant consumerism (the latter seen most prominently in discussions of women choosing caesareans for convenience – see, for example, Beckett 2005).

A version of the culture wars can also be seen playing out here, with women who choose childbirth interventions or formula feed (who are largely from working-class and minority ethnic groups) presented as ignorant and lazy or at best in need of education (which feeds racist and classist stereotypes – see Millner 2012). A generous formulation is that women lack the confidence to give birth without technology and need to be educated to trust themselves (Romano and Lothian 2008). For instance, Kennedy and Shannon (2004: 556) highlight American midwives' frustration with women who 'do not believe in their own strength'. Less judiciously, British activist the Alpha Parent (2011) blogs that formula companies 'exploit the lazy' – women who 'can't be bothered' – by claiming their products are convenient. There is a large group of lay 'experts' and professionals on hand to help women make the right choices, from lactation consultants to doulas to national and international organizations. Unfortunately, however, their activities often play into broader class and 'race' antagonisms in which the white middle classes judge other social groups as 'lacking' and attempt, through education and occasionally through ridicule, to force them into the dominant mode (see, for example, McRobbie 2004). This invisibilizes the important role of economic, social and cultural capitals: being able to choose a home birth, for example, often takes time and research and carries expense; and breastfeeding is not easily combined with paid work or other responsibilities. These factors perhaps explain why the most vocal advocates are extremely privileged women in western countries – in parts of the world with high rates of maternal mortality (and where most women deliver at home), activists are demanding more medical intervention (Johnson 2008). Choice, then, is inextricably linked to privilege.

Conclusion

In this chapter, I have introduced what I see as the new reproductive 'regimes of truth': the consensus around 'normal birth' and 'breast is best' which dominates policy, academia and the activist field. I have argued that these ideas have partly become hegemonic due to their strong connections with neoconservative and neoliberal rationalities, and that agendas which began in feminist efforts to empower women have now been transformed into messages which can put pressure on mothers in a number of different ways while excluding other caregivers. In my analysis, I have attempted to apply the principle of intersectionality: seeing the new reproductive activism as largely a politics of white, middle-class women with abundant cultural, social and economic capitals, I have explored how such agendas might intersect with the politics of class and 'race' and access to economic, social and cultural resources.

The new 'intensive motherhood' dovetails well with both neoconservative gender traditionalism and the neoliberal politics of personal responsibility. 'Natural' birth and breastfeeding are seen as defining characteristics of (biological) motherhood and a route to personal empowerment and bonding, with women who do not engage in such practices positioned as immature or lazy, or suffering from a false consciousness. In the absence of engagement with structural factors which hinder the achievement of 'intensive' or 'natural' motherhood, such ideas serve to reinforce neoconservative notions of motherhood as the route to women's self-actualization and their primary responsibility, and neoliberal agendas in which (biological) mothers are tasked with managing risk and ensuring their children's health through prescribed practices. This is linked to western middle-class 'healthism', which emphasizes personal accountability for health and disease prevention and often incorporates a suspicion of the medical and an allegiance to 'alternative' and non-western practices, through which the new 'natural motherhood' can be carried out. Such models rely on an uncritical acceptance of the idea of the 'natural', as well as a romanticization of 'primitive' and 'traditional' cultures which often flies in the face of evidence related to maternal and child mortality in international and developing contexts. Furthermore and perhaps paradoxically, the new reproductive agendas are highly achievement-focused, and natural birth and extended breastfeeding can be conceptualized as 'body projects' which are supported by a plethora of products and commercialized services. This feeds the identity politics which can be distinguished in this arena, with 'natural' parents being positioned against an Other associated with practices such as formula feeding and birth interventions. Furthermore, although birth and breastfeeding activists have a tendency to present themselves as counter-cultural, and identify themselves with global Others in their appropriation of 'traditional' practices, there is little attention paid to the stigmatizing effect this might have upon our own social Others, the working-class and minority ethnic women who may choose birth interventions or infant formula for a variety of structural reasons. Indeed, the discourse of 'informed choice' which underpins birth and breastfeeding politics largely ignores such factors, positioning 'wrong' choices as an effect of lack of education at best, or personal failure at worst. Such debates incorporate an element of coercion and ignore the fact that choice is to a large extent a function of privilege. The behavioural rhetoric which underpins natural birth and breastfeeding advocacy, in the absence of solid structural supports for mothers (and indeed, all parents), serves to vilify those with less access to resources and raises questions about the movement's concept of itself as being concerned with empowerment for all women.

Conclusion

This book has used a variety of different case studies and primary and secondary data to analyse sociologically the contemporary field of debate around four important issues in the politics of the body. In chapter 2, the cases of Julian Assange, Dominique Strauss-Kahn and Roman Polanski provided a way into the contemporary terrain of sexual violence politics. I identified a suspicion of victimhood and reluctance to moralize on the political and academic Left which chimes well with neoliberal individualism, and which has developed at least in part in response to the association of radical feminism with neoconservative agendas around crime and social control. I also highlighted two related backlashes: the right-wing backlash against feminism and the left-wing backlash against the United States, both of which I linked to left-wing ambivalence around feminist sexual violence politics. I acknowledged problems of positioning for feminism in relation to honouring the experience of sexual violence without playing into judgemental expressions of morality or punitive forms of regulation. This discussion resonated with the material presented in chapter 3, which examined the two main frameworks in the contemporary debate around gender and Islam. I uncovered similar challenges for feminist thought and activism faced with contemporary imperialisms which manifest themselves in an Orientalist construction of the 'Muslim woman' as an eternal victim, used in the service of neoconservative political projects. I explored these right-wing discourses and the answering tendency within academia and the activist and political Left to focus on women's agency and resistance and celebrate cultural difference, with the attendant risk of invisibilizing gender-based oppression. I argued that on both sides there is dogma and essentialism, and that they share a number of themes drawn from the contemporary neoliberal context: a politics of recognition (and anti-recognition), which is homogenizing in its effects, and a rational-individualistic formulation of 'choice'.

These ideas were also situated as central to the sex radicalism explored in chapter 4 as the dominant extant political and intellectual framework around the sex industry. I again identified the influence of the neoliberal paradigm in shifting concerns about sexual freedom towards ideas about commodity choice and 'rational' decision making. I examined an emergent politics of recognition around sex work as an identity, which can be seen as a form of Orientalism in its fetishization of the 'marginal' but which also draws much from mainstream sexualized consumer culture. There are continued difficulties here in relation to radical feminisms which have become identified with neoconservative discourses in the debate around trafficking in particular. However, the postmodern and 'third wave' feminisms which underpin contemporary sex radicalism are also problematic in their associations with neoliberal rationalities and embodiment of privilege: those with economic and cultural resources are more likely to be able to choose to participate in sex work and also dominate the 'sex work glitterati' who are the principal representatives of the industry in activism, politics, academia and popular culture. Ideas about privilege also underpinned the discussion in chapter 5, which focused on the contemporary orthodoxy around natural childbirth and exclusive breastfeeding. I exposed resonances between these ideas, neoconservative gender essentialisms and the neoliberal politics of personal responsibility, and argued that agendas which originally developed in feminist attempts to empower have now become

normalizing discourses. I also argued that the practices they pre-
scribe are largely the preserve of a class and ethnic elite, being
resource-heavy and linked to western middle-class 'healthism', and
that they exclude social Others while romanticizing global Others
in their recognition politics around the 'traditional' and 'primitive'.
The notion of 'informed choice' central to these debates was critiqued for being a coercive device which can produce shame and
feelings of failure in women unable to make the 'right' choices for
structural reasons. The themes explored in all four of these chapters
are also evident in other arenas of body politics, for instance disability, where an emergent identity politics has set the concerns
of disability rights activists against feminist formulations of choice
(often overly rationalist) in the debate around abortion, or the
beauty industry, where radical feminist condemnations of practices
such as cosmetic surgery are juxtaposed with facile celebrations of
women's agency which draw on both neoliberal and neoconservative discourses in their tendency to take normative femininities and
capitalist structures as given.

All these debates are shaped in some way by marketized and
individual-rational formulations of choice, associated with neoliberalism and its attendant politics of personal responsibility. In
a neoliberal context, we are all responsible for creating our own
destinies within a free market and we are also at fault in relation
to our 'failures': this produces the contemporary populist suspicion of claims of victimization identified in relation to many of
the issues discussed here. This contemporary individualism and
emphasis on self-creation, regardless of one's social or economic
position or experiences, conflates with the more progressive
and postmodern intellectual preoccupations with agency that set
themselves against the neoconservative appropriation of victimized women in the service of social and political control. The
right-wing monopoly on morality and tendency to normalizing
judgement shapes an answering inclination to relativize: however,
this means that choice is often valorized as an end in itself, regardless of context, content or effect. The result is a focus on choices
abstracted from the social structures which frame and constrain
how women choose, for instance to commodify their bodies in the

sex industry or to cover them according to particular religious or cultural practices. Choice, then, exists only between a predefined set of alternatives set by structures such as the market or religious institutions, which are reified and taken as given. This is a rather minimalistic and consumerist formulation of agency which does not allow for discussion of how to improve the situations in which women choose, or to create alternative choices. Ironically, this also sometimes means that, in the current context, any choice made by a woman can be a feminist one.

The retreat of the structural can also be seen in the dominant political register of recognition, evident in the identity politics observed in many of the debates in this book. In general, a progressive and left-wing disposition towards the counter-cultural and marginal can be observed, which produces some rather contradictory alliances, for instance the radical Left's simultaneous support of 'sex positive' feminism and radical Islam. The oppressive strands of communitarianism which Fraser (1995, 2000) has identified are also in operation, for instance in the sex-radical personalization and psychologization of critique or the positioning of some Muslim feminists as traitors who have sold out to the West. A politics of 'voice' and 'authenticity' characterizes many of the issues, with ethnographic research, experiential narratives and lay expertise reigning supreme. It sometimes appears that the feminist adage 'the personal is political' has shifted from its original meaning – that personal experiences are framed by broader political structures – to now denote that personal stories are political in themselves, often devoid of any overarching analytical framework. As Fraser (1995, 2000) predicted, this often has a silencing function in relation to those seen as unqualified to speak. Although this is understandable given the history of dubious and ill-informed interventions into all the fields discussed, particularly on the part of neoconservatives and some radical feminists, it is unsound when one considers that 'voice' often continues to be the property of the privileged, whose claims to speak for a variety of others have been problematized by empirical evidence. Indeed, using an intersectional frame for analysis undermines many of the orthodoxies explored in this book.

Of course, some generalizations can and should be made: as Mohanty argued in 2002, globalized capitalism is a structure which impacts upon most if not all of us, and it certainly makes its presence known in all the issues covered here. The core of my structural analysis is constituted by the economic and political rationalities and practices of neoliberalism and neoconservatism: the hegemony of this contemporary coalition can be observed in all the debates in this book, particularly as it impacts upon left-wing and progressive academic and political discourses. I have identified a backlash on the Left against neoconservative frameworks, which maps onto other dichotomies, for instance between oppression and freedom, and victimization and agency, and has embraced other political movements which share its anti-imperial stance. This has led to some contradictory political alliances, and the gender essentialism of the neoconservative framework and its focus on women's victimization as a tool of social control has produced gender-blindness among some of its opponents, and a defensible yet risky refusal to engage with issues around women's oppression in contexts where this might feed neo-imperialist projects. The convergence between neoconservatism and radical feminist politics and activism around issues such as sexual violence and sex work has also produced, in areas of the Left, a reversion to backlash constructions of feminism as anti-sex, anti-men, anti-fun and pro-censorship. This positioning of 'feminism' (or sometimes radical feminism) as bogeyman in different ways within various contexts, which often involves the attribution of psychological hang-ups or dubious motives to individual feminists, is proof enough that the backlash has had significant reach.

This book is entitled *The Politics of the Body*: however, it often seems that women's bodies and experiences are lost in this shifting and frequently fraught discursive terrain. Positions taken in the contemporary political field regularly appear dictated by oppositional logics, rather than underpinning value or conceptual systems, and 'women's issues' are caught up in broader political struggles, in particular that between the Left and the neoconservative Right. Indeed, although throughout this book I have used the terminology 'Left' and 'Right' to facilitate description and analysis, these terms are problematic, and it is evidenced in all the debates covered that positions in terms of gender cannot be clearly articulated in relation to this political dichotomy. This brings to mind Duggan's (2003) assertion that contemporary progressives have been pushed by neoliberalism into bitterly opposing camps, while failing to recognize that which divides them. It can also be argued that the hegemony of the contemporary neoconservative/neoliberal political coalition is such that attempts to distance from one of these rationalities often involves the mobilization of the other: arguments against neoconservatism frequently collapse into neoliberalized formulations of 'choice' as an end in itself, the politics of personal responsibility or apolitical ideas about difference, set against right-wing co-optations of women's victimhood. This can be observed in contemporary feminist frameworks such as the postmodern, postcolonial and 'third wave', where attempts to reclaim and celebrate women's agency can sometimes veer into facile voluntarism or consumerist notions.

This is an incredibly challenging political context in which to operate, and this book undoubtedly asks more questions than it answers. However, I hope it has offered an analytical framework for a number of key contemporary issues to do with women's bodies which might facilitate reflection and discussion in arenas both activist and academic. In terms of ways forward, I am afraid I do not have a clear programme to offer: however, I have always found feminism to be an incredibly reflexive political and academic movement and hope that attempting to foster contemplation upon its contemporary discursive and ideological positionings might germinate alternative languages and concepts. Furthermore, although the recent resurgence of youth feminist debate and activism in a number of countries worldwide (Baumgardner and Richards 2010; Pedersen and Salib 2013; Redfern and Aune 2013) has already become ensnared by the neoliberal/neoconservative dialectic in some instances (seen here for example in the discussion of Slutwalk), its simultaneous promise of fresh ideas, dialogues and relationships gives me plenty of hope for the future.

For Fraser (2013), the current international crisis of neoliberal capitalism offers opportunities for feminism. This is a cheering thought – perhaps some neoliberal certainties will be (or already have been) shaken, and feminists may find a position of opposition to neoconservative regulation which does not automatically play into market-based conceptualizations of freedom. Such a position would create spaces for the articulation of values which do not slip into unhelpful moralizing but which also move away from consumerist formulations of choice. It would pay attention to the context of choices and also their effects, understood in a non-individualistic sense: how economic, social and cultural structures both shape our agency and are shaped by it. For me, this is the work of reinserting politics into feminism in a moment in which issues of identity have taken centre stage. This does not mean jettisoning the intersectionality principle; far from it: instead, it requires attempting to understand this as a structural, as well as an experiential and performative, dynamic, as shown by the application of ideas of economic and social privilege to many of the issues in this book. Perhaps something can be learned here from feminism in non-neoliberal settings, for example Venezuelan Chavismo, where the 'feminization of resistance' is rooted in the structural conditions of women's lives and a participatory collectivist politics which is explicitly opposed to neoliberal individualism and competition and thus attempts to subvert, often from within, capitalist social relations (Fernandes 2007; Motta 2013). It is important not to romanticize such examples and to remember that the influence of the neoliberal/neoconservative dialectic can probably be felt across the globe. We must also not forget, as shown in this book, that socialism is not immune from misogyny. However, examining pockets of resistance which are not wholly determined by neoliberal/neoconservative rationalities could provide potential ways in which to revitalize the feminist politics of the body, reconnecting the personal with the political, instead of positioning it as an end in itself.

Notes

Introduction

1 Although all the issues in this book involve and affect men, contemporary debates continue to focus disproportionately on women, which is an insight into the heavy politicization of women's bodies. As a result, I have chosen to give emphasis to discourses around women's bodies in this volume.

Chapter 1 Neoliberalism and Neoconservatism

1 What Brown terms 'conservative feminism' encompasses radical feminism, which is not always defined as a conservative philosophy.

Chapter 2 Sexual Violence and the Politics of Victimhood

1 As I write this book, some of this support has now fallen away (Khan 2013): however, the coalition around Assange was originally a very committed group.
2 Such work has not confined itself to understanding resilience as an individual attribute but has also explored the social conditions that

promote it (Walklate 2011: 180). However, this has not yet entered common policy or therapeutic parlance.

3 Trans* is an umbrella term which attempts to include all non-cisgender identities, such as transgender, transsexual, transvestite, genderqueer, genderfluid, non-binary, genderless, agender, third gender, two-spirit, bigender, as well as trans man and trans woman.

Chapter 3 Gender and Islam in a Neoconservative World

1 The quotation marks around this term denote that it has been problematized in many different ways, and can often be used pejoratively or to create homogeneity where none exists.

2 Again, the quotation marks denote that this is a problematic term.

3 This term is used as though all 'Muslim women' were the same, erasing differences of nationality, cultural and ethnic background, social class and other factors.

4 This was also observed in 1990s' India under Hindutva (see Rajan 1993; Oza 2001).

5 Indeed, the evidence which has recently emerged about hundreds of historic cases of abuse of girls and young women by high-profile men at the BBC suggests that all the perpetrators were white: however, as Harker (2013) points out, this has not been interpreted as the product of an inherent cultural deficit.

6 More recently in the UK, there have been moves to deal with the issue of forced marriage, but within a rather clumsy criminal justice framework which, some groups have argued, may actually dissuade women from coming forward.

Chapter 4 The Commodified Politics of the Sex Industry

1 Although 'prostitute' is now widely regarded as a pejorative term, the term is used here to denote the particular sector of the sex industry characterized by the sale of sexual acts (in contrast to erotic dancing or pornography, for instance) in the absence of alternative terminology.

2 1970s' political organizing made use of this term and it is in this context that it is being used here.

3 However, this union has been criticized for being dominated by pimps,

escort agency owners and male users of sexual services, rather than representing sex workers themselves (Elliot 2009).

4 There are also critiques being put forward within other contemporary popular feminist works which draw upon liberal and radical feminisms (see, for example, Levy 2005; Banyard 2010; Walter 2010).

5 There has also recently been a revival of anti-pornography feminism in Britain, seen in campaigns by groups such as UK Feminista and Object (Long 2012).

6 The Sexual Freedom Coalition is a UK alliance of a large number of LGBT, libertarian, disability and sex work groups, including BiCon, Striporama, Campaign Against Censorship, COYOTE, Outrage!, Outsiders, the International Union of Sex Workers and the Libertarian Alliance. It characterizes itself as a group of 'freedom fighters' which has 'made Britain sexier'.

7 Sexonomics ® is a registered trademark of Dr Adalbert Lallier, and appears in the title of his book, *Sexonomics: The Golden Triangle: Sexuality, Money, Power –*, in which he presents sexonomics as a fifth social science which uses economic reasoning to 'understand and predict the complexity of human sexual interaction'.

Chapter 5 The New Reproductive Regimes of Truth

1 These critiques owed much to Dick Grantly-Read's *Childbirth Without Fear* (1959), originally published in 1933 as *Natural Childbirth*: this text will be discussed later in the chapter.

2 A number of interventions were permissible within this definition, such as augmentation of labour, opioid pain medications such as pethidine, electronic fetal monitoring and managed third stage (delivery of the placenta) (Maternity Care Working Party 2007: 3).

3 However, a Breastfeeding Rights Amendment to the EU Pregnant Workers' Directive, which required legislated breastfeeding breaks at work, was passed in the European Parliament but opposed by the Council of Ministers, with the UK government very active in this process. In addition, plans to require employers to provide facilities for breastfeeding mothers to express and store milk, included in the 2010 UK Public Health White Paper (DirectGov 2012), did not proceed (information from Maternity Action UK).

4 See also Kitzinger 1979, 1984 for earlier similar constructions.

5 For instance, in a convergence of attachment theory and the 'new brain science', such models linked formula feeding to 'impaired bonding' between mother and infant and future psychological difficulties for the child, even positioning this as causal in the origin of social problems such as criminality and violence, for all of which there was no credible scientific basis (Wolf 2007; Lee 2008).

6 Such models are not supported by all 'natural childbirth' activists: the Bradley method, for example, markets itself as 'husband coached' (this, of course, is extremely heteronormative).

7 Since 1981, 84 countries have enacted legislation implementing all or many of the provisions of the Code (UNICEF 2012).

Bibliography

References (primary and secondary sources)

Abbott, Stephen, Renfrew, Mary J. and McFadden, Alison (2006) '"Informal" learning to support breastfeeding: local problems and opportunities'. *Maternal & Child Nutrition* 2(4): 232–8.

Abel, Jennifer (2009) 'Selling sex with a smile', *The Guardian*, 30 October, available online at www.guardian.co.uk/commentisfree/cifamerica/2009/oct/28/sex-work-superfreakonomics, accessed 7 August 2013.

Abu-Lughod, Lila (1990) 'The romance of resistance: tracing transformations of power through Bedouin women'. *American Ethnologist* 17(1): 41–55.

Abu-Lughod, Lila (2002) 'Do Muslim women really need saving? Anthropological reflections on cultural relativism and its Others'. *American Anthropologist* 104(3): 783–90.

Adams, Richard (2010) '#MooreandMe: the hashtag that roared', *The Guardian*, 28 December, available online at www.guardian.co.uk/commentisfree/cifamerica/2010/dec/28/michael-moore-mooreandme-twitter, accessed 7 August 2013.

Addley, Esther (2011) 'Julian Assange "would face bias in Sweden"', retired judge says', *The Guardian*, 7 February.

Agustín, Laura (2007a) 'Introduction to the cultural study of commercial sex'. *Sexualities* 10(4): 403–7.

Agustín, Laura (2007b) *Sex at the Margins: Migration, Labour Markets and the Rescue Industry*. London: Zed Books.

Agustín, Laura (2010) 'Is rape rampant in gender-equal Sweden? Re Assange and Wikileaks'. Posted 8 December, available online at www.lauraagustin.com/is-rape-rampant-in-gender-equal-sweden, accessed 8 August 2013.

Ahlborg, Tone, Dahlöf, Lars-Gösta, and Hallberg, Lillemor R.-M. (2005) 'Quality of the intimate and sexual relationship in first-time parents six months after delivery'. *The Journal of Sex Research* 42(2): 167–74.

Alcoff, Linda Martín (2011) 'When culture, power and sex collide', *The New York Times Opinionator* 8 June, available online at http://opinionator.blogs.nytimes.com/2011/06/08/when-culture-power-and-sex-collide/, accessed 8 August 2013

Alpha Parent, The (2011) '15 tricks of formula companies', available online at www.thealphaparent.com/2011/10/15-tricks-of-formula-companies.html, accessed 19 August 2013.

Altman, Dennis (2004) 'Sexuality and globalization'. *Sexuality Research & Social Policy* 1(1): 63–8.

American Academy of Pediatrics (2012) 'Breastfeeding and the use of human milk'. *Pediatrics* 129(3): e827–e841.

Amnesty International News (2010) 'France votes to ban full-face veils', available online at www.amnesty.org.

Anthias, Floya (2002) 'Beyond feminism and multiculturalism: locating difference and the politics of location'. *Women's Studies International Forum* 25(3): 275–394.

Aradau, Claudia (2004) 'The perverse politics of four-letter words: risk and pity in the securitisation of human trafficking'. *Millennium: Journal of International Studies* 33(2): 251–77.

Associated Press (2010a) 'Belgium ban burqa-type dress; law cites public security, securing emancipation of women', posted April 29.

Attwood, Feona (2009) 'The sexualization of culture', in F. Attwood (ed.), *Mainstreaming Sex: The Sexualization of Western Culture*. London: I. B. Tauris, pp. xiii–xxiv.

AuthentiCity (2012) 'Authenticity website'. Available online at www. authenticitytravel.com, accessed 7 August 2013.

Avishai, Orit (2008) '"Doing religion" in a secular world: women in conservative religions and the question of agency'. *Gender & Society* 22(4): 409–33.

Axelsson, Katrin (2010) 'Rape claims, WikiLeaks and internet freedom', *The Guardian*, letters page, 8 December.

Axelsson, Katrin and Longstaff, Lisa (2012) 'We are women against rape but we do not want Julian Assange extradited', *The Guardian*, 23 August.

Ayers, Susan and Ford, Elizabeth (2009) 'Birth trauma: widening our knowledge of postnatal mental health'. *The European Health Psychologist* 11: 16–19.

Ayotte, Kevin T. and Husain, Mary E. (2005) 'Securing Afghan women: neocolonialism, epistemic violence, and the rhetoric of the veil'. *NWSA Journal* 17(3): 112–33.

Babble (2012) '9 celebrity moms who opted for natural childbirth'. Available online at http://blogs.babble.com/famecrawler/2010/02/02/9-cele brity-moms-who-opted-for-natural-childbirth/, accessed 8 August 2013.

Babyworld (2012) Celebrity Breastfeeding Mothers. Available online at http://babyworld.co.uk/2009/05/celebrity-breastfeeding-mothers/, accessed 8 August 2013.

Badcock, Elly (2012) 'That's not what a feminist looks like', *Counterfire*, 9 August, available online at www.counterfire.org/index.php/arti cles/78-womens-liberation/15951-femen-protest-sharia-law-tower-br idge, accessed 15 August 2013.

Badinter, Elisabeth (2010) *The Conflict: How Modern Motherhood Undermines the Status of Women*. New York: Metropolitan Books.

Baker, Brent (2008) 'Flashback: Stephanopoulos scolded critic of Bonior and McDermott', Newsbusters, 26 March, available online at http://newsbusters.org/blogs/brent-baker/2008/03/26/flashback-stephanopoulos-scolded-critic-bonier-mcdermott, accessed 8 August 2013.

Baker, Joanne (2009) 'Young mothers in late modernity: sacrifice, respectability and the transformative neo-liberal subject'. *Journal of Youth Studies* 12(3): 275–88.

Baker, Joanne (2010) 'Claiming volition and evading victimhood: post-feminist obligations for young women'. *Feminism & Psychology* 20(2): 186–204.

Balko, Radley (2002) 'Targeting the social drinker is just MADD', *The Los Angeles Times*, 9 December.

Banyard, Kat (2010) *The Equality Illusion: The Truth About Women and Men Today*. London: Faber and Faber.

Barston, Suzanne (2012) *Bottled Up: How the Way We Feed Babies has Come to Define Motherhood, and Why it Shouldn't*. Los Angeles, CA: University of California Press.

Bartick, Melissa and Reinhold, Arnold (2010) 'The burden of suboptimal breastfeeding in the United States: a pediatric cost analysis'. *Pediatrics* 125(5): 1048–56.

Bartlett, Alison (2005) 'Maternal sexuality and breastfeeding'. *Sex Education* 5(1): 67–77.

Barton, Bernadette (2002) 'Dancing on the Möbius Strip: challenging the sex war paradigm'. *Gender & Society* 16(5): 585–602.

Bartowski, John P. and Read, Jen'nan Ghazal (2003) 'Veiled submission: gender, power and identity among evangelical and Muslim women in the United States'. *Qualitative Sociology* 26(1): 71–92.

Basen, Ira (2012) 'Monetizing mommy-hood', broadcast on CBC radio on 3 January.

Bassiouny, Mostafa (2012) 'Unity against generals' attempted coup in Egypt', *Socialist Worker*, 23 June.

Batha, Emma (2012) 'UK to examine failure to try genital mutilation crimes', *TrustLaw*, 26 September, available online at www.trust.org/item/20121126190100-a51ur/, accessed 8 August 2013.

Bauman, Zygmunt (1992) *Intimations of Postmodernity*. London: Routledge.

Baumgardner, Jennifer and Richards, Amy (2010) *Manifesta: Young Women, Feminism, and the Future* (10th anniversary edn). New York: Farrar, Straus and Giroux.

BBC News (2007) 'Schools allowed to ban face veils', posted online 20 March, available at http://news.bbc.co.uk/1/hi/education/6466221.stm, accessed 8 August 2013.

BBC News (2011a) 'Dominique Strauss-Kahn: "Doubts" on maid's credibility'. BBC News, 1 July, available online at www.bbc.co.uk/news/world-us-canada-13986970, accessed 8 August 2013.

BBC News (2011b) 'Strauss-Kahn sex case: French inquiry dropped'. BBC News, 13 October, available online at www.bbc.co.uk/news/world-europe-15296244, accessed 8 August 2013.

BBC News (2012a) 'Protest greets Dominique Strauss-Kahn talk in Cambridge'. BBC News, 10 March, available online at www.bbc.co.uk/news/uk-england-cambridgeshire-17311867, accessed 8 August 2013.

BBC News (2012b) 'Galloway clarifies "rape" comments amid growing storm', BBC News, 21 August, available online at www.bbc.co.uk/news/uk-politics-19334598, accessed 8 August 2013.

Beck, Ulrich and Beck-Gernsheim, Elisabeth (2002) *Individualization: Institutionalized Individualism and its Social and Political Consequences.* London: Sage.

Beckett, Clare and Macey, Marie (2001) 'Race, gender and sexuality: the oppression of multiculturalism'. *Women's Studies International Forum* 24(3/4): 309–19.

Beckett, Katherine (2005) 'Choosing cesarean: feminism and the politics of childbirth in the United States'. *Feminist Theory* 6(3): 251–75.

Beckett, Katherine and Hoffman, Bruce (2005) 'Challenging medicine: law, resistance, and the cultural politics of childbirth'. *Law & Society Review* 39(1): 125–70.

Belknap, Joanne (2012) 'Rape: too hard to report and too easy to discredit victims'. *Violence Against Women* 16(2): 1335–44.

Belle de Jour (2005) *The Intimate Adventures of a London Call Girl.* London: Phoenix.

Belle de Jour (2006) *The Further Adventures of a London Call Girl.* London: Phoenix.

Belle de Jour (2008) *Playing the Game.* London: Phoenix.

Bennett, Catherine (2010) 'Polanski's "genius" is only a defence to the morally vacuous', *The Observer*, 18 July.

Bernstein, Elizabeth (1999) 'What's wrong with prostitution? What's right with sex work? Comparing markets in female sexual labor'. *Hastings Women's Law Journal* 10(1): 91–117.

Bernstein, Elizabeth (2001) 'The meaning of the purchase: desire, demand and the commerce of sex'. *Ethnography* 2(3): 389–420.

Bernstein, Elizabeth (2007a) 'Sex work for the middle classes'. *Sexualities* 10(4): 473–88.

Bernstein, Elizabeth (2007b) *Temporarily Yours: Intimacy, Authenticity, and the Commerce of Sex*. London: The University of Chicago Press.

Betts, Hannah (2013) 'We need to face up to hatred of prostitutes – among feminists, too', *The Guardian*, 5 March.

Bhattacharyya, Gargi (2008) *Dangerous Brown Men: Exploiting Sex, Violence and Feminism in the War on Terror*. London: Zed Books.

Bilge, Sirma (2010) 'Beyond subordination vs. resistance: an intersectional approach to the agency of Muslim women'. *Journal of Intercultural Studies* 31(1): 9–28.

Birthplace in England Collaborative Group (2011) 'Perinatal and maternal outcomes by planned place of birth for healthy women with low risk pregnancies: the Birthplace in England national prospective cohort study'. *British Medical Journal* 343: 1–13.

Black Women's Blueprint (2011) 'An open letter from black women to the Slutwalk', posted on Facebook, 23 September, available at www.facebook.com/notes/blackwomens-blueprint/an-open-letter-from-black-women-to-the-slutwalk/232501930131880, accessed 8 August 2013.

Blackman, Lisa and Venn, Couze (2010) 'Affect'. *Body and Society* 16(1): 7–28.

Boas, Taylor C. and Gans-Morse, Jordan (2009) 'Neoliberalism: from New Liberal philosophy to anti-liberal slogan'. *Studies in Comparative International Development* 44(2): 137–61.

Boffey, Daniel (2013a) 'Breastfeeding figures fall as NHS budget is cut', *The Guardian*, 22 June.

Boffey, Daniel (2013b) 'Breastfeeding shunned as new mums deem it "unnatural and abnormal"', *The Guardian*, 22 June.

Boot, Martjin (2012) 'Does global spread of liberal democracies promote consensus on justice?' *Ritsumeikan Studies in Language and Culture* 23: 85–102.

Boseley, Sarah (2011) 'Breastfeeding awareness week dropped by Department of Health', *The Guardian*, 17 June.

Boucher, Geoff (2006) 'The politics of performativity: a critique of Judith Butler'. *Parrhesia* 1: 112–41.

Bourdieu, Pierre (1984 [1979]) *Distinction: A Social Critique of the Judgment of Taste*. London: Routledge.

Boyd, Anne (2006) 'A childbirth educator speaks out for increased advocacy for normal birth'. *The Journal of Perinatal Education* 15(1): 8–10.

Braiker, Brian (2012) 'Ecuador's free speech record at odds with Julian Assange's bid for openness', *The Guardian*, 19 June.

Breastfeeding.com (2012) 'Celebrity update: a roundup of famous breastfeeding moms'. Available online at www.breastfeeding.com/reading_room/celebrity_update.html

Brents, Barbara G. and Hausbeck, Kathryn (2007) 'Marketing sex: US legal brothels and late capitalist consumption'. *Sexualities* 10(4): 425–39.

Brents, Barbara G. and Sanders, Teela (2010) 'Mainstreaming the sex industry: economic inclusion and social ambivalence'. *Journal of Law and Society* 37(1): 40–60.

Brickell, C. (2005) 'Masculinities, performativity, and subversion: a sociological reappraisal'. *Men and Masculinities* 8: 24–43.

Broadcasters' Audience Research Board (2007) *Weekly Viewing Figures: Secret Diary of a Call Girl.* Accessed at www.barb.co.uk, accessed 8 August 2013.

Brooks, Libby (2010) 'No one gains from this "rape-rape" defence of Julian Assange', *The Guardian*, 9 December.

Brown, Wendy (1995) *States of Injury: Power and Freedom in Late Modernity.* Princeton, NJ: Princeton University Press.

Brown, Wendy (2006) 'American nightmare: neoliberalism, neoconservatism, and de-democratization'. *Political Theory* 34(6): 690–714.

Brubaker, Sarah Jane (2007) 'Denied, embracing and resisting medicalization: African-American teen mothers' perceptions of formal pregnancy and childbirth care'. *Gender and Society* 21(4): 528–52.

Bumgarner, Norma Jane (2000) *Mothering Your Nursing Toddler.* Schaumburg, IL: La Leche League International.

Bumiller, Kristin (2008) *In an Abusive State: How Neoliberalism Appropriated the Feminist Movement against Sexual Violence.* Durham, NC: Duke University Press.

Burns, John F. and Somaiya, Ravi (2010) 'Under "high-tech house arrest", WikiLeaks founder takes the offensive', *The New York Times*, 22 December.

Butler, Judith (1988) 'Performative acts and gender constitution: an essay in phenomenology and feminist theory'. *Theatre Journal* 40(4): 519–31.

Butler, Judith (1999) *Gender Trouble*. New York: Routledge.

Butler, Judith (2004) *Undoing Gender*. London: Routledge.

Cahill, Ann (2001) *Rethinking Rape*. London: Cornell University Press.

Call, J. E., Nice, D. and Talarico, S. M. (1991) 'Analysis of state rape shield laws'. *Social Science Quarterly* 72(4): 774–88.

Cameron, Deborah (2010) 'Gender, language and the new biologism'. *Constellations* 17(4): 526–39.

Cammu, Hendrick, Martens, Guy and Keirse, Marc J. N. C. (2011) 'Mothers' level of education and childbirth interventions: a population-based study in Flanders, Northern Belgium'. *Birth* 38(3): 191–9.

Campbell, Denis (2009) 'It's good for women to suffer the pain of a natural birth, says medical chief', *The Observer*, 12 July.

Carolan, Mary (2005) 'The conspicuous body: capitalism, consumerism, class and consumption'. *Worldviews: Global Religions, Culture, and Ecology* 9(1): 82–111.

Carolan, Mary (2010) 'The good midwife: commencing students' views'. *Midwifery* 27: 503–8.

Cashmore, Ellis (2006) *Celebrity/Culture*. London: Routledge.

Caton, Donald (1996) 'Who said childbirth is natural? The medical mission of Grantly Dick-Read'. *Anesthesiology* 84(4): 955–64.

Chalmers, Beverley and Porter, Richard (2001) 'Assessing effective care in normal labor: the Bologna score'. *Birth* 28(2): 79–83.

Chan, Emily (2013) 'Julian Assange to address Oxford Union', in *Varsity Online*, 9 January, available at www.varsity.co.uk/news/5392, accessed 8 August 2013.

Chancellor, Cristal Williams (2012) 'Gloria Steinem, women's media center denounce hustler attack on conservative commentator.' Press release issued 23 May.

Chancer, Lynn S. (1996) 'Feminist offensives: "Defending pornography" and the splitting of sex from sexism'. *Stanford Law Review* 48(3): 739–60.

Chancer, Lynn S. (2000) 'From pornography to sadomasochism: reconciling feminist differences'. *The ANNALS of the American Academy of Political and Social Science* 571: 77–88.

Chaudhry, Yahya (2010) 'Roman Polanski is a "rape-rape" rapist', *Indiana Daily Student*, 14 July, available online at www.idsnews. com.

Cheyney, Melissa J. (2008) 'Homebirth as systems-challenging praxis: knowledge, power, and intimacy in the birthplace'. *Qualitative Health Research* 18(2): 254–67.

Choi, Chong Ju and Berger, Ron (2010) 'Ethics of celebrities and their increasing influence in 21st century society'. *Journal of Business Ethics* 91: 313–18.

Chrisafis, Angelique (2011a) 'Dominique Strauss-Kahn's return could be a threat to Nicolas Sarkozy', *The Guardian*, 2 July.

Chrisafis, Angelique (2011b) 'Muslim women protest on first day of France's veil ban', *The Guardian*, 11 April.

Ciclitira, Karen (2004) 'Pornography, women and feminism: between pleasure and politics'. *Sexualities* 7(3): 281–301.

Clarke, D. A. (2004) 'Prostitution for everyone: feminism, globalisation and the "sex" industry', in R. Whisnant and C. Stark (eds), *Not for Sale: Feminists Resisting Prostitution and Pornography*. Melbourne: Spinifex, pp. 149–205.

Clarke, Gemma (2010) 'Uncomfortable territory? The relationship between gender, intoxication, and rape', in G. Clarke, F. McQueen, M. Pnacekova and S. Sahli (eds), *Examining Aspects of Sexualities and the Self*. Oxford: Inter-disciplinary Press.

Coleman, Doriane Lambelet (1996) 'Individualizing justice through multiculturalism: the liberals' dilemma'. *Columbia Law Review* 96(5): 1093–167.

Coulmont, Baptiste and Hubbard, Phil (2010) 'Consuming sex: socio-legal shifts in the space and place of sex shops'. *Journal of Law and Society* 37(1): 189–209.

Crunk Feminist Collective (2011) 'Slutwalks v. ho strolls', Crunk Feminist Collective blog, 23 May, available online at www.crunk feministcollective.com/2011/05/23/slutwalks-v-ho-strolls, accessed 8 August 2013.

CNN (2011) 'In the arena (debate on face veils)', broadcast 11 April.

CNN Wire Staff (2011) 'Lowe's pulls advertising from TLC's "All-American Muslim"', CNN Online, 12 December, available at www. cnn.co.uk.

Cochrane, Kira (2011) 'When men behave badly', *The Guardian*, 19 May.

Cohen, Nick (2012) 'Stieg Larsson was an extremist, not a feminist', *The Observer*, 8 January.

Cole, Alyson (1999) '"There are no victims in this class": on female suffering and anti-"victim feminism"'. *NWSA Journal* 11(1): 72–96.

Cole, Teju (2012) 'The white savior industrial complex', *The Atlantic*, 21 March, available online at www.theatlantic.com.

Conover, Patrick W. (1975) 'An analysis of communes and intentional communities with particular attention to sexual and genderal relations'. *The Family Coordinator* 24(4): 453–64.

Convery, Alison (2006) 'No victims, no oppression: feminist theory and the denial of victimhood'. Paper presented to the Australasian Political Studies Association Conference, 25–27 September.

Coulter, Ann (2009) *Guilty: Liberal 'Victims' and Their Assault on America*. New York: Three Rivers Press.

Crossley, Michele L. (2009) 'Breastfeeding as a moral imperative: an autoethnographic study'. *Feminism & Psychology* 19(1): 71–87.

Crul, Maurice and Vermeulen, Hans (2003) 'The second generation in Europe'. *International Migration Review* 37(4): 965–86.

Curtis, Adam (2012) 'He's behind you: how Colonel Gaddafi and the western establishment together created a pantomime world', BBC Newsblogs, 21 October, available online at www.bbc.co.uk/blogs/adamcurtis/posts/hes_behind_you, accessed 8 August 2013.

Daily Mail (2011a) 'Feminists are ruining good clean fun, says former Playboy bunny', 27 May.

Daily Mail (2011b) 'Not too posh to breastfeed: Victoria plans to feed her new daughter naturally for the first time', 4 July.

Daily Telegraph (2011) 'Posh spices up women's birth choices', 30 July.

Daily Telegraph (2012) 'Parents jailed for attacking daughter because she had black boyfriend', 6 August.

Daly, Kathleen (2006) 'Feminist engagement with restorative justice'. *Theoretical Criminology* 10(1): 9–28.

Danahar, Paul (2012) 'Egyptian revolution "failing to deliver for women"', BBC News, 17 July, available online at www.bbc.co.uk/news/world-middle-east-18861958, accessed 16 August 2013.

Dangers of Baby Training, The (2012) 'The dangers of baby training Facebook page', available online at https://www.facebook.com/T.D.o.B.T/info.

DasGupta, Sayantani (2012) '"Your women are oppressed, but ours are awesome": how Nicholas Kristof and half the sky use women against each other'. *Racialicious*, 8 October, available online at www.racialicious.com, accessed 18 August 2013.

Davids, M. F. (2009) 'The impact of Islamophobia'. *Psychoanalytic History* 11(2): 175–91.

Davies, Caroline (2011) 'Harrods "ladies code" drives out sales assistant', *The Guardian*, 1 July. Available at: www.guardian.co.uk/law/2011/jul/01/harrods-dress-code-sales assistant, accessed 8 November 2012.

Davies, Caroline, Jones, Sam and Hirsch, Afua (2010) 'Julian Assange denied bail over sexual assault allegations', *The Guardian*, 7 December.

Davis, Kathy (2004) 'Responses to W. Njambi's "Dualisms and female bodies in representations of African female circumcision: a feminist critique": Between moral outrage and cultural relativism'. *Feminist Theory* 5(3): 305–23.

Davis, Lucy (2009) 'Hugh Hefner: interview on Playboy', *The Daily Telegraph*, 27 October, www.telegraph.co.uk/culture/books/6397504/Hugh-Hefner-interview-on-Playboy.html, accessed 8 August 2013.

Daviss, Betty-Anne (2001) 'Reforming birth and (re)making midwifery in North America', in R. G. de Vries (ed.), *Birth by Design: Pregnancy, Maternity Care, and Midwifery in North America and Europe*. London: Routledge, pp. 70–86.

Davis-Floyd, Robbie (1999) 'The technocratic body: American childbirth as cultural expression'. *Social Science and Medicine* 38(8): 1125–40.

Day, Sophie (2007) *On the Game: Women and Sex Work*. London: Pluto Press.

Deacon, Michael (2009) 'Yet another celebrity who's glad Roman Polanski escaped justice', *The Daily Telegraph*, 14 October.

Democracy Now! (2010) 'Naomi Wolf vs. Jaclyn Friedman: feminists debate the sexual allegations against Julian Assange', *Democracy Now!* Broadcast 20 December.

Delacoste, Frédérique and Alexander, Priscilla (1988) *Sex Work: Writings by Women in the Sex Industry*. London: Virago.

Dershowitz, Alan M. (2011) 'The trouble with rape prosecutions', *The Daily Beast*, 1 July, available online at www.thedailybeast.com.

DiNardo, John (2006) 'Freakonomics: scholarship in the service of story-telling'. *American Law and Economics Review* 8(3): 615–26.

DirectGov (2012) *Statutory Maternity Leave: Returning to Work*. Available online at www.direct.gov.uk/en/Parents/Moneyandworkentitle ments/WorkAndFamilies/Pregnancyandmaternityrights/DG_065153, accessed 11 August 2013.

Ditum, Sarah (2012) 'What is Slutwalk London doing lining up behind Julian Assange?', *The Guardian*, 28 September.

Doezema, Jo (2000) 'Ouch! Western feminists' "wounded attachment" to the "third world prostitute"'. *Feminist Review* 67: 16–38.

Dogba, Maman and Fournier, Pierre (2009) 'Human resources and the quality of emergency obstetric care in developing countries: a system-atic review of the literature'. *Human Resources for Health* 7(7), available online at www.human-resources-health.com/content/7/1/7, accessed 15 August 2013.

Donna, Sylvie (2011) 'Introduction', *Promoting Normal Birth: Research, Reflections and Guidelines*. Chester le Street: Fresh Heart Publishing.

Donnelly, Laura (2009) 'Maternity guru Sheila Kitzinger says "fairytale" expectations of childbirth end with dashed hopes for women', *The Daily Telegraph*, 14 November.

Donnelly, Laura (2011) 'Middle class boom in private home births', *The Daily Telegraph*, 14 August.

Draper, Janet (1997) 'Whose welfare in the labour room? A discussion of the increasing trend of fathers' birth attendance'. *Midwifery* 13: 132–8.

Duggan, Lisa (2003) *The Twilight of Equality? Neoliberalism, Cultural Politics, and the Attack on Democracy*. Boston, MA: Beacon Press.

Dumoulin, Frederick (2010) 'French Parliament adopts ban on full-face veil'. Agence France-Presse, posted 14 September.

Dupré, John (2010) 'The human genome, human evolution, and gender'. *Constellations* 17(4): 540–8.

Dustin, Moira and Phillips, Anne (2008) 'Whose agenda is it? Abuses of women and abuses of "culture" in Britain'. *Ethnicities* 8(3): 405–24.

Eden, Richard (2012) 'Dominique Strauss-Kahn books date with British students', *The Daily Telegraph*, 15 January.

Edinburgh Eye (2012) 'Naomi Wolf says sorry . . . sort of', posted online 7 September, at http://edinburgheye.wordpress.com/2012/09/07/naomi-wolf-says-sorry-sort-of/, accessed 15 August 2013.

Edwards, S. D. (2004) 'Disability, identity and the "expressivist objection"'. *Journal of Medical Ethics* 30: 418–20.

Egan, R. Danielle (2006) 'The phenomenology of lap dancing', in R. D. Egan, K. Frank and M. L. Johnson (eds), *Flesh for Fantasy: Producing and Consuming Exotic Dance*. New York: Thunder's Mouth Press, pp. 19–34.

Egan, R. Danielle, Frank, Katherine and Johnson, Merri Lisa (2006) 'Third wave strippers: flesh for feminist fantasy', in R. D. Egan, K. Frank and M. L. Johnson (eds), *Flesh for Fantasy: Producing and Consuming Exotic Dance*. New York: Thunder's Mouth Press, pp. xi–xxxiii.

Eisenstein, Hester (2010) *Feminism Seduced: How Global Elites Use Women's Labor and Ideas to Exploit the World*. Boulder, CO: Paradigm Publishers.

El-Hameed, Dalia Abd (2012) 'Get an Arab woman to say it for you', on the Egyptian Initiative for Personal Rights blog, available online at http://eipr.org/en/blog/post/2012/04/26/1406, accessed 8 August 2013.

El-Hamel, C. (2002) 'Muslim diaspora in Western Europe: the Islamic headscarf (hijab), the media and Muslims' integration in France'. *Citizenship Studies* 6(3): 293–308.

Elliott, Cath (2009) 'The great IUSW con', posted online at http://toomuchtosayformyself.com/2009/01/09/the-great-iusw-con/, accessed 11 August 2013.

Ellison, Jesse (2011) 'DSK maid fights back', *The Daily Beast*, 6 July, available online at www.thedailybeast.com/articles/2011/08/22/dominique-strauss-kahn-case-maid-asks-to-remove-prosecutors.html, accessed 8 August 2013.

El Saadawi, Nawal (1997) *The Nawal el Saadawi Reader*. London: Zed Books.

Eltahawy, Mona (2012) 'Why do they hate us? The real war on women is in the Middle East'. *Foreign Policy*, May/June.

England and Wales High Court (2011) 'Assange v Swedish Prosecution Authority [2011] EWHC 2849 (Admin). Decision published 2 November.

Ensler, Eve (2011) 'Dominique Strauss-Kahn: so much for us to learn', *The Guardian*, 1 July, available online at www.guardian.co.uk/commentisfree/2011/jul/01/dominique-strauss-kahn-dialogue-rape, accessed 8 August 2013.

Eriksson, Marianne (2004) *Report on the Consequences of the Sex Industry in the European Union*. Brussels: European Parliament.

Erlandsson, Kerstin and Lindgren, Helena (2011) 'Being a resource for both mother and child: fathers' experiences following a complicated birth'. *Journal of Perinatal Education* 20(2): 91–9.

Erlanger, Steven (2010) 'Parliament moves France closer to a ban on facial veils', *The New York Times*, 13 July.

Evans, Kate (2010) 'Equality bill won't protect breastfeeding', *The Guardian*, 8 March.

Evans, Peter (2005) 'Sufferings of the great seducer', *The Times*, 24 July.

Evans, Adrienne and Riley, Sarah (2012) 'Immaculate consumption: negotiating the sex symbol in postfeminist celebrity culture'. *Journal of Gender Studies*, 1–14, available online at www.tandfonline.com/doi/abs/10.1080/09589236.2012.658145#.UgttqWTTVho, accessed 15 August 2013.

Faircloth, Charlotte (2013) *Militant Lactivism? Attachment Parenting and Intensive Motherhood in the UK and France*. Oxford: Berghahn Books.

Faludi, Susan (1992) *Backlash: The Undeclared War against Women*. London: Vintage.

Farm, The (2012) 'The Farm website', available online at http://www.thefarm.org/.

Fassin, Eric (2011) 'The symbolic politics of DSKgate', *The Guardian*, 23 May, available online at www.guardian.co.uk/commentisfree/cifamerica/2011/may/23/dominique-strauss-kahn-race, accessed 8 August 2013.

Fausto-Sterling, Anne (1992) *Myths of Gender: Biological Theories about Women and Men*. USA: Basic Books.

Featherstone, Mike (1991) *Consumer Culture and Postmodernism*. London: Sage.

Fensterstock, Allison (2006) 'How you got here', in R. D. Egan, K. Frank and M. L. Johnson (eds), *Flesh for Fantasy: Producing and Consuming Exotic Dance*. New York: Thunder's Mouth Press, pp. 63–84.

Fernandes, Sujatha (2007) 'Barrio women and popular politics in Chávez's Venezuela'. *Latin American Politics and Society* 49(3): 97–127.

Fernandez, Sonya (2009) 'The crusade over the bodies of women'. *Patterns of Prejudice* 43(3): 269–86.

Fewtrell, Mary, Wilson, David C., Booth, Ian and Lucas, Alan (2011) 'When to wean? How good is the evidence for six months' exclusive breastfeeding?' *British Medical Journal* 342 (22 January): 209–12.

Fine, Michelle (2012) 'Troubling calls for evidence: A critical race, class and gender analysis of whose evidence counts'. *Feminism & Psychology* 22(1): 3–19.

Flynt, Larry and Eisenbach, David (2011) *One Nation Under Sex: How the Private Lives of Presidents, First Ladies and Their Lovers Changed the Course of American History*. Basingstoke: Palgrave Macmillan.

Ford, Elizabeth and Ayers, Susan (2009) 'Stressful events and support during birth: the effect on anxiety, mood and perceived control'. *Journal of Anxiety Disorders* 23: 260–8.

Forty Shades of Grey (2011) 'Occupations, safe spaces, and the privilege-denying left', in Forty Shades of Grey blog, 17 October, available online at http://fortyshadesofgrey.blogspot.co.uk/2011/10/occupations-safe-spaces-and-privilege.html, accessed 8 August 2013.

Foucault, Michel (1973[1963]) *The Birth of the Clinic*. London: Tavistock Press.

Foucault, Michel (1976) *The History of Sexuality Volume 1: The Will to Knowledge* (this text is available in many editions).

Foucault, Michel (1977) *Discipline and Punish: The Birth of the Prison* (this text is available in many editions).

Foucault, Michel (1980) *Power/Knowledge: Selected Interviews and Other Writings 1972–1977* (trans. C. Gordon, L. Marshall, J. Mepham and K. Soper). New York: Pantheon Books.

Foucault, Michel (1988a) 'Truth, power, self: an interview with Michel Foucault', in L. H. Martin, H. Gutman, and P. H. Hutton (eds), *Technologies of the Self*. Amherst, MA: University of Massachusetts Press, pp. 9–15.

Foucault, Michel (1988b) 'Technologies of the self', in L. H. Martin, H.

Gutman and P. H. Hutton (eds), *Technologies of the Self*. Amherst, MA: University of Massachusetts Press, pp. 16–49.

Fraser, Christian (2011) 'View from France', BBC News, 1 July, available online at www.bbc.co.uk/news/world-us-canada-13986970, accessed 15 August 2013.

Fraser, Nancy (1995) 'Recognition or redistribution? A critical reading of Iris Young's *Justice and the Politics of Difference*'. *The Journal of Political Philosophy* 3(2): 166–80.

Fraser, Nancy (2000) 'Rethinking recognition'. *New Left Review* 3: 107–20.

Fraser, Nancy (2009) 'Feminism, capitalism and the cunning of history'. *New Left Review* 56: 97–117.

Fraser, Nancy (2013) *Fortunes of Feminism: From State-managed Capitalism to Neoliberal Crisis*. London: Verso.

Fraser, Nancy and Gordon, Linda (1994) 'A genealogy of dependency: tracing a keyword of the US Welfare State'. *Signs* 19(2): 309–36.

Fraser, Nancy and Honneth, Axel (2003) *Redistribution or Recognition? A Political Philosophical Exchange*. London: Verso.

Freedman, M. A., Gay, G. A., Potrzebowski, P. W. and Rothwell, C. J. (1988) 'The 1989 revisions of the US Standard Certificates of live birth and death and the US Standard Report of fetal death'. *American Journal of Public Health* 78(2): 168–72.

Frost, Julia, Pope, Catherine, Liebling, Rachel and Murphy, Deirdre (2006) 'Utopian theory and the discourse of natural birth'. *Social Theory & Health* 4: 299–318.

F Word, The (2012) 'There's nothing radical about transphobia', *The F Word*, 17 May, available at www.thefword.org.uk/blog/2012/05/theres_nothing, accessed 8 August 2013.

Furry Girl (2011) 'My call for a "working" class uprising against inaccessible discourse and the over-representation of dabblers', posted on Feminisnt, 17 January, available online at www.feminisnt.com, accessed 16 August 2013.

G, Helen (2012) 'Trans inclusion and Reclaim the Night', *The F Word*, 24 October, available online at www.thefword.org.uk/blog/2012/10/update_trans_inclusion_rtn, accessed 8 August 2013.

Gall, Gregor (2006) *Sex Worker Union Organizing: An International Study*. Basingstoke: Palgrave Macmillan.

Gaskin, Ina May (1976) *Spiritual Midwifery*. Summertown, TN: Book Publishing Company.

Gastaldo, Denise (1997) 'Is health education good for you? Re-thinking health education through the concept of bio-power', in A. R. Petersen and R. Bunton (eds), *Foucault, Health and Medicine*. London: Routledge, pp. 113–33.

Gavey, Nicola (1999) '"I wasn't raped, but . . ." Resisting definitional problems in sexual victimization', in S. Lamb (ed.), *New Versions of Victims: Feminists Struggle with the Concept*. New York: New York University Press, pp. 57–81.

Gee, Clare (2010) *Hooked: Confessions of a London Call Girl*. Edinburgh: Mainstream Publishing.

Geller, Pamela (2011) '"Enlightened" leftwing barbarity: Honour killings adjective angers liberal Trudeau: "There needs to be a little bit of an attempt at responsible neutrality"', *Atlas Shrugs*, 15 March, available online at http://atlasshrugs2000.typepad.com/atlas_shrugs/2011/03/enlightened-leftwing-barbarity-honour-killings-adjective-angers-liberal-trudeau-there-needs-to-be-a-.html, accessed 15 August 2013.

Gibson, Faith (2011) 'Traveling through time to normal birth'. *Birth* 38(3): 266–8.

Giddens, Anthony (1991) *Modernity and Self-Identity: Self and Society in the Late Modern Age*. Cambridge: Polity Press.

Gilbert, Neil (1991) 'The phantom epidemic of sexual assault'. *Public Interest* 103 (Spring): 54–65.

Gilbert, Neil (1995) *Was it Rape? An Examination of Sexual Assault Statistics*. MenloPark, CA: Henry J. Kaiser Family Foundation.

Gill, Aisha (2006) 'Patriarchal violence in the name of "honour"'. *International Journal of Criminal Justice Sciences* 1(1): 1–12.

Gill, Aisha (2009) 'Honor killings and the quest for justice in black and minority ethnic communities in the United Kingdom'. *Criminal Justice Policy Review* 20(4): 475–94.

Gill, Rosalind C. (2007) 'Critical respect: the difficulties and dilemmas of agency and "choice" for feminism'. *European Journal of Women's Studies* 14(1): 69–80.

Gill, Aisha and Mitra-Kahn, Trishima (2012) 'Modernising the other: assessing the ideological underpinnings of the policy discourse on forced marriage in the UK'. *Policy and Politics* 40(1): 104–19.

Gill, Rosalind, Henwood, Karen and McLean, Carl (2005) 'Body projects and the regulation of normative masculinity'. *Body & Society* 11(37): 37–62.

Gilligan, Carol (1982) *In a Different Voice: Psychological Theory and Women's Development*. Cambridge, MA and London: Harvard University Press.

Gira Grant, Melissa (2011) 'Rape charges, libel suits, hooker headlines: the trial by media of Dominique Strauss-Kahn's accusers', *Alternet*, 7 July, available online at www.alternet.org/story/151562/rape_charges,_libel_suits,_hooker_headlines%3A_the_trial_by_media_of_dominique_strauss-kahn's_accusers, accessed 13 August 2013.

Gira Grant, Melissa (2013) 'The war on sex workers', *Reason*, February, available online at http://reason.com/archives/2013/01/21/the-war-on-sex-workers.

Glantz, J. Christopher (2011) 'Commentary: "The Times, They are a-Changin'"'. *Birth* 38(2): 140–1.

Goer, Henci (1999) *The Thinking Woman's Guide to a Better Birth*. New York: Perigee Books.

Goldin, Rebecca, Smyth, Emer and Foulkes, Andrea (2006) 'What science really says about the benefits of breast-feeding (and what the *New York Times* didn't tell you)'. *Stats*, 20 June, available online at http://stats.org/stories/breast_feed_nyt_jun_20_06.htm, accessed 8 August 2013.

Gray, John (1992) *Men are from Mars and Women are from Venus: A Practical Guide for Improving Communication and Getting What You Want in Relationships*. New York: HarperCollins.

Green, David Allen (2012) 'The desperation of Julian Assange', *The New Statesman*, 19 June.

Greenhalgh, Trisha and Wessley, Simon (2004) '"Health for me": a sociocultural analysis of healthism in the middle classes'. *British Medical Bulletin* 69: 197–213.

Gruber, Aya (2009) 'Rape, feminism and the war on crime'. *Washington Law Review* 84: 581–660.

Guindi, Fadwa El (1999) *Veil: Modesty, Privacy and Resistance*. Oxford: Berg.

Gupta, Nabanita Datta, Smith, Nina and Verner, Mette (2008) 'The impact of Nordic countries' family friendly policies on employment, wages and children'. *Review of Economics of the Household* 6(1): 65–89.

Gyte, Natalie (2013) 'Why I won't support One Billion Rising', *The Huffington Post*, 14 February, available online at www.huffing tonpost.co.uk/natalie-gyte/one-billion-rising-why-i-wont-support_b _2684595.html, accessed 8 August 2013.

Haddad, Yvonne Yazbeck (2007) 'The post 9/11 *Hijab* as icon'. *Sociology of Religion* 68(3): 253–67.

Haines, Joe (2011) 'The right to know is not absolute'. *British Journalism Review* 22(1): 27–32.

Hakim, Catherine (2000) *Work–Lifestyle Choices in the 21st Century: Preference Theory*. Oxford: Oxford University Press.

Hakim, Catherine (2003) 'Public morality versus personal choice: the failure of social attitude surveys'. *British Journal of Sociology* 54(3): 339–45.

Hall, S. (1988) 'Brave new world'. *Marxism Today* (October): 24–9.

Hallett, Stephanie (2011) 'Does the reaction to IMF rape charges show progress?' *MS. Magazine*, Blog, 17 May, available online at http://msmagazine.com/blog/blog/2011/05/17/does-the-reaction-to-imf-rape-charges-show-progress/, accessed 8 August 2013.

Haraway, Donna J. (1989) *Primate Visions*. London: Routledge.

Harcourt, C. and Donovan, B. (2005) 'The many faces of sex work'. *Sexually Transmitted Infections* 81: 201–6.

Harding, Kate (2010) 'The rush to smear Assange's rape accuser', Salon. com, 7 December, available online at www.salon.com/2010/12/07/julian_assange_rape_accuser_smeared, accessed 15 August 2013.

Hari, Johann (2011) 'Larry Flynt: freedom fighter, pornographer, monster?' *The Independent*, 27 May.

Harker, Jonathan (2013) 'It's time to face up to the problem of sexual abuse in the white community', *The Guardian*, 6 May.

Harris, Anita (2003) *Future Girl: Young Women in the Twenty-first Century*. London: Routledge.

Harvey, David (1990) *The Condition of Postmodernity*. Oxford: Blackwell Publishing.

Harvey, David (2005) *A Brief History of Neoliberalism*. Oxford: Oxford University Press.

Hasan, Medhi (2012) 'British Muslims must step outside this anti-war comfort zone', *The Guardian*, 2 April.

Hausman, Bernice L. (2004) 'The feminist politics of breastfeeding'. *Australian Feminist Studies* 19(45): 273–85.

Hendrix, Els (2011) 'Routine interventions during normal labour and birth: are they really necessary?' *Promoting Normal Birth: Research, Reflections and Guideline*. Chester le Street: Fresh Heart Publishing.

Henley-Einion, Alyson (2009) 'The medicalisation of childbirth', in C. Squire (ed.), *The Social Context of Birth*. Abingdon: Radcliffe Publishing, pp. 180–90.

Henry, Astrid (2004) 'Orgasms and empowerment: Sex and the City and the third wave feminism', in K. Akass and J. McCabe (eds), *Reading Sex and the City*. London: I. B. Tauris, pp. 65–82.

Hildingsson, Ingegard, Radestad, Ingela and Lindgren, Helena (2010) 'Birth preferences that deviate from the norm in Sweden: planned home birth versus planned Caesarean section'. *Birth* 37(4): 288–95.

Hirschkind, Charles and Mahmood, Saba (2002) 'Feminism, the Taliban, and politics of counter-insurgency'. *Anthropological Quarterly* 75(2): 339–54.

Hochschild, Arlie (1983) *The Managed Heart: Commercialisation of Human Feeling*. Berkeley, CA: University of California Press.

Hochschild, Arlie (2000) 'The chain of love', in W. Hutton and A. Giddens (eds), *On the Edge: Living with Global Capitalism*. London: Jonathan Cape.

Hoddinott, Pat, Tappin, David and Wright, Charlotte (2008) 'Breast feeding'. *British Medical Journal* 336: 881–7.

Hoff-Sommers, Christina (1994) *Who Stole Feminism? How Women Have Betrayed Women*. New York: Touchstone.

Holland, Samantha and Attwood, Feona (2009) 'Keeping fit in six-inch heels: the mainstreaming of pole dancing', in F. Attwood (ed.), *Mainstreaming Sex: The Sexualization of Western Culture*. London: I. B. Tauris, pp. 165–82.

Holmes, Linda (2011) 'The bizarre pitch for "The Playboy Club": It's all about female empowerment?' Available online at www.npr. org/blogs/monkeysee/2011/08/02/138924658/the-bizarre-pitch-for-the-playboy-club-its-all-about-female-empowerment, accessed 8 August 2013.

Holsopple, Kelly (1999) 'Pimps, tricks, and feminists'. *Women's Studies Quarterly* 27(1/2): 47–52.

Hoodfar, Homa (2003) 'More than clothing: veiling as an adaptive strategy', in S. Alvi, H. Hoodfar and S. McDonough (eds), *The Muslim Veil in North America*. Toronto: The Women's Press, pp. 3–40.

Hotelling, Barbara A. (2009a) 'From psychoprophylactic to orgasmic birth'. *The Journal of Perinatal Education* 18(4): 45–8.

Hotelling, Barbara A. (2009b) 'Teaching normal birth, normally'. *The Journal of Perinatal Education* 18(1): 51–5.

Hughes, Mark (2012) 'Julian Assange could be in London embassy for ten years, warns Ecuadorian minister', *The Daily Telegraph*, 27 September.

Humenick, Sharron S. (2006) 'The life-changing significance of normal birth'. *The Journal of Perinatal Education* 15(4): 1–3.

Hundal, Sunny (2012) 'The left cannot remain silent over "honour killings"', *The New Statesman* blog, 4 August, available online at www.newstatesman.com/blogs/politics/2012/08/left-cannot-remain-silent-over-honour-killings, accessed 15 August 2013.

Huntington, Samuel P. (1993) 'The clash of civilizations?' *Foreign Affairs* 72(3): 22–49.

Hursh, David (2007) 'Assessing No Child Left Behind and the rise of neoliberal education policies'. *American Educational Research Journal* 44(3): 493–518.

Hussein, Shakira (2007) 'The limits of force/choice discourses in discussing Muslim women's dress codes'. *Transforming Cultures eJournal* 2(1): 1–15.

Indo Asian News Service (2010) 'Veil empowers women, says UK minister', 19 July, available online at www.ndtv.com/article/world/veil-empowers-women-says-uk-minister-38414, accessed 8 August 2013.

Indoors (2010) *Indoor Sex Work*. Marseille: Autres Regards.

InFact Canada (2006) *Risks of Formula Feeding*. Toronto: InFact Canada.

Italiano, Laura (2011) 'Maid cleaning up as "hooker"', *The New York Post*, 2 July.

Jacobsen, Christine M. and Stenvoll, Dag (2010) 'Muslim women and foreign prostitutes: victim discourse, subjectivity and governance'. *Social Politics* 17(3): 270–94.

Jamet, Constance (2010) 'Législation sur la burqa: ce qui se fait ailleurs en Europe', *Le Figaro*, 15 June.

Jeffreys, Elena (2011) 'Why feminists should listen to sex workers'. Available online at www.thescavenger.net/feminism-a-pop-culture/why-feminists-should-listen-to-sex-workers-732.html, accessed 8 October 2013.

Johnson, Candace (2008) 'The political "nature" of pregnancy and childbirth'. *Canadian Journal of Political Science* 41(4): 889–913.

Jones, Owen (2011) 'Why I've joined the Workers' Revolutionary Party', on his blog, 1 April, available online at http://owenjones.org/, accessed 8 August 2013.

Jong, Erica (2010) 'Mother madness', *The Wall Street Journal*, 6 November.

Jouili, Jeanette and Amir-Moazami, Schirin (2006) 'Knowledge, empowerment and religious authority among pious Muslim women in France and Germany'. *The Muslim World* 96(4): 617–42.

Kamnitzer, Ruth (2009) 'Breastfeeding in the land of Genghis Khan', *Mothering Magazine* 155, July–August.

Keirse, Marc J. N. C. (2010) 'Home birth: gone away, gone astray, and here to stay'. *Birth* 37(4): 341–6.

Kelly, Jon (2012) 'The rise and fall of lap dancing', on BBC News online 8 February, available at www.bbc.co.uk/news/magazine-16869029, accessed 8 August 2013.

Kelly, Liz (2012) 'The (in)credible words of women: false allegations in European rape research'. *Violence Against Women* 16(2): 1345–55.

Kennedy, Holly P. and Shannon, Maureen T. (2004) 'Keeping birth normal: research findings on midwifery care during childbirth'. *Journal of Obstetric, Gynecologic, and Neonatal Nursing* 33(5): 554–60.

Kingsley, Patrick (2013) 'Muslim Brotherhood backlash against UN declaration on women's rights', *The Guardian*, 15 March.

Kinkade, Kathleen (1974) 'Power and the utopian assumption'. *Journal of Applied Behavioral Science* 10(3): 402–14.

Kinnell, Hilary (2008) *Violence and Sex Work in Britain*. Devon: Willan Publishing.

Kitzinger, Sheila (1972) *The Experience of Childbirth*. Harmondsworth: Penguin.

Kitzinger, Sheila (1978) *Women as Mothers*. London: Fontana.

Kitzinger, Sheila (1979) *The Experience of Breastfeeding*. Harmondsworth: Penguin.

Kitzinger, Sheila (1984) 'The psychology of breast-feeding'. *Breastfeeding Review* 5: 45–7.

Kitzinger, Sheila (2011 [1980]) *The New Pregnancy and Childbirth: Challenges and Choices* (4th edn). London: Dorling Kindersley.

Knegt, Peter (2009) 'Over 100 in film community sign Polanski petition', *IndieWire*, 29 September, available online at www.indiewire. com/article/over_100_in_film_community_sign_polanski_petition, accessed 8 August 2013.

Koon-Magnin, Sarah (2008) 'Adolescent sexual activity and statutory rape: a multi-method investigation'. Thesis submitted to the MA Crime, Law and Justice at Pennsylvania State University.

Kotiswaran, Prabha (2010) 'Labours in vice or virtue? Neo-liberalism, sexual commerce, and the case of Indian bar dancing'. *Journal of Law and Society* 37(1): 105–24.

Kukla, Rebecca (2006) 'Ethics and advocacy in breastfeeding campaigns'. *Hypatia* 21(1): 157–80.

Kurien, Prema (2003) 'To be or not to be South Asian: contemporary Indian-American politics'. *Journal of Asian American Studies* 6(3): 261–88.

Kvåle, Gunnar, Olsen, Bjørg Evjen, Hinderaker, Sven Gudmund, Ulstein, Magnar and Bergsjø, Per (2005) 'Maternal deaths in developing countries: a preventable tragedy'. *Norsk Epidemiologi* 15(2): 141–9.

La Leche League (2010) *The Womanly Art of Breastfeeding* (8th edn). New York: Random House.

La Leche League (2012) *La Leche League International*. Available online at http://www.llli.org/.

Lamaze (2011) *Year in Review, 2010–11*. Washington, DC: Lamaze International.

Lamb, Sharon (1999) 'Constructing the victim: popular images and lasting labels', in S. Lamb (ed.), *New Versions of Victims: Feminists Struggle with the Concept*. New York: New York University Press, pp. 108–38.

Lamb, Sharon (2010) 'Porn as a pathway to empowerment? A response to Petersen's commentary'. *Sex Roles* 62(3): 314–17.

Lather, Patti (2009) 'Against empathy, voice and authenticity', in A. Y. Jackson and L. A. Mazzei (eds), *Voice in Qualitative Inquiry: Challenging Conventional, Interpretive and Critical Conceptions in Qualitative Research*. Abingdon: Routledge, pp. 17–26.

Lauren, Jillian (2010) *Some Girls: My Life in a Harem*. New York: Plume.

Lauwers, Judith and Swisher, Anna (2011) *Counseling the Nursing Mother: A Lactation Consultant's Guide*. Sudbury, MA: Jones and Bartlett Publishers.

Leaky Boob (2011) 'Unsupportive support: stories of breastfeeding

doom and gloom', available online at http://theleakyboob.com/2011/
11/unsupportive-support-stories-of-breastfeeding-doom-and-gloom,
accessed 8 August 2013.

Lee, Ellie J. (2008) 'Living with risk in the age of "intensive mother-hood": maternal identity and infant feeding'. *Health, Risk & Society* 10(5): 467–77.

Leonard, Lori (2000) '"We did it for pleasure only": hearing alternative tales of female circumcision'. *Qualitative Inquiry* 6(2): 212–28.

Levitt, Steven D. and Dubner, Stephen J. (2005) *Freakonomics: A Rogue Economist Explores the Hidden Side of Everything*. London: Allen Lane.

Levitt, Steven D. and Dubner, Stephen J. (2009) *Superfreakonomics: Global Cooling, Patriotic Prostitutes and Why Suicide Bombers Should Buy Life Insurance*. London: Allen Lane.

Levy, Andrew (2012) 'Cambridge students told to bar Strauss-Kahn from union debate', *The Daily Mail*, 28 February.

Levy, Ariel (2005) *Female Chauvinist Pigs: Women and the Rise of Raunch Culture*. London: Pocket Books.

Lévy, Bernard-Henri (2011) 'Bernard-Henri Lévy defends accused IMF director', *The Daily Beast*, 16 May, available online at www.thedai lybeast.com/articles/2011/05/16/bernard-henri-lvy-the-dominique-strauss-kahn-i-know.html, accessed 8 October 2013.

Liberal Conspiracy (2012) 'Benn sorry for dismissing Assange rape alle-gations', *Liberal Conspiracy* 18 September, available online at http://liberalconspiracy.org/2012/09/18/tony-benn-sorry-for-dismissing-as sange-rape-allegations/, accessed 8 August 2013.

Lim, Lin Lean (1998) *The Sex Sector: The Economic and Social Bases of Prostitution in Southeast Asia*. Geneva: International Labour Office.

Livia, Anna and Hall, Kira (1997) '"It's a girl!": Bringing performativ-ity back to linguistics', in A. Livia and K. Hall (eds), *Queerly Phrased: Language, Gender and Sexuality*. New York: Oxford University Press, pp. 3–18.

Long, Julia (2012) *Anti-Porn: the Resurgence of Anti-Pornography Feminism*. London: Zed Books.

Longhurst, Robyn (2009) 'YouTube: a new space for birth?' *Feminist Review* 93: 46–63.

Lopez, Lori Kido (2009) 'The radical act of "mommy blogging": redefining motherhood through the blogosphere'. *New Media & Society* 11(5): 729–47.

Lothian, Judith (2006) 'Birth plans: the good, the bad, and the future'. *Journal of Obstetric, Gynecologic and Neonatal Nursing* 35(2): 295–303.

Lothian, Judith (2007) 'Selling normal birth: six ways to make birth easier'. *The Journal of Perinatal Education* 16(3): 44–6.

Lyotard, Jean-François (1979) *The Postmodern Condition: A Report on Knowledge*. Manchester: Manchester University Press.

M, Sarah (2012) 'To the would-be sex work abolitionist, or "ain't I a woman?"', rabble.ca, available online at http://rabble.ca/news/2012/02/would-be-sex-work-abolitionist-or-aint-i-woman, accessed 8 August 2013.

MacDonald, Margaret (2006) 'Gender expectations: natural bodies and natural births in the new midwifery in Canada'. *Medical Anthropology Quarterly* 20(2): 235–56.

MacDonald, Margaret (2011) 'The art of medicine: the cultural evolution of natural birth'. *The Lancet* 378: 394–5.

MacDorman, Marian F., Declerq, Eugene and Menacker, Fay (2010) 'Trends and characteristics of home births in the United States by race and ethnicity, 1990–2006'. *Birth* 38(1): 17–23.

MacIntyre, Alasdair (1984) *After Virtue*. Notre Dame, IN: University of Notre Dame Press.

Maddison, Stephen (2010) 'Online obscenity and myths of freedom: dangerous images, child porn, and neoliberalism', in F. Attwood (ed.), *Porn.com: Making Sense of Online Pornography*. Oxford: Peter Lang, pp. 17–33.

Magnanti, Brooke (2012) *The Sex Myth: Why Everything We're Told is Wrong*. London: Weidenfeld & Nicolson.

Mahmood, Saba (2001) 'Feminist theory, embodiment, and the docile agent: some reflections on the Egyptian Islamic revival'. *Cultural Anthropology* 16(2): 202–36.

Mahmood, Saba (2005) *The Politics of Piety: The Islamic Revival and the Feminist Subject*. Princeton, NJ: Princeton University Press.

Majid, Anouar (1998) 'The politics of feminism in Islam'. *Signs* 23(2): 321–61.

Malik, Kenan (2007) 'The failures of multiculturalism', available online at www.kenanmalik.com/papers/engelsberg_mc.html, accessed 8 August 2013.

Malik, Nesrire (2012) 'Do Arab men hate women? It's not that simple', *The Guardian*, 25 April.

Malkin, Michelle (2003) 'Roman Polanski and R. Kelly: pedophilic celebrities are above the law', *Capitalism Magazine*, 26 February, available online at http://capitalismmagazine.com/2003/02/roman-polan ski-and-r-kelly-pedophilic-celebrities-are-above-the-law/, accessed 8 August 2013.

Manaster, Shelly (2006) 'Treading water: an autoethnographic account(ing) of the lap dance', in R. D. Egan, K. Frank and M. L. Johnson (eds), *Flesh for Fantasy: Producing and Consuming Exotic Dance*. New York: Thunder's Mouth Press, pp. 3–18.

Marcus, Sharon (1992) 'Fighting bodies, fighting words, a theory and politics of rape prevention,' in J. Butler and J. W. Scott (eds), *Feminists Theorize the Political*. London: Routledge, pp. 385–403.

Mardorossian, C. M. (2002) 'Toward a new feminist theory of rape'. *Signs: Journal of Women in Culture and Society* 27(3): 744–75.

Marsh, David, Hart, Paul 't and Tindall, Karen (2010) 'Celebrity politics: the politics of the late modernity?' *Political Studies Review* 8(3): 322–40.

Martino, Wayne and Rezai-Rashti, Goli M. (2008) 'The politics of veiling, gender and the Muslim subject: on the limits and possibilities of anti-racist education in the aftermath of September 11'. *Discourse: Studies in the Cultural Politics of Education* 29(3): 417–31.

Maternity Care Working Party (2007) *Making Normal Birth a Reality: Consensus Statement from the Maternity Care Working Party; Our Shared Views about the Need to Recognise, Facilitate and Audit Normal Birth*. Available online at www.rcog.org.uk/womens-health/clinical-guid ance/making-normal-birth-reality, accessed 8 August 2013.

McCaffrey, Dawn (1998) 'Victim feminism/victim activism'. *Sociological Spectrum* 18(3): 263–84.

McColgan, Aileen (1996) *The Case for Taking the 'Date' Out of Rape*. London: Pandora/HarperCollins.

McDaniel, Jequita Potts (2009) 'Exploration of ecological identity and natural childbirth'. Unpublished PhD thesis available from Union Institute and University at http://www.myunion.edu/.

McEwan, Melissa (2010) 'Michael Moore doubles down on rape

apologia', *Shakesville*, 15 December, available online at www.shakesville. com/2010/12/michael-moore-doubles-down-on-rape.html, accessed 15 August 2013.

McLennan, Natalie (2008) *The Price: My Rise and Fall as Natalia, New York's #1 Escort*. Beverly Hills, CA: Phoenix Books.

McNair, Brian (2002) *Striptease Culture: Sex, Media and the Democratization of Desire*. New York: Routledge.

McRobbie, Angela (2004) 'Notes on "what not to wear" and post-feminist Symbolic violence'. *The Sociological Review* 52(s2): 97–109.

McRobie, Heather (2011) 'Ken Clarke, Strauss-Kahn, Yale and Slutwalks: rape, consent and agency'. *50.50 Inclusive Democracy*, 26 May, available online at www.opendemocracy.net/5050/heather-mcrobie/ken-clarke-strauss-kahn-yale-and-slutwalks-rape-consent-and-agency, accessed 8 August 2013.

Meetoo, Veena and Mirza, Heidi Safia (2007) 'There is nothing honourable about honour killings: gender, violence and the limits of multiculturalism'. *Women's Studies International Forum* 30(3): 187–200.

Melzack, Ronald (1984) 'The myth of painless childbirth'. *Pain* 19(4): 321–37.

Menacker, Fay P. H. (2005) 'Trends in Cesarean rates for first births and repeat Cesarean rates for low-risk women: United States, 1990–2003'. *National Vital Statistics Reports* 54(4): 1–8.

Meyers, Diana Tietjens (2000) 'Feminism and women's autonomy: the challenge of female genital cutting'. *Metaphilosophy* 31(5): 469–91.

Miles, Emily (2011) 'OCCUPY LSX sexual harassment', *LSE Engenderings*, blog, 5 December, available online at http://blogs.lse.ac.uk/gender/2011/12/05/occupy-lsxual-harrassment/, accessed 8 August 2013.

Millner, Denene (2012) 'Why latch on NYC is not the answer to low breastfeeding rates', *Parenting*, 2 August, available online at www.parenting.com/blogs/show-and-tell/denene-millner-mybrownbaby/guest-blog-why-latch-nyc-not-answer-low-breastfeeding, accessed 15 August 2013.

Miriam, Kathy (2005) 'Stopping the traffic in women: power, agency and abolition in feminist debates over sex-trafficking'. *Journal of Social Philosophy* 36(1): 1–17.

Miriam, Kathy (2010) 'Feminism or barbarism: the patriarchy papers

2010', available online at http://kmiriam.wordpress.com/feminism-or-barbarism-the-patriarchy-papers-2010, accessed 8 August 2013.

Misra, Joya, Budig, Michelle and Boeckmann, Irene (2011) 'Work–family policies and the effects of children on women's employment hours and wages'. *Community, Work & Family* 14(2): 139–57.

Miss S (2007) *Confessions of a Working Girl.* London: Penguin.

Mkrtchyan, Gayane (2011) 'Infant rights: NA considers bill on breastfeeding', *Armenia Now*, 31 October, available online at http://armenian ow.com/social/health/32796/armenia_bill_breastfeeding, accessed 8 August 2013.

Modood, Tariq (2003) 'Muslims and the politics of difference'. *The Political Quarterly* 74(s1): 100–15.

Moghadam, Valentine M. (2001) 'Feminism and Islamic fundamentalism: a secularist approach'. *Journal of Women's History* 13(1): 42–5.

Moghissi, Haideh (1999) *Feminism and Islamic Fundamentalism: The Limits of Postmodern Analysis.* London: Zed Books.

Mohanty, Chandra Talpade (1984) 'Under western eyes: feminist scholarship and colonial discourses'. *Boundary* 2, 12(3): 333–58.

Mohanty, Chandra Talpade (2002) '"Under western eyes" revisited: feminist solidarity through anticapitalist struggles'. *Signs: Journal of Women in Culture and Society* 28(2): 499–535.

Moore, Ellouise (2008) *Girl in High Heels: Intimate Confessions of a London Stripper.* London: Ebury Publishing.

Morton, James (2005) 'Celebrities and juries'. *Journal of Criminal Law* 69(5): 365–6.

Mosucci, O. (2003) 'Holistic obstetrics: the origins of "natural childbirth" in Britain'. *The Postgraduate Medical Journal* 79: 168–73.

Motsoaledi, Aaron (2011) Media Statement by the South African Minister of Health on Breastfeeding, available online at www.doh.gov.za/show.php?id=3045, accessed 15 August 2013.

Mott, Rebecca (2011) 'Thoughts on chosen work for the prostituted class.' Note posted on Facebook, 15 June, available online at www.facebook.com/notes/rebecca-mott/thoughts-on-chosen-work-for-the-prostituted-class/361760799968.

Motta, Sara C. (2013) '"We are the ones we have been waiting for": the feminization of resistance in Venezuela'. *Latin American Perspectives* 40(4): 35–54.

Mottershead, N. (2006) 'Hypnosis: removing the labour from birth'. *The Practising Midwife* 9(3): 26–9.

Moynihan, Colin (2012) 'Strauss-Kahn sues housekeeper, saying she hurt his career', *The New York Times*, 15 May.

Mullally, Siobhán (2011) 'Civic integration, migrant women and the veil: at the limits of rights?' *The Modern Law Review* 74(1): 27–56.

Murray, Craig (2011) 'Another vicious, ugly-souled feminist', 28 July, available online at www.craigmurray.org.uk/.

Murray, David (2012) 'Australian Breastfeeding Association class told baby formula was "like AIDS"', *The Sunday Mail*, 26 August.

Murshed, Syed Mansoob and Pavan, Sara (2009) 'Identity and Islamic radicalization in Western Europe'. Economics of Security Working Paper 14. Berlin: Economics of Security.

Mustafa, Zubeida (2011) 'The burka debate', in Dawn.com, 12 October, available online at www.zubeidamustafa.com/the-burka-debate, accessed 15 August 2013.

Napier, Jessica Renee (2011) 'IMF chief's arrest offers teachable moment', *Public Affairs*, 17 May, available online at www.calcasa.org/blog/imf-chiefs-arrest-offers-teachable-moment, accessed 15 August 2013.

Narayan, Uma (1998) 'Essence of culture and a sense of history: a feminist critique of cultural essentialism'. *Hypatia* 13(2): 86–106.

National Childbirth Trust (2010) *Normal Birth as a Measure of the Quality of Care: Evidence on Safety, Effectiveness and Women's Experiences*. London: NCT.

National Conference of State Legislatures (2011) *Breastfeeding Laws*. Available online at www.ncsl.org/issues-research/health/breastfeeding-state-laws.aspx, accessed 15 August 2013.

National Health Service (2008) *Breastfeeding and Work: Information for Employees and Employers*. Department of Health.

National Health Service (2010) *High Impact Actions for Nursing and Midwifery: The Essential Collection*. London: NHS.

Nettleton, Sarah (2006) *Sociology of Health and Illness*. Cambridge: Polity Press.

Newburn, Mary (2011) 'NCT response to birthplace in England study findings'. Press release available online at www.nct.org.uk/press-release/nct-response-birthplace-england-study-findings, accessed 8 August 2013.

Niala, Claire (2012) 'Why African babies don't cry', available online from www.incultureparent.com/2010/12/why-african-babies-dont-cry/, accessed 13 August 2013.

Norman, Julian (2012a) 'Assange, the European Arrest Warrant, and the Supreme Court', *The F Word*, 30 May, available online at http://www.thefword.org.uk/blog/2012/05/assange_the_eur, accessed 21 August 2013.

Norman, Julian (2012b) 'Rochdale rape ring: on political correctness versus survivor's credibility', *The F Word* blog, 10 May, available online at www.thefword.org.uk/.

North, Anna (2012) 'The anti-Nicholas Kristof backlash'. *Buzzfeed*, available online at www.buzzfeed.com/annanorth/the-anti-nicholas-kristof-backlash, accessed 9 August 2013.

Norton, Anne (2004) *Leo Strauss and the Politics of American Empire*. New Haven, CT: Yale University Press.

Odent, Michel (1984) *Birth Reborn*. New York: Pantheon.

O'Keefe, Theresa (2012) 'Flaunting our way to freedom? SlutWalks, gendered protest and feminist futures', available online at http://eprints.nuim.ie/3569/1/Flaunting_2012-1.pdf, accessed 16 August 2013.

Okin, Susan Moller (2011) 'Is multiculturalism bad for women?', in S. Moller Okin (ed.), *Is Multicultualism Bad for Women?* Princeton, NJ: Princeton University Press, pp. 9–26.

O'Neill, Maggie (2001) *Prostitution and Feminism: Towards a Politics of Feeling*. Cambridge: Polity Press.

Orr, Deborah (2011a) 'End this cowardice over forced marriages', *The Guardian*, 19 May.

Orr, Deborah (2011b) 'Newspapers don't put a brake on sexual antics: they fuel them', *The Guardian*, 19 May, available online at www.guardian.co.uk/commentisfree/2011/may/19/newspapers-fuel-sexual-excess, accessed 9 August 2013.

Oza, Rupal (2001) 'Showcasing India: gender, geography and globalization'. *Signs* 26(4): 1067–95.

Paasonen, Susanna, Nikunen, Kaarina and Saarenmaa, Laura (2007) 'Pornification and the education of desire', in S. Paasonen, K. Nikunen and L. Saarenmaa (eds), *Pornification: Sex and Sexuality in Media Culture*. Oxford: Berg, pp. 1–20.

Palm Beach Post (2012) 'Man who killed wife in jealous rage gets 25 year sentence', *The Palm Beach Post*, 17 April.

Palmer, Gabrielle (1988) *The Politics of Breastfeeding*. London: Pandora Press.

Parashar, Swati (2012) 'The silent feminism', posted on the Gender in Global Governance Net-work 24 December, available online at http://genderinglobalgovernancenet-work.net/comment/the-silent-fe minism/, accessed 9 August 2013.

Parvez, Z. Fareen (2011) 'Debating the burqa in France: the antipolitics of Islamic revival'. *Qualitative Sociology* 34: 287–312.

Pedersen, Jennifer and Salib, Monalisa (2013) 'Women of the Arab Spring'. *International Feminist Journal of Politics*, available at www.tandfon line.com/doi/abs/10.1080/14616742.2013.796218#.UhRsvdKmguc/, accessed 21 August.

Pedwell, Carolyn (2007) 'Theorizing "African" female genital cutting and "western" body modifications: a critique of the continuum and analogue approaches'. *Feminist Review* 86: 45–66.

Pendlebury, Richard (2010) 'The Wikileaks sex files: How two one-night stands sparked a worldwide hunt for Julian Assange', *The Daily Mail*, 6 December.

Penny, Laurie (2010) 'Tell me what a rapist looks like', *The New Statesman*, 9 December, available online at www.newstatesman.com/blogs/laurie-penny/2010/12/julian-assange-rape-women, accessed 9 August 2013.

Penny, Laurie (2012) 'This strange neo-Victorian desire to save prostitutes and porn actresses', *The New Statesman*, 13 December, available online at www.newstatesman.com/society/2012/12/strange-neo-victorian-desire-save-prostitutes-and-porn-actresses, accessed 9 August 2013.

Penttinen, Elina (2010) 'Imagined and embodied spaces in the global sex industry'. *Gender, Work and Organization* 17(1): 28–44.

PhD in Parenting (2011) 'Infant formula advertising *does* influence mothers', available online at www.phdinparenting.com/2011/11/20/infant-formula-advertising-does-influence-mothers/#.T6udop9YvG8, accessed 9 August 2013.

Phipps, Alison (2009) 'Review of Laura Agustín's sex at the margins'. *Journal of Ethnic and Migration Studies* 35(6): 1054–5.

Phipps, Alison (2013) 'Violence against sex workers in the UK', in

L. McMillan and N. Lombard (eds), *Violence Against Women (Research Highlights in Social Work Series)*. London: Jessica Kingsley Publishers, pp. 87–102.

Phoenix, Ann (2006) 'Editorial: intersectionality'. *European Journal of Women's Studies* 13(3): 187–92.

Pietrykowski, B. (1994) 'Consuming culture: postmodernism, post-Fordism, and economics'. *Rethinking Marxism: A Journal of Economics, Culture & Society* 7(1): 62–80.

Poirier, Agnès (2010) 'The prurient hounding of Roman Polanski is over at last', *The Guardian*, 12 July, available online at www.guardian.co.uk/commentisfree/cifamerica/2010/jul/12/roman-polanski-extradite-swiss-us, accessed 9 August 2013.

Pollitt, Katha (2010) 'On rape, the left still doesn't get it', *The Guardian*, 27 December, available online at www.guardian.co.uk/commentisfree/2010/dec/27/rape-left-julian-assange-swedish-law-wikileaks, accessed 9 August 2013.

Pollitt, Katha (2012) 'Attachment parenting: more guilt for mothers', *The Guardian*, 18 May.

Porton, Richard (2012) 'In new Roman Polanski documentary, an odd evasion of rape controversy', *The Daily Beast*, 17 May, available online at www.thedailybeast.com/articles/2012/05/17/in-new-roman-polanski-documentary-an-odd-evasion-of-rape-controversy.html, accessed 9 August 2013.

Power, Carla (2009) 'The politics of women's head coverings', *Time Magazine*, 13 July.

Pritchard, Jane (2010) 'The sex work debate', *International Socialism* 125, available online at www.isj.org.uk/?id=618, accessed 9 August 2013.

Puar, Jasbir K. (2007) *Terrorist Assemblages: Homonationalism in Queer Times*. Durham, NC: Duke University Press.

Purdy, Laura (2001) 'Medicalization, medical necessity, and feminist medicine'. *Bioethics* 15(3): 248–61.

Quan, Tracy (2005) *Diary of a Manhattan Call Girl*. London: Harper Perennial.

Quan, Tracy (2006) *Diary of a Married Call Girl*. London: Harper Perennial.

Quan, Tracy (2008) *Diary of a Jetsetting Call Girl*. London: Harper Perennial.

Quan, Tracy (2010) 'Julian Assange, chick magnet?' *The Daily Beast*, 13 December.

Queen, Carol (2001) 'Sex radical politics, sex-positive feminist thought, and whore stigma', in B. Ryan (ed.), *Identity Politics in the Women's Movement*. New York: New York University Press, pp. 92–102.

Quinn, Ben (2012) 'Salma Yaqoob quits as Respect party leader', *The Guardian*, 12 September.

Rajan, Rajeswari Sunder (1993) *Real and Imagined Women: Gender, Culture and Postcolonialism*. London: Routledge.

Rana, Junaid (2011) 'Clothing the "terrifying Muslim": Q&A with Junaid Rana', in *Racialicious*, 12 May, available online at www.racialicious. com/2011/05/12/clothing-the-terrifying-muslim-qa-with-junaid-rana, accessed 9 August 2013.

Rawlinson, Kevin (2013) '"I was targeted after I made Assange sex crime claim" says accuser of Wikileaks founder', *The Independent*, 13 May.

Ray, Audacia (2012) 'Things I once valued but now think are massively problematic', available online at http://audaciaray.tumblr.com/post/17593622586/things-i-once-valued-but-now-think-are-massively/, accessed 21 August 2013.

Rayner, Lisa and Easthope, Gary (2001) 'Postmodern consumption and alternative medications'. *Journal of Sociology* 37(2): 157–76.

Readings, George (2010) 'Female genital mutilation cannot be defended as part of Islam', *The Guardian*, 15 October.

Reddy, Rupa (2008) 'Gender, culture and the law: approaches to "honour crimes" in the UK'. *Feminist Legal Studies* 16: 305–21.

Redfern, Catherine, and Aune, Kristin (2013) *Reclaiming the F-Word: The New Feminist Movement* (rev. edn). London: Zed Books.

Reuters (2013) 'Venezuela considers banning baby bottle feeding', *The Daily Telegraph*, 14 June.

Rich, Adrienne (1980) 'Compulsory heterosexuality and lesbian existence'. *Signs: Journal of Women in Culture and Society* 5(4): 631–60.

Rich, Adrienne (1986 [1976]) *Of Woman Born: Motherhood as Experience and Institution*. New York: W. W. Norton.

Righard, Lennart (2001) 'Making childbirth a normal process'. *Birth* 28(1): 1–4.

Ringrose, Jessica and Renold, Emma (2012) 'Slut-shaming, girl power and "sexualisation": thinking through the politics of the international SlutWalks with teenage girls'. *Gender and Education* 24(3): 333–43.

Roberts, Celia, Satchwell, Candice and Tyler, Imogen (2011) *Report on Childbirth Organisations UK.* Deliverable for the EPOKS (European Patient Organisations in Knowledge Society) Project, unpublished.

Roberts, Paul Craig (2010) 'What the Wiki-saga teaches us', *Counterpunch*, 2 December, available online at www.counterpunch.org/2010/12/02/what-the-wiki-saga-teaches-us/, accessed 9 August 2013.

Rochman, Bonnie (2012) 'Celebrities breast-feeding: why it matters', *Time*, 14 March.

Roiphe, Katie (1994) *The Morning After: Sex, Fear and Feminism.* London: Hamish Hamilton.

Romano, A. M and Lothian, J. A. (2008) 'Promoting, protecting and supporting normal birth: a look at the evidence'. *Journal of Obstetric, Gynecologic, and Neonatal Nursing* 37(1): 94–105.

Romero, Mary (2012) 'The real help'. *Contexts* 11: 54–6.

Rothschild, Nathalie (2009) 'We're all traffickers now', *Spiked*, 26 August, available online at www.spiked-online.com/index.php/site/article/7312/, accessed 9 August 2013.

Royal Islamic Strategic Studies Centre (2009) *The 500 Most Influential Muslims in the World.* Georgetown: Royal Islamic Strategic Studies Centre.

Ruddick, Sara (1989) *Maternal Thinking: Toward a Politics of Peace.* Boston, MA: Beacon Press.

Saedi, Goal Auzeen (2011) 'Is the Lowe's anti-Muslim controversy about cognitive distortions?' *Psychology Today*, 13 December.

Saharso, Sawitri (2003) 'Feminist ethics, autonomy and the politics of multiculturalism'. *Feminist Theory* 4(2): 199–215.

Said, Edward (1978) *Orientalism.* New York: Pantheon.

Salecl, Renata (2010) 'Motherhood: from rights to choices'. *Studies in the Maternal* 2(1), available online at www.mamsie.bbk.ac.uk/salecl.html, accessed 21 August 2013.

Sanders, Teela (2005) *Sex Work: A Risky Business.* Cullompton: Willan Publishing.

Sanders, Teela (2006) 'Behind the personal ads: the indoor sex markets in Britain', in R. Campbell and M. O'Neill (eds), *Sex Work Now.* Cullompton: Willan Publishing, pp. 92–115.

Sanders, Teela (2007) 'Protecting the health and safety of female sex workers: the responsibility of all'. *British Journal of Obstetrics and Gynaecology* 114: 791–3.

Sanders, Teela (2008a) *Paying for Pleasure: Men Who Buy Sex*. Cullompton: Willan Publishing.

Sanders, Teela (2008b) 'Selling sex in the shadow economy'. *International Journal of Social Economics* 35(10): 704–16.

Saner, Emine (2013) 'Are we getting childbirth wrong?' *The Guardian*, 11 January.

Satz, Debra (2010a) 'Ethics, economics, and markets: an interview with Debra Satz', *Erasmus Journal for Philosophy and Economics* 3(1): 68–88.

Satz, Debra (2010b) *Why Some Things Should Not Be For Sale: The Moral Limits of Markets*. Oxford: Oxford University Press.

Saunders, Debra J. (2012) 'DSK and the return of conspiracy theories', *SFGate*, 8 May, available online at blog.sfgate.com.

Savage, Mike, Barlow, James, Dickens, Peter and Fielding, Tony (1992) *Property, Bureaucracy and Culture: Middle-Class Formation in Contemporary Britain*. London: Routledge.

Savage, Wendy (1986) *A Savage Enquiry: Who Controls Childbirth?* London: Virago.

Schaffauser, Thierry (2010) 'Whorephobia affects all women', *The Guardian*, 23 June.

Schmied, Virginia and Lupton, Deborah (2001) 'Blurring the boundaries: breastfeeding and maternal subjectivity'. *Sociology of Health & Illness* 23(2): 234–50.

Schmied, Virginia, Beake, Sarah, Sheehan, Athena, McCourt, Christine and Dykes, Fiona (2011) 'Women's perceptions and experiences of breastfeeding support: a metasynthesis'. *Birth* 38(1): 49–60.

Scotsman (2011) 'Woman is raped at anti-capitalism camp', *The Scotsman*, 27 October.

Scott, Joan Wallach (2007) *The Politics of the Veil*. Princeton, NJ: Princeton University Press.

Scoular, Jane (2004) 'The "subject" of prostitution: interpreting the discursive, symbolic and material position of sex/work in feminist theory'. *Feminist Theory* 5(3): 343–55.

Scoular, Jane and Sanders, Teela (2010) 'Introduction: The changing social and legal context of sexual commerce: why regulation matters'. *Journal of Law and Society* 37(1): 1–11.

Seidel, Beth (2012) 'What makes the difference?' *The Pekin Daily Times*, 3 April.

Sere, Adriene (2004) 'Sex and feminism: Who is being silenced?' in R. Whisnant and C. Stark (eds), *Not for Sale: Feminists Resisting Prostitution and Pornography*. Melbourne: Spinifex, pp. 269–74.

Sex Worker Literati (2001) *Hos, Hookers, Call Girls, and Rent Boys*. Available online at http://hoshookerscallgirlsrentboys.com/, accessed 9 August 2013.

Shakespeare, Tom (2006) *Disability Rights and Wrongs*. New York: Routledge.

Shamir, Israel and Bennett, Paul (2010) 'Assange: the amazing adventures of Captain Neo in blonde land', *Counterpunch*, 27–29 August.

Shaw, Rebecca and Kitzinger, Celia (2005) 'Calls to a home birth helpline: empowerment in childbirth'. *Social Science & Medicine* 61(11): 2374–83.

Shilling, Chris (1993) *The Body and Social Theory*. London: Sage.

Shiner, Larry (1982) 'Reading Foucault: Anti-method and the genealogy of power-knowledge'. *History and Theory* 21(3): 382–98.

Sholkamy, Hania (2009) 'Islam and feminism', *Contestations: Dialogues on Women's Empowerment* 1(1), available online at www.contestations.net/issues/issue-1/religion-and-gender-justice/, accessed 9 August 2013.

Shuval, Judith T. and Gross, Sky E. (2008) 'Midwives practice CAM: feminism in the Delivery Room'. *Complementary Health Practice Review* 13(1): 46–62.

Silverleib, Alan (2011) 'Dominique Strauss-Kahn: A brilliant career, a stunning accusation', *CNN World Politic*, 16 May, available online at www.cnn.com/2011/WORLD/europe/05/16/france.strauss.kahn/index.html/, accessed 21 August 2013.

Smart, Sarah (2012) 'Feeling uncomfortable: young people's emotional responses to neo-liberal explanations for economic inequality'. *Sociological Research Online* 17(3): 1.

Smith, Andrew (2008) 'Review essay: working lives: cultural control, collectivism, karoshi'. *Sociology* 42(1): 179–85.

Smyth, Lisa (2012) 'The social politics of breastfeeding: norms, situations and policy implications'. *Ethics and Social Welfare* 6(2): 182–94.

Snitow, Ann (1992) 'Feminism and motherhood: an American reading'. *Feminist Review* 40: 32–51.

Soares, Andre (2013) 'Roman Polanski Petition', in Alt Film Guide, 17 January, available online at www.altfg.com/blog/directors/roman-polanski-petition/, accessed 19 August 2013.

Socialist Unity (2012) 'Time for the left to stand up for Galloway', posted on *Socialist Unity* blog, 5 September, available online at www.socialistunity.com.

Spelvin, Georgina (2009) 'The accidental hooker', in D. H. Sterry (ed.), *Hos, Hookers, Call Girls, and Rent Boys: Professionals Writing on Life, Love, Money, and Sex*. Brooklyn, NY: Soft Skull Press, pp. 38–43.

Spencer, Robert (2007) 'Cultural abdication: western feminists hesitate to decry female genital mutilation', *Jihadwatch*, 26 August, available online at www.jihadwatch.org.

Spivak, Gayatri (1988) *In Other Worlds: Essays in Cultural Politics*. New York: Routledge.

Spivak, Gayatri Chakravorty (1993) *Outside in the Teaching Machine*. New York: Routledge.

Sprinkle, Annie (2009) '40 reasons why whores are my heroes', in D. H., Sterry (ed.), *Hos, Hookers, Call Girls, and Rent Boys: Professionals Writing on Life, Love, Money, and Sex*. Brooklyn, NY: Soft Skull Press, pp. 10–11.

Squire, Corinne (2001) 'The public life of emotions'. *International Journal of Critical Psychology* 1: 27–38.

Stein, Ben (2011) 'Presumed innocent, anyone?' *The American Spectator*, 17 May, available online at www.spectator.org.

Sterry, David Henry (2009) 'Introduction', in D. H. Sterry (ed.), *Hos, Hookers, Call Girls, and Rent Boys: Professionals Writing on Life, Love, Money, and Sex*. Brooklyn, NY: Soft Skull Press, pp. 1–6.

Stevenson, C. and Cutcliffe, J. (2006) 'Problematizing special observation in psychiatry: Foucault, archaeology, genealogy, discourse and power/knowledge'. *Journal of Psychiatric and Mental Health Nursing* 13: 713–21.

Stivens, Maila (2006) '"Family values" and Islamic revival: gender, rights and state moral projects in Malaysia'. *Women's Studies International Forum* 29(4): 354–67.

Story (2011) 'Research proves men come to strip clubs to relax', *Tits and Sass: one big service piece*, 2 August. Available online at http://titsandsass.com/?p=3942, accessed 9 August 2013.

Strudwick, Patrick (2012) '"Homophobia" and "Islamophobia" are the right words for the job', *The Guardian*, 27 November.

Suarez, Eliana and Gadalla, Tahany M. (2010) 'Stop blaming the victim: a meta-analysis on rape myths'. *Journal of Interpersonal Violence* 25(11): 2010–35.

Sutherland, Kate (2004) 'Work, sex, and sex-work: competing feminist discourses on the international sex trade'. *Osgoode Hall Law Journal* 42(1): 1–28.

Symon, Andrew, Winter, Clare, Donnan, Peter T. and Kirkham, Mavis (2010) 'Examining autonomy's boundaries: a follow-up review of perinatal mortality cases in UK independent midwifery'. *Birth* 37(4): 280–7.

Tadros, Mariz (2009) 'Feminism through safe Islam?' *Contestations: Dialogues on Women's Empowerment* 1(1), available online at www. contestations.net/issues/issue-1/religion-and-gender-justice-feminism -through-safe-islam/, accessed 21 August 2013.

Tatchell, Peter (2009) 'Not all cultures are equally valid and commendable', *The Independent*, 3 November.

Temkin, Jennifer (1995) *Rape and the Criminal Justice System*. Brookfield, VT: Dartmouth Publishing Company.

Thebes, Molly (2012) 'The prospect of extraditing Julian Assange', *North Carolina Journal of International Law and Commercial Regulation* 37(3): 889–915.

Thomson, Rachel, Kehily, Mary Jane, Hadfield, Lucy and Sharpe, Sue (2011) *Making Modern Mothers*. Bristol: The Policy Press.

Tissot, Sylvie (2011) 'Excluding Muslim women: from hijab to niqab, from school to public space'. *Public Culture* 23(1): 39–46.

Turchik, Jessica and Edwards, Kate (2012) 'Myths about male rape: a literature review'. *Psychology of Men & Masculinity* 13(2): 211–26.

Turner, Beverly (2013) '10 reasons why breastfeeding is out of fashion', *The Daily Telegraph*, 24 June.

Turner, Bryan (1984) *The Body and Society: Explorations in Social Theory*. London: Basil Blackwell Publishing.

Ullman, Sarah E. (2010) *Talking about Sexual Assault: Society's Response to Survivors*. Washington, DC: American Psychological Association.

UNFPA, UNICEF, WHO, World Bank (2012) *Trends in Maternal Mortality: 1990–2010*. Geneva: World Health Organization.

UNICEF (2012) *International Code of Marketing of Breast-milk Substitutes.* Available online at www.unicef.org/nutrition/index_24805.html, accessed 11 August 2013.

Valenti, Jessica (2011) 'Slutwalks and the future of feminism', *The Washington Post*, 3 June.

Vallely, Paul (2013) 'The Oxford child sex abuse verdict highlights a cultural problem, but not a specifically Muslim one', *The Independent*, 15 May.

Vance, Carole (2013) 'What is wrong with this picture?' *Kafila*, 18 February, available online at http://kafila.org/2013/02/18/what-is-wrong-with-this-picture-carole-vance-2/, accessed 21 August 2013.

Vaswani, Karishma (2010) 'New Indonesia breastfeeding law stokes controversy'. Available online at www.bbc.co.uk/news/world-asia-pacific-11586719, accessed 9 August 2013.

Villegas, Laura, McKay, Katherine, Dennis, Cindy-Lee and Ross, Lori E (2011) 'Postpartum depression among rural women from developed and developing countries: A systematic review'. *The Journal of Rural Health* 27(3): 278–88.

Vogel, Shane (2011) 'The new queer essentialism'. *American Literature* 83(1): 175–84.

Volpp, Leti (2000) 'Blaming culture for bad behaviour'. *Yale Journal of Law and the Humanities* 12: 89–116.

Volpp, Leti (2001) 'Feminism versus multiculturalism'. *Columbia Law Review* 101(5): 1181–218.

Walby, Sylvia (2011) *The Future of Feminism*. Cambridge: Polity Press.

Walby, Sylvia, Armstrong, Jo and Strid, Sofia (2012) 'Intersectionality: multiple inequalities in social theory'. *Sociology* 46(2): 224–40.

Walklate, Sandra (2011) 'Reframing criminal victimization: finding a place for vulnerability and resilience'. *Theoretical Criminology* 15(2): 179–94.

Wall, Glenda (2001) 'Moral constructions of motherhood in breastfeeding discourse'. *Gender & Society* 15(4): 592–610.

Walter, Natasha (2010) *Living Dolls: The Return of Sexism*. London: Virago.

Waters, Malcolm (1995) *Globalization*. London: Routledge.

Webster, Fiona (2000) 'The politics of sex and gender: Benhabib and Butler debate subjectivity'. *Hypatia* 15(1): 1–22.

Weinberg, Bill (2012) 'Will American left betray heroine Malala Yousafzai?', World War 4 Report, 12 October, available online at http://ww4report.com/node/11598/, accessed 21 August 2013..

Weitz, Rose (1998) *The Politics of Women's Bodies: Sexuality, Appearance, and Behavior.* Oxford: Oxford University Press.

Weitzer, Ronald (2009) 'Sociology of sex work'. *Annual Review of Sociology* 35: 213–34.

Weitzer, Ronald (2010) 'The mythology of prostitution: advocacy research and public policy'. *Sexuality Research and Social Policy* 7: 15–29.

White, Michael (2011) 'Ken Clarke and Dominique Strauss-Kahn: a tale of two cultures', *The Guardian*, 19 May, available online at www.guardian.co.uk/politics/blog/2011/may/19/ken-clarke-dominique-strauss-kahn-tale-two-cultures, accessed 8 August 2013.

White, Michael (2012) 'Sex grooming: no good comes from looking the other way', *The Guardian*, 9 May.

Wilde-Blatavsky, Adele (2012) 'When anti-racism becomes anti-woman: the "privileging" of race over gender', *The Huffington Post*, 1 May, available online at www.huffingtonpost.co.uk/.

Williams, Zoe (2011a) 'Dominique Strauss-Kahn finds sympathy in Paris', *The Guardian*, 20 May.

Williams, Zoe (2011b) 'Come back "Superwoman": the lost ideal of combining motherhood and work', *The Guardian*, 17 September.

Williams, Paul (2012) 'Jihad: the last refuge of the scoundrel', in his blog *Freedom in the 21st Century*, 14 January, available online at http://freedominthe21st.blogspot.co.uk/.

Willitts, Philippa (2011) 'We are the 49%?', *The F Word*, 16 October, available at www.thefword.org.uk.

Willitts, Philippa (2012) 'Slutwalk and Assange: can it be salvaged?' *The F Word*, 1 October, available at www.thefword.org.uk.

Willsher, Kim (2011) 'Dominique Strauss-Kahn to face fresh sex assault complaint', *The Guardian*, 16 May.

Wing, Adrien Katherine and Smith, Monica Nigh (2005) 'Critical race feminism lifts the veil? Muslim women, France, and the headscarf ban'. *UC Davis Law Review* 39(3): 743–90.

Winter, Bronwyn (2001) 'Fundamental misunderstandings: issues in feminist approaches to Islamism'. *Journal of Women's History* 13(1): 9–41.

Wolf, Joan B. (2007) 'Is breast really best? Risk and total motherhood in the National Breastfeeding Awareness Campaign'. *Journal of Health Politics, Policy and Law* 32(4): 595–636.

Wolf, Joan B. (2011) *Is Breast Best? Taking on the Breastfeeding Experts and the New High Stakes of Motherhood*. New York: New York University Press.

Wolf, Naomi (1994) *Fire with Fire: The New Female Power and How to Use It*. London: Vintage.

Wolf, Naomi (2010) 'Julian Assange captured by world's dating police', in *The Huffington Post*, 7 December.

Wolf, Naomi (2011) 'Julian Assange's sex-crime accusers deserve to be named', *The Guardian*, 5 January.

Women's Resource Centre (2007) 'Uncovering women's inequality in the UK: statistics'. London: Women's Resource Centre.

Woodhead, Charlotte and Wessley, Simon (2010) 'What interventions work with victims of conflict-related rape?' *British Medical Journal* 341: 1253.

World Health Organization (1981) *International Code of Marketing of Breast-milk Substitutes*. Geneva: World Health Organization.

World Health Organization (1996) *Care in Normal Birth: A Practical Guide*. Geneva: Department of Reproductive Health and Research, World Health Organization.

World Health Organization (2003) *Kangaroo Mother Care: A Practical Guide*. Geneva: World Health Organization.

World Health Organization and UNICEF (2009) *Baby Friendly Hospital Initiative: Revised, Updated and Expanded for Integrated Care*. Geneva: World Health Organization.

World Health Organization/UNICEF (1989) *Protecting, Promoting and Supporting Breast-feeding: The Special Role of Maternity Services*. Geneva: World Health Organization.

World News Australia (2012) 'Assange gets Aboriginal passport', on *World News Australia*, 15 September, available online at www.sbs.com.au/news/article/1692865/Assange-gets-Aboriginal-passport, accessed 7 August 2013.

Wu, Joyce (2004) 'Left Labor in bed with the sex industry', in R. Whisnant and C. Stark (eds), *Not for Sale: Feminists Resisting Prostitution and Pornography*. Melbourne: Spinifex, pp. 206–9.

Yerkes, Mara (2010) 'Diversity in work: the heterogeneity of women's employment patterns'. *Gender, Work and Organization* 17(6): 696–720.

Yuval-Davis, Nira (2006) 'Intersectionality and feminist politics'. *European Journal of Women's Studies* 13(3): 193–209.

Zeisler, Andi (2010) 'Douchebag Decree: WFT, Naomi Wolf?' *Bitch Magazine*, 9 December, available online at http://bitchmagazine.org/post/douchebag-decree-wtf-naomi-wolf, accessed 8 October 2013.

Zupan, Jelka (2005) 'Perinatal mortality in developing countries'. *New England Journal of Medicine* 352(20): 2047–8.

Further Reading

This bibliography contains details of both primary and secondary sources which have not been directly cited in the text but which have informed the analysis.

Addley, Esther (2012) 'Muslim men accused of hate crime over anti-gay leaflet', *The Guardian*, 10 January 2012.

Addley, Esther and Sabbagh, Dan (2012) 'Jimmy Savile: police investigate alleged rape and sex abuse on a "national scale"', *The Guardian*, 9 October.

African Sex Worker Alliance (2011) African Sex Worker Alliance. Available online at http://africansexworkeralliance.org/.

Afshar, Haleh (1994) 'Growing up with real and imaginary values amidst conflicting views of self and society', in M. Afshar and M. Maynard (eds), *The Dynamics of Race and Gender in Britain*. London: Taylor & Francis, pp. 127–45.

Afshar, Haleh (1998) *Islam and Feminisms: An Iranian Case Study*. Basingstoke: Palgrave Macmillan.

Afshar, Haleh, Aitken, Rob and Franks, Myfanwy (2005) 'Feminisms, Islamophobia and identities'. *Political Studies* 53(2): 262–83.

Agustín, Laura (2005) 'The cultural study of commercial sex'. *Sexualities* 8(5): 618–31.

Agustín, Laura (2011) 'Sex offenders and clients of sex workers: creating monsters'. 25 October 2011, available online at www.lauraagustin.com/male-sex-offenders-and-clients-of-sex-workers-our-current-monsters/.

Agustín, Laura (2011) Naked Anthropologist | Laura Agustín | Migration | Trafficking | Sex. Available online at www.lauraagustin.com/.

Ahmed, Leila (1992) *Women and Gender in Islam: Historical Roots of a Modern Debate*. New Haven, CT: Yale University Press.

Alcoff, Linda (1996) 'Dangerous pleasures: Foucault and the politics of pedophilia', in S. Hekman (ed.), *Feminist Interpretations of Michel Foucault*. University Park, PA: The Pennsylvania State University Press.

Alibhai-Brown, Yasmin (1998) 'God's own vigilantes', *The Independent*, 12 October.

Alpha Parent, The (2012) 'The alpha parent', available online at www.thealphaparent.com, accessed 8 August 2013.

Amin, A. (2000), 'Post-Fordism: models, fantasies and phantoms of transition', in A. Amin (ed.), *Post-Fordism: A Reader*. Oxford: Blackwell.

Asia Pacific Network of Sex Workers (2011) apnsw << Asia Pacific Network of Sex Worker$. Available online at http://apnswdollhouse.wordpress.com/.

Asorson, April (2012) 'My Natural Childbirth Story', available online at http://mynaturalchildbirth.org/my-natural-childbirth-story/.

Associated Press (2010b) 'French parliament adopts ban on full-face veil', 14 September.

Association of Radical Midwives (2012) 'Midwifery Matters', available online at http://www.midwifery.org.uk/.

Attachment Parenting International (2012) 'Welcome to Attachment Parenting International', available online at http://www.attachment-parenting.org/.

Ayers, Susan (2007) 'Thoughts and emotions during traumatic birth: A qualitative study'. *Birth* 34(3): 253–63.

Badinter, E. (2006) *Dead End Feminism*. Cambridge: Polity Press.

Bartkowski, J. and Ghazal-Read, J. (2003) 'Veiled submission: gender, power, and identity among evangelical and Muslim women in the United States'. *Qualitative Sociology* 26(1): 71–92.

BBC (2010) 'Transcript: the Assange interview', 21 December, available online at http://news.bbc.co.uk/today/hi/today/newsid_93090 00/9309320.stm.

BBC (2011) 'Is breast best? Cherry Healey investigates', broadcast at 9 pm on BBC Three, 12 April.

BBC News (2010) 'Model's breastfeeding law apology'. Available online at www.bbc.co.uk/news/health-10878803, accessed 8 August 2013.

BBC News (2012) 'Dominique Strauss-Kahn on formal sex ring investigation'. *BBC News*, 26 March, available online at www.bbc.co.uk/news/world-europe-17518628.

Blackburn, Jen (2012) 'Dressing down for film lothario Russell Brand', *The Sun*, 3 August.

Breastfeeding Moms Unite (2012) 'Breastfeeding Moms Unite', available online at http://www.breastfeedingmomsunite.com/, accessed 8 August 2013.

Brems, Eva (1997) 'Enemies or allies? Feminism and cultural relativism as dissident voices in human rights discourse'. *Human Rights Quarterly* 19: 136–64.

British Doulas (2012) 'British Doulas', available online at www.britishdoulas.co.uk/.

Brooke Magnanti (2011) Brooke Magnanti: author, scientist, former call girl. Available online at http://belledejour-uk.blogspot.com/.

Brooke Magnanti (2011) 'Sexonomics'. Available online at http://sexonomics-uk.blogspot.com/.

Brown, Wendy (2006b) *Regulating Aversion: Tolerance in the Age of Identity and Empire*. Princeton, NJ: Princeton University Press.

Brubaker, Sarah Jane and Dillaway, Heather E. (2009) 'Medicalization, natural childbirth and birthing experiences'. *Sociology Compass* 3(1): 31–48.

Bunnyranch.com (2010) *Bunny Ranch*. Available online at www.bunnyranch.com.

Cáceres, C., Cueto, M., and Palomino, N. (2008) 'Policies around sexual and reproductive health and rights in Peru: conflict, biases and silence'. *Global Public Health* 3(1): 39–57.

Cairney, Kathleen F. (1995) 'Recognizing acquaintance rape in potentially consensual situations: a re-examination of Thomas Hardy's *Tess of the D'Urbervilles*', *The American University Journal of Gender, Social Policy and Law* 3(2): 301–31.

Calderone, Michael (2010) 'Wikileaks' Assange fires back at *The Guardian* to competitor', *The Cutline*, 21 December, available online at http://news.yahoo.com/blogs/cutline/wikileaks-assange-fires-back-guardian-competitor-20101221-070416-841.html.

Callinicos, A. (1989) *Against Postmodernism: A Marxist Perspective*. Cambridge: Polity Press.

Campbell, Denis (2010) 'Too scared to push: big rise reported in birth trauma', *The Observer*, 14 November.

Carbajosa, Ana (2011) 'Gazan youth issue manifesto to vent their anger with all sides in this conflict', *The Guardian*, 2 January.

Carney, Terri (2011) 'Still hungover: Todd Philips and rape culture'. *Bright Lights Film Journal* 73.

Carpentier, Megan (2012) 'Rapists rape because they like raping (the Dominique Strauss-Kahn example)', *The Raw Story*, 4 May, available online at www.rawstory.com.

Carter, Kate (2011) 'Cashing in on new mums', *The Guardian*, 22 August, available at www.guardian.co.uk/lifeandstyle/the-womens-blog-with-jane-martinson/2011/aug/22/childbirth-women.

Caryl, Christian (2011) 'Why WikiLeaks changes everything', *The New York Review of Books*, 13 January.

Center for Healthcare Quality and Payment Reform (2013) 'How to save $5 billion in healthcare spending for employers and taxpayers', 7 January, posted online at http://chqpr.org.

Cesario, AnneMarie and Chancer, Lynn (2009) 'Sex work: a review of recent literature'. *Qualitative Sociology* 32: 213–20.

Channel 4 (2011) *WikiLeaks: Secrets and Lies*. Broadcast on Channel 4, 10 pm, 29 November.

Charles, Nickie (2000) *Feminism, the State and Social Policy*. Basingstoke: Macmillan Press Ltd.

CNN.com (2003) Live from the headlines: interview with Dennis Hof, Genevieve Wood. Broadcast 27 June, 20.29 (transcript available at http://transcripts.cnn.com/TRANSCRIPTS/0306/27/se.15.html, accessed 8 August 2013).

Collective of Sex Workers and Supporters (2011) COSWAS. Available online at http://coswas.org/.

Committee for the Civil Rights of Prostitutes (2011) luccioleon-line – CURRICULUM VITAE. Available online at http://www.lucciole.org/content/view/18/9/Collective of Sex Workers and Supporters (2011) COSWAS. Available online at http://coswas.org/.

Committee for the Civil Rights of Prostitutes (2011) luccioleonline

– CURRICULUM VITAE. Available online at http://www.lucciole. org/content/view/18/9/.

Coronel, Gustavo (2011) 'Epidemics of despicable global leaders', published by the Cato Institute at http://www.cato.org/publications/ commentary/epidemics-despicable-global-leaders.

Cotter, D., Hermsen, J. M. and Vanneman, R. (2011) 'The end of the gender revolution? Gender role attitudes from 1977 to 2008'. *American Journal of Sociology* 116(4): 1–31.

Coulter, Kristine and Meyer, David S. (2010) 'High profile rape trials and policy advocacy'. Paper presented at the annual meeting of the American Political Science Association, September 3, Washington, DC.

COYOTE LA (2011) Index page. Available online at www.coyotela. org/.

Crosley-Corcoran, Gina (2012) 'The feminist breeder: where edgy feminism meets modern motherhood', available online at http://thefeminist breeder.com/.

Cybermummy (2012) 'Sponsors – cybermummy', available online at www.cybermummy.com/sponsors.

Das, Veena (1996) 'Sexual violence, discursive formations and the state'. *Economic and Political Weekly* (September): 2411–23.

Davis, Erik (2008) 'Sundance review: Roman Polanski: wanted and desired', Moviefone, 20 January, available online at blog.moviefone. com.

Department for Work and Pensions (2008) *Consultation Document: Accepting and Advertising Employer Vacancies from within the Adult Entertainment Industry by Jobcentre Plus.* London: Department for Work and Pensions.

De Rode Draad (the red thread) (2011) De Rode Draad: English. Available online at http://rodedraad.nl/other-languages/english.html.

Desiree Alliance (2011) *Desiree Alliance: Welcome!* Available online at http://www.desireealliance.org/.

Devreinot, Tom (2011) 'DSK, the maid from Guinea and "agency"', *Africa is a Country*, 18 July, available online at www.africasacountry. com.

Dick-Read, Grantly (1959) *Childbirth Without Fear: the Principles and Practice of Natural Childbirth.* New York: Harper and Row.

Dickerson, Justin (2010) 'Celebrity justice and victims' rights initiatives', available at Social Science Research Network, online at http://papers.ssrn.com/sol3/papers.cfm?abstract_id=1828022.

Dines, Gail (2010) *Pornland: How Porn has Hijacked our Sexuality.* Boston, MA: Beacon Press.

Dirtygirl Diaries (2011) *dirtygirl diaries.* Available online at http://thedirtygirldiaries.com/.

Doezema, J. (1999) 'Loose women or lost women? The re-emergence of the myth of white slavery in contemporary discourses of trafficking in women'. *Gender Issues* 18(1): 23–50.

DONA International (2012) 'DONA International – welcome', available online at http://www.dona.org/.

Durbar (2011) Durbar Mahila Samanwaya Committee. Available online at www.durbar.org/.

Dustin, Holly (2012) 'Where is the feminist voice in the porn debate?' *The Guardian*, 6 September.

Ehrenreich, Nancy and Barr, Mark (2005) 'Intersex surgery, female genital cutting, and the selective condemnation of "cultural practices"'. *Harvard Civil Rights-Civil Liberties Law Review* 40: 71–140.

El Saadawi, Nawal (1980) *The Hidden Face of Eve.* London: Zed Press.

Ellen, Barbara (2012) 'Shafilea Ahmed's death was not the fault of liberal lefties', *The Observer*, 5 August.

Eltahawy, Mona (2010) 'From liberals and feminists, unsettling silence on the Muslim veil', *The Washington Post*, 17 July.

Eltahawy, Mona (2010) 'Let me, a Muslim feminist, confuse you', writing on her blog, December 11.

Empower Foundation (2011) 'Empower foundation'. Available online at www.empowerfoundation.org/index_en.html.

Fadil, Nadia (2011) 'not-/unveiling as an ethical practice', *Feminist Review* 98: 83–109.

Farsides, Calliope (1994) 'Autonomy, responsibility and midwifery', in S. Budd and U. Sharma (eds), *The Healing Bond: The Patient–Practitioner Relationship and Therapeutic Responsibility.* London: Routledge, pp. 42–62.

Fegan, Eileen V. (2002) 'Recovering women: intimate images and legal strategy'. *Social and Legal Studies* 11(2): 155–83.

Figes, Kate (2012) 'Postnatal depression: the pressures new mothers face, now more than ever', *The Guardian*, 3 November.

Flanders, Laura (2010) 'Since when does Interpol care about sexual assault?' *Alternet*, 7 December, available online at www.alternet.org.

Foucault, M. (1984) *The Foucault Reader* (ed. P. Rabinow). Harmondsworth: Pantheon Books.

Frank, Katherine (2007) 'Thinking critically about strip club research'. *Sexualities* 10(4): 501–17.

Freeman, Hadley (2011) 'DSK: a trial of the accuser not the accused', *The Guardian*, 23 August, available online at www.guardian.co.uk/commentisfree/2011/aug/23/dsk-trial-accuser-not-accused.

Galeotti, Anna Elisabetta (2007) 'Relativism, universalism and applied ethics: the case of female circumcision'. *Constellations* 14(1): 91–111.

Geimer, Samantha (2003) 'Judge the movie, not the man', *The Los Angeles Times*, 23 February.

Glass, Robert L (2012) 'All about Julian Assange'. *Information Systems Management* 29(2): 165–8.

Gov.uk (2012) *Married Couples Allowance.* [online] (last updated 22.10.2012) Available at: www.gov.uk/married-couples-allowance/overview, accessed 1 November 2012.

Green Left TV (2012) 'David Hicks speaks out for Julian Assange and WikiLeaks', on Green Left TV, 1 June, available online at http://www.greenleft.org.au.

Greer, Germaine (1999) *The Whole Woman*. London: Doubleday.

Guardian (2011) 'Dominique Strauss-Kahn tried to claim diplomatic immunity', *The Guardian*, 17 June.

Guardian (2011) 'Julian Assange extradition appeal hearing – Tuesday 12 July 2011'. Available online at www.guardian.co.uk/media/2011/jul/12/julian-assange-extradition-live-coverage.

Guardian (2012) 'Jealous teenager who stabbed girlfriend 60 times jailed for life', *The Guardian*, 7 September.

Gunning, Isabelle R. (1991–2) 'Arrogant perception, world-travelling and multicultural feminism: the case of female genital surgeries'. *Columbia Human Rights Law Review* 23: 189–248.

Hakim, Catherine (2011) *Honey Money: the Power of Erotic Capital.* London: Allen Lane.

Hakim, Catherine (2012) 'The sex myth: why everything we're told is wrong by Brooke Magnanti – review', *The Guardian*, 15 April.

Hamel, Chouki El (2002) 'Muslim diaspora in Western Europe: the Islamic headscarf (Hijab), the media and Muslims' integration in France'. *Citizenship Studies* 6(3): 293–308.

Hamid, Shadi (2011) 'The rise of the Islamists: How Islamists will change politics, and vice versa'. *Foreign Affairs* 90(3): 40–7.

Harris, Molly Laura Boeder (2010) 'Transnational feminism and gender-based violence: Exploring the relationship between feminist theory and V-Day,' De Paul University Theses and Dissertations. Paper 63, available at http://via.library.depaul.edu/etd/63/.

Hasan, Md. Mahmudul (2012) 'Feminism as Islamophobia: a review of misogyny charges against Islam', *Intellectual Discourse* 20(1): 55–78.

Hassan, Narin (2010) 'Milk markets: technology, the lactating body, and new forms of consumption'. *Women's Studies Quarterly* 38(3/4): 209–28.

Hausbeck, K and Brents, B 'McDonaldization of the sex industry?' in G. Ritzer (ed.), *McDonaldization: The Reader*. Thousand Oaks, CA: Sage.

Henry, Julie (2012) 'Trust drops "evangelical" breastfeeding message', *The Daily Telegraph*, 22 January.

Hodnett, E. D., Downe, S., Walsh, D. and Weston, J. (2010) 'Alternative versus conventional institutional settings for birth', Cochrane Database of Systematic Reviews 2010, Issue 9. Art. No.: CD000012. DOI: 10.1002/14651858.CD000012.pub3.

Hymowitz, Kay S (2003) 'The feminist silence about Islam'. *Policy Magazine* 19(1): 29–33.

Independent Midwives UK (2012) 'Independent midwives UK', available online at www.independentmidwives.org.uk/.

International Committee on the Rights of Sex Workers in Europe (2011). ICRSE Home. Available online at www.sexworkeurope.org/.

International Confederation of Midwives (2012) 'International Confederation of Midwives', available online at www.international midwives.org/.

International Prostitutes Collective (2011) *International Prostitutes Collective*. Available online at www.prostitutescollective.net/.

International Union of Sex Workers (2011). *International Union of Sex Workers*. Available online at www.iusw.org/.

Invisible Midwife (2012) 'Invisible midwives – home', available online at www.invisiblemidwives.co.uk/.

Jardin, Xeni (2010) 'Assange: "I'm not a player, I just crush a lot"', Boingboing.net, 21 December, available online at www.boingboing. net/.

Jensen, Tracey (2010) 'Warmth and wealth: re-imagining social class in taxonomies of good parenting'. *Studies in the Maternal* 2(1), available online at www.mamsie.bbk.ac.uk/back_issues/issue_three/docume nts/jensen.pdf, accessed 15 August 2013.

Judge, Anthony (2011) 'Pre-judging an institution's implicit strategy by the Director's private behaviour', available online at www.laetusin praesens.org/musings/imfimag.php/.

Keller, Bill (2011) 'Dealing with Assange and the WikiLeaks secrets'. *The New York Times*, January 26.

Kelly, Liz (1988) *Surviving Sexual Violence*. Cambridge: Polity Press.

KellyMom (2012) 'Kelly Mom: evidence-based breastfeeding and parenting', available online at http://kellymom.com/.

Khan, Jemima (2010) 'Why did I back Julian Assange? It's about justice and fairness', *The Guardian*, 12 December.

Khan, Jemima (2013) 'Jemima Khan on Julian Assange: how the Wikileaks founder alienated his allies', *The New Statesman*, 6 February.

Khan, Sara (2012) 'Muslim marriages like George Galloway's should be registered', *The Guardian*, 4 May.

Kipnis, Laura (2011) 'Leaking all over the page'. *PMLA* 126(4): 1085–91.

Kitzinger, Sheila (2011) 'Letter from Europe: kick-starting the uterus'. *Birth* 38(3): 269–70.

Kramer, Anne-Marie (2009) 'The Polish parliament and the making of politics through abortion'. *International Feminist Journal of Politics* 11(1): 81–101.

Lallier, Adalbert (1989) Sexonomics website. Available online at http:// www.sexonomics.com/.

Lamaze (2012) Lamaze International website. Available online at www. lamaze.org/.

Lentin, Alana (2009) 'Liberals, the hijab and the denial of full equality', on her blog, 7 July, available online at http://www.alanalentin.net/.

Levenson, Ellie (2009) *The Noughtie Girl's Guide to Feminism*. London: Oneworld.

Lewis, Helen (2012) 'How Belle de Jour got her figures wrong', *The New Statesman*, 26 April.

Linkins, Jason (2011) 'Dominique Strauss-Kahn defended witlessly by Bernard-Henri Levy and Ben Stein', *The Huffington Post*, 18 May, available online at www.huffingtonpost.com.

London Sex Worker Open University (2011) London Sex Worker Open University. Available online at www.sexworkeropenuniversity. com/.

Lothian, Judith (2001) 'Back to the future: trusting birth'. *Journal of Perinatal and Neonatal Nursing* 15(3): 13–22.

Lothian, Judith (2008) 'Childbirth education at the crossroads'. *The Journal of Perinatal Education* 17(2): 45–9.

Love Your Hooker and Pay Them Well (2011) Love Your Hooker and Pay Them Well (Facebook Page). Available online at www.facebook. com/pages/Love-your-hooker-Pay-them-well/294019263919/.

Maréchal, Nathalie R. (2011) 'Hackers, Heavies and Heroes: Dissent and Control in Cyberworld'. Unpublished Masters thesis, School of International Service, American University.

Marks, Monica (2011) 'Can Islamism and feminism mix?', *The New York Times*, 26 October.

Martin, Emily (2001) *The Woman in the Body: A Cultural Analysis of Reproduction*. Boston, MA: Beacon Press.

Martin-Weber, Jessica (2012) 'The leaky boob', available online at http://theleakyboob.com/.

McEwan, Melissa (2011) 'Today in Feminist Rape Apologia', in *Shakesville*, 5 January, available online at http://shakespearessister. blogspot.com/.

McGrath, Melanie (2012) 'The Sex Myth by Brooke Magnanti: review', *The Daily Telegraph*, 24 April.

Meer, Nasar, Dwyer, Claire and Modood, Tariq (2010) 'Embodying Nationhood? Conceptions of British national identity, citizenship, and gender in the "veil affair"'. *The Sociological Review* 58(1): 84–111.

Mendoza, Breny (2011) 'The role of the law in the rule of law of the new oligarchies: a Latin American feminist perspective', *feminists@law* 1(1), available at http://journals.kent.ac.uk/index.php/feministsatlaw/ index/.

Merali, Arzu (2012) 'All quiet on the western front: the loss of radical

Islamic feminism at the hands of Euro-Islam', *Sons of Malcolm* blog, 30 September, available online at http://sonsofmalcolm.blogspot.co.uk/.

Midwives' Alliance of North America (2012) 'Midwives' Alliance of North America', available online at http://mana.org/.

Moenne, María Elena Acuña (2005) 'Embodying memory: women and the legacy of the military government in Chile'. *Feminist Review* 79: 150–61.

Mogahed, Dalia (2012) 'Arab women and men see eye to eye on religion's role in law', report available at Gallup World: www.gallup.com/poll/155324/Arab-Women-Men-Eye-Eye-Religion-Role-Law.aspx/.

Mom 2.0 Summit (2012) 'Mom 2.0 Summit', available online at www.mom2summit.com/.

Moore, Michael (2010) 'Why I'm posting bail money for Julian Assange', available online at www.michaelmoore.com/words/mike-friends-blog/why-im-posting-bail-money/.

Moran, Caitlin (2011) *How to be a Woman*. London: Ebury Press.

Mulla, Sameena (2011) 'Review essay: on sexual violence'. *Political and Legal Anthropology Review* 34(1): 204–9.

My Mystic Mama (2012) 'milestone | My Mystic Mama', available online at www.mymysticmama.com/tag/milestone/.

My Mystic Mamma (2012) 'Breastfeeding badges', available online at www.mymysticmama.com/mamas/breastfeeding-badges/.

National Childbirth Trust (2012) NCT website. Available online at www.nct.org.uk/.

The Natural Child Project (2012) 'The Natural Child Project', available online at http://www.naturalchild.org/.

The Natural Mummy Files (2012) 'The Natural Mummy Files: our natural parenting and home education journey', available online at www.thenaturalmummyfiles.co.uk/.

Nayar, Pramod K (2010) 'WikiLeaks, the new information cultures, and digital parrhesia'. *Economic and Political Weekly* XLV (52): 27–30.

Network of Women Sex Workers of Latin America and the Caribbean (2011) *RedTraSex: Red de Mujeres Trabajadoras Sexuales de Latinoamérica y el caribe*. Available online at www.redtrasex.org.ar/.

New Zealand Prostitutes Collective (2011) Homepage. Available online at www.nzpc.org.nz/index.php/.

Newsweek (2011) 'The Maid's Tale', in *Newsweek Magazine*, 25 July.

Njambi, Wairimu Ngaruiya (2004) 'Dualisms and female bodies in representations of African female circumcision: a feminist critique'. *Feminist Theory* 5(3): 281–303.

Oakley, Ann (1980) *Women Confined: Towards a Sociology of Childbirth*. New York: Schocken Books.

O'Connell Davidson, Julia (1998) *Prostitution, Power and Freedom*. Cambridge: Polity Press.

Odeh, Lama Abu (1993) 'Postcolonial feminism and the veil: thinking the difference'. *Feminist Review* 43: 26–37.

Odent, Michel (2008) 'A top obstetrician on why men should NEVER be at the birth of their child', *The Daily Mail*, 15 April.

O'Keefe, Theresa (2011) 'Flaunting our way to freedom? Slutwalks, gendered protest and feminist futures'. Conference paper presented at New Agendas in Social Movement Studies, November 2011, National University of Ireland Maynooth.

Oksala, Johanna (2011) 'Sexual experience: Foucault, phenomenology, and feminist theory'. *Hypatia* 26(1): 207–23.

OneWorld Birth (2012) 'One world birth | save birth, one world', available online at http://www.oneworldbirth.net/.

Orgasmic Birth (2012) 'Orgasmic birth movie', available online at http://www.orgasmicbirth.com/.

Part of Me (2012) 'Part of Me', available online at http://partofmeintro.blogspot.co.uk/, accessed 8 August 2013.

Patel, Pragna (2012) 'The use and abuse of honour-based violence in the UK', on opendemocracy.net, 6 June, available online at www.opendemocracy.net/.

Pedwell, Carolyn (2008) 'Weaving relational webs: theorizing cultural difference and embodied practice'. *Feminist Theory* 9(1): 87–107.

Petchesky, Rosalind (2011) 'Phantom empire: a feminist reflection ten years after 9/11'. *Women's Studies Quarterly* 39(3/4): 288–94.

PhD in Parenting (2010) 'I won't ask you why you didn't breastfeed', available online at http://www.phdinparenting.com/2010/07/01/i-wont-ask-you-why-you-didnt-breastfeed/#.T6uiRZ9YvG.

Philadelphoff-Puren, Nina (2004) 'The mark of refusal: sexual violence and the politics of recontexualization'. *Feminist Theory* 5(3): 243–56.

Phipps, Alison (2006) 'Girls of the future? Extended review'. *British Journal of Sociology of Education* 27(3): 409–15.

Porter, Henry (2012) 'Islam must embrace reason and responsibility', *The Observer*, 23 September.

Positive Birth Stories (2012) 'Positive birth stories', available online at www.positivebirthstories.com/.

Primitive Mommy (2012) 'Primitive Mommy: instinctual eating, parenting and living', available online at http://primitivemommy.com/.

Punternet (2011) *PunterNet UK: reviews and listings of UK escorts and massage parlours*. Available online at http://www.punternet.com/index1.html/.

Quan, Tracy (2011) ~*Tracy Quan*~. Available online at http://tracy quan.net/index.php.

Regents Midwifery Practice (2012) 'Regent's Independent Midwifery Practice', available online at www.regentsmidwife.co.uk/.

Reimers, Eva (2007) 'Representations of an honor killing: intersections of discourses on culture, gender, equality, social class, and nationality'. *Feminist Media Studies* 7(3): 239–55.

Roberts, Dorothy E. (2003) 'The future of reproductive choice for poor women and women of color', in R. Weitz (ed.), *The Politics of Women's Bodies: Sexuality, Appearance & Behaviour*. Oxford: Oxford University Press, pp. 282–7.

Romano, Amy M. (2008) 'Research summaries for normal birth'. *The Journal of Perinatal Education* 17(1): 48–52.

Rundle, Guy (2010) 'Assange accuser may have ceased co-operating', in *Crikey*, 9 December 2010, available online at www.crikey.com.au.

Ryan, Erin Gloria (2012) 'Breastfeeding moms plan massive, unnecessary protest', *Jezebel*, 8 May.

Saunders, Candida L. (2012) 'The truth, the half-truth and nothing like the truth: reconceptualizing false allegations of rape'. *British Journal of Criminology* 52(6): 1152–71.

Save the Children (2013) *Superfood for Babies: How Overcoming Barriers to Breastfeeding Will Save Children's Lives*. London: Save the Children.

Scarlet Alliance (2011) Scarlet Alliance Homepage. Available online at www.scarletalliance.org.au/.

Schneider, Elizabeth M. (1993) 'Feminism and the false dichotomy of victimhood and agency'. *New York Law School Review* 38: 387–99.

Sex Professionals of Canada (2011) SPOC. Available online at www. spoc.ca/.

Sex Work Activists, Allies and You (2011) SWAAY. Available online at www.swaay.org/index.html.

Sex Workers' Rights Advocacy Network in Central and Eastern Europe and Central Asia (2011) Main page | SWAN. Available online at http://swannet.org/.

Sexual Freedom Coalition (2011) Sexual Freedom Coalition. Available online at www.sfc.org.uk/.

Shahryar, Josh (2012) 'The myth of how the hijab protects women against sexual assault', *Women Under Siege* blog, 6 September, available online at www.womenundersiegeproject.org/.

Sheehan, Lindsey M. (2012) 'The sex myth: why everything we're told is wrong', *The F Word*, 5 May, available online at www.thefword.org. uk/reviews/2012/05/thesexmyth/.

Sheldon, Sally and Wilkinson, Stephen (1998) 'Female genital mutilation and cosmetic surgery: regulating non-therapeutic body modification'. *Bioethics* 12(4): 263–85.

Siddique, Haroon (2011) 'Muslim women: beyond the stereotype', *The Guardian*, 29 April.

Smith, Joan (2012) 'Strong religious belief is no excuse for intimidation', *The Independent*, 22 January.

Solnit, Rebecca (2011) 'When institutions rape nations', 22 May, at www.tomdispatch.com/blog/175395/.

Solomon, Deborah (2010) 'Sex and the single man (interview with Hugh Hefner)', *The New York Times Magazine*, 7 July, available online at www.nytimes.com/2010/07/11/magazine/11fob-q4-t.html/.

Stan, A. (1995) *Debating Sexual Correctness: Pornography, Sexual Harassment, Date Rape, and the Politics of Sexual Equality*. New York: Delta.

Stewart, Sheree (2012) 'Birthsong', available online at http://www. birthsong.com.au/

Stone Age Parenting (2012) 'Stone age parenting', available online at www.stoneageparenting.com/.

Storksen, Hege Therese, Eberhard-Gran, Malin, Garthus-Niegel, Susan and Eskild, Anne (2012) 'Fear of childbirth: the relation to anxiety and depression'. *Acta Obstetrica et Gynecologica Scandinavia* 91(2): 237–42.

SWEAT (2011) SWEAT website. Available online at www.sweat.org.za/.

Tyler, Imogen (2009) 'Introduction: birth'. *Feminist Review* 93: 1–7.

Urban, Annie (2012) 'PhD in parenting blog', available online at www. phdinparenting.com/.

Valenti, Jessica (2007) *Full Frontal Feminism: a Young Woman's Guide to Why Feminism Matters*. Emeryville, CA: Seal Press.

Vanderlaan, Jennifer (2012) 'Birthing naturally', available online at www. birthingnaturally.net/.

Vandermassen, Griet (2011) 'Evolution and rape: a feminist Darwinian perspective'. *Sex Roles* 64: 732–47.

Viloria, Hida (2012) 'Clinton's pronouncements against female genital mutilation don't go far enough', *The Global Herald*, 23 February.

Wade, Lisa (2012) 'Black face, racial caricature, and cake: raising awareness about "female genital mutilation"'? *Sociological Images*, 18 April, available online at www.thesocietypages.org/.

Walley, Christine J (1997) 'Searching for "voices": feminism, anthropology, and the global debate over female genital operations'. *Cultural Anthropology* 12(3): 405–38.

Wannamaker, Julie (2012) 'Natural childbirth education', available online at http://naturalchildbirthedu.com/.

Warshaw, R (1988) *I Never Called it Rape: the MS Report on Recognizing, Fighting and Surviving Date and Acquaintance Rape*. New York: Harper Perennial.

Werbner, Pnina (2007) 'Veiled interventions in pure space: honour, shame and embodied struggles among Muslims in Britain and France'. *Theory, Culture and Society* 24(2): 161–86.

Williams, Juliet (2011) 'Diary of a chambermaid?' *MS. Blog*, 18 May, available online at http://msmagazine.com/blog/blog/2011/05/18/diary-of-a-chambermaid/, accessed 8 August 2013.

Winnett, Robert (2012) 'Britain being overtaken by "militant secularists" says Baroness Warsi', *The Daily Telegraph*, 13 February.

Winter, Bronwyn (1994) 'Women, the law, and cultural relativism in France: the case of excision'. *Signs* 19(4): 939–74.

Woodhouse, Laura (2011) 'Assange', *The F Word*, 17 July, available online at www.thefword.org.uk/.

World Health Organization/UNICEF (2012) 'World Breastfeeding Week', available online at http://worldbreastfeedingweek.org/.

Xifra, Jordi (2012) 'Sex, lies and post-trial publicity: the reputation repair strategies of Dominique Strauss-Kahn'. *Public Relations Review* 38(3): 477–83.

Young, Diony (2011) '"Gentle Cesareans": Better in some respects, but fewer cesareans are better still'. *Birth* 38(3): 183–4.

Zechenter, Elizabeth M. (1997) 'In the name of culture: cultural relativism and the abuse of the individual'. *Journal of Anthropological Research* 53(3): 319–47.

Zeedyk, Suzanne (2007) 'The science of rape: (mis)constructions of women's trauma in evolutionary theory'. *Feminist Review* 86: 67–88.

Index